George Ross

Patriotic recitations and Arbor Day exercises

George Ross

Patriotic recitations and Arbor Day exercises

ISBN/EAN: 9783337303853

Printed in Europe, USA, Canada, Australia, Japan

Cover: Foto ©Suzi / pixelio.de

More available books at **www.hansebooks.com**

No pupil or teacher in the Province of Ontario is obliged to purchase this volume as a text-book for School purposes.

PATRIOTIC RECITATIONS

AND

ARBOR DAY EXERCISES

Awake, my country, the hour of dreams is done
Doubt not, nor dread the greatness of thy fate,
Tho' faint souls fear the keen, confronting sun
And fain would bid the morn in splendor wait!
Tho' dreamers wrapt in starry visions cry
"Lo, yon thy future, yon thy faith, thy fame!"
And stretch vain hands to stars. Thy fame is nigh,
Here in Canadian hearth, and home and name;
This name which yet shall grow till all the nations know
Us for a patriot people, heart and hand,
Loyal to our native hearth, our native land.

—ROBERTS.

GEORGE W. ROSS, LL.D.
Minister of Education, Ontario

PRICE: $1.00.

TORONTO:
WARWICK BROS. & RUTTER, 68 AND 70 FRONT ST. WEST.
1893

THIS VOLUME

IS DEDICATED

TO THE TEACHERS OF CANADA.

"We owe to our schools the thankful task of strengthening the feeling that we are all Germans."

—BISMARCK.

PREFACE.

The first part of this volume contains suggestions which the teacher might find useful in preparing his pupils for properly appreciating the purposes of a national holiday and other important events in the history of the country. The teacher should explain to his pupils the main features of our system of government from the administration of the school section in which he lives to the Government of the Empire to which he belongs. Although these suggestions are not intended to be a treatise on Civics, yet if properly developed they will practically amount to that.

The pupil should be encouraged to ascertain for himself the functions of the various persons concerned in the government of the country, and, where his knowledge fails, the teacher need have no difficulty in supplying the information after consultation with any intelligent ratepayer in the section or with the ordinary histories at his command. In many cases the terms to be explained can be better understood by making the lesson a practical illustration of the subject under consideration. If the school is turned into a meeting of Parliament, or into a municipal meeting, or a school meeting, the place and duties of each officer become at once apparent, and the pupil who is asked for the time being to act the part of chairman, or returning officer, or school trustee, as well as the pupils who look on, will obtain a better idea of the duties of these officers in one such lesson than from many hours of explanation.

The patriotic selections are of two kinds—Canadian and general. The greater number of the Canadian selections appear for the first time for the purpose of recitation. They breathe a genuine Canadian spirit and are, moreover, generally of high literary merit. Many of the other selections have become common property for the purpose of public declamation. They have not, however, lost their value either as exercises in elocution or as the embodiment of a substantial and stirring patriotic sentiment.

The fourth division of the volume contains suggestions respecting Arbor Day. It is to be hoped, in addition to the comfort and pleasure to be derived from planting school grounds with suitable shade trees and otherwise improving them, that Arbor Day will be used by the teacher to foster in his pupils a love for the beautiful and grand in nature.

Should the publishers see fit to issue a second edition of these selections, an effort will be made to find a place for quotations from several prominent writers and speakers who were not able to supply material in time for this edition.

Grateful acknowledgments are hereby tendered to authors and publishers who have permitted the use of their productions for this volume.

G. W. R.

TORONTO, October, 1893.

CONTENTS.

PART I.

PART II.

PART III.

PART IV.

2

PART I.

A TALK WITH TEACHERS.

PART I.

A TALK WITH TEACHERS.

THE QUEEN'S BIRTHDAY.

A national holiday, while the occasion for recreation and pleasure-seeking, should be used by the teacher for impressing upon the minds of his pupils such facts and circumstances as would foster a national spirit. The birthday of Her Majesty, the Queen, furnishes an excellent opportunity for this purpose. As memory is always aided by association, the events which transpired during her reign might be clustered around the holiday to which the pupils so eagerly look forward; and thus a more intelligent conception obtained of the greatness of the Empire and of the grounds on which loyalty to the sovereign is founded.

To this end the teacher should spend half an hour every afternoon, for two or three weeks before the Queen's Birthday, in familiar conversations on the most important events of Her Majesty's reign. The extent of the British Empire might be shown upon the map and its vast area impressed upon the memory by comparisons with the extent and population of other important countries. The relations of Canada with the Empire, politically and historically, should be considered. Though far removed from the capital, and although in many respects differing in our habits, laws, and modes of thought from our kinsmen in the British Isles, yet we are of the same race and equally interested in the prosperity and honor of the Empire.

The teacher might also explain that whatever the Empire has achieved in statesmanship, or in literature, or in invention, Canadians, as subjects of the Empire or as descendants of the same ancestry, share in the honor of all such achievements.

The essential unity of the Empire should be duly emphasized. Notwithstanding the number of its colonies and their distance from the capital and from each other, they all acknowledge the sovereignty of one Queen—a Queen whose personal qualities, apart from the dignity of her position, have won for her the unqualified affection and allegiance of her subjects and the respect of all the nations of the world.

The teacher might point out that the flag which floats from the schoolhouse on Her Majesty's birthday is a symbol of national unity, and that in every colony of the Empire, in Australia, in South Africa, in Hindostan,—on every fortress guarded by British soldiers and on every ship manned by British sailors, the same flag proclaims universal allegiance to one sovereign and universal fealty to one Empire.

The teacher might then give a brief sketch of the Monarchical form of Government as compared with an Absolute Monarchy or a Republic, explaining clearly that under a Limited Monarchy the Queen acts on the advice of Parliament, and that she is as much bound by the Constitution of the country as any of her subjects. Reference might be made to the impartiality with which she has discharged her functions as a sovereign, to the great measures passed during her reign, such as the Repeal of the Corn Laws, the extension of the Franchise, Acts for the improvement of the laboring classes, the different Reform Bills, the Education Act, etc.

Then might follow a number of familiar talks or essays on:

(1) *The great wars of the Victorian Era*—such as the Russian War, the Indian Mutiny, the Egyptian War, the War of the Soudan, etc.

(2) *The great statesmen of her reign*—Sir Robert Peel, Daniel O'Connell, John Bright, Richard Cobden, the Duke of Wellington, Lord Beaconsfield, Lord Salisbury, W. E. Gladstone, etc.

(3) *The great philosophers and literary men of her reign*—Darwin, Murchison, Sir Humphrey Davy, Sir John Simpson, Wordsworth, Browning, Tennyson, Matthew Arnold, Thomas Carlyle, Ruskin, etc.

(4) *The material and scientific improvements of her reign*—Railroads, steam navigation, gas, electricity, the reaping machine, penny postage, etc.

(5) *The great educational and moral reforms of her reign*—Mechanics' institutes, free libraries, free schools, compulsory education, industrial schools, missionary enterprises, factory laws, limitations of capital punishment, hospitals and charities, etc.

(6) *The progress of Canada during her reign*—The railways and canals built, the telegraph, telephone, free schools, the British North America Act of 1867, the ballot, the opening of the North-west, etc.

An entertainment might be given on the afternoon preceding the Queen's Birthday, to which the parents and friends of the pupils should be invited. In such cases a programme might be prepared as outlined below. This programme may be varied as the judgment of the teacher and the circumstances render necessary.

Programme for Queen's Birthday.

Prayer.

Chorus by the Pupils - "Rule Britannia."

Recitation - Tennyson's "Ode to the Queen."

Address - One Flag, one Empire, one Queen.

Song - - "The Red, White and Blue."

Recitation - "To the Queen"—by Joseph Howe.

Song - - "The Maple Leaf for Ever."

Essay - - The Extent of the British Empire.

Recitation - - - "The Loyal Brigade."

God Save the Queen.

DOMINION DAY.

Every pupil in the schools of Canada should be thoroughly instructed in Canadian history and made fully acquainted with the extent and resources of his own country. The suggestions given with regard to the Queen's birthday apply with even greater force to our national holiday, and no teacher should allow such an occasion to pass without arousing the deepest interest of every pupil in the prosperity of Canada. A Canadian sentiment we must have, if we are to develop the great forces which make for national life. To minimize our status as a people, or to repine at the obstacles which retard our prosperity, or to shrink from the place which our wealth and natural resources entitle us to assume, is to anticipate that obscurity which such a course would deserve and to which it would inevitably lead. The teacher, of all others, has opportunities for preventing such a calamity. Our past history says we need have no fear, politically. Our resources, our native energy and our wealth say we need have no fear, financially. Our system of schools, our universities and colleges, surpassed by no people, say we need have no fear, educationally. And, if these things are properly impressed upon the children attending our schools, an impetus will be given to Canadian patriotism and an intelligent interest will be taken in Canadian affairs which will place the future of the country beyond all doubt.

"They must be free or die
Who speak the language Shakespeare spoke."

The following topics should be considered by the teacher in half-hour-talks with his pupils, for several weeks prior to the first of July:

(1) *Early history of Canada*—Its discovery by Jacques Cartier, in 1535, the explorations and adventures of Champlain, La Salle and Father Henepin, the Indian tribes who occupied the country, the trade carried on with the Indians in furs and the misfortunes or perils through which the early settlers passed in obtaining a foothold in the country.

(2) *Early settlement of Canada*—A familiar talk on the early settlement of Canada, the hardships of emigrants from the British Isles in battling with the forest and in making homes for themselves in the wilderness, their difficulties in providing for their families, a description of the log cabins in which they dwelt and the variety of ways in which they were compelled to obtain subsistence, the kind of roads they travelled, the scarcity of a market for their products, the want of schools and of churches, etc.

(3) *The wars of Canada*—The conquest of Canada in 1759 by General Wolfe, the efforts made by the Americans during the Revolutionary War to capture the country, the war of 1812, Sir Isaac Brock, Queenston Heights, the burning of Toronto, the capture of Detroit, battles of Stony Creek, Chateauguay, Lundy's Lane, Batoche, etc.

(4) *The constitutional development of the country*—The Quebec Act of 1774, the Constitutional Act of 1791 and the meeting of the First Parliament of the Province, the Union Act of 1841, and the British North America Act of 1867.

(5) *The extent of Canada*—Area of the Dominion of Canada, 3,315,647 square miles; length from east to west, 3,500 miles; length from north to south, 1,400 miles. Area of the different Provinces: British Columbia, 382,-300 square miles; Manitoba, 64,066; New Brunswick, 28,100; Nova Scotia, 20,550; Ontario, 219,650; Prince Edward Island, 2,000; Quebec, 227,500; the Territories, 2,371,481; total, 3,315,647 square miles. For purposes of comparison the following figures might be used: Area of United Kingdom of Great Britain and Ireland, 121,481 square miles; British India, 1,068,314; France, 246,000; Italy, 110,623; Russia, 2,095,504; Spain, 194,744; German Empire, 208,738; United States, 3,499,027; Europe, 3,555,000. From these comparisons it will be seen that, geographically, we possess almost as much territory as the United States, nearly thirty times the area of Great Britain and Ireland, fifteen times the area of France or Germany, and only 200,000 square miles less than the whole Continent of Europe.

(6) *Commercial advantages of Canada*—Our eastern seaports looking towards Europe, western seaports looking towards Asia, large rivers affording communication with the interior of the country—the St. Lawrence, together with the lakes it drains, extending inland 2,384 miles, giving access to many of the large cities of Canada and the United States, the advantages of commerce and shipping, extent of our shipping, where and how ships are built. Illustrate from the map.

(7) *The resources of Canada*—The wheat fields of Canada, the fertility of the soil, the productiveness of Manitoba, and the North-west Territories, the ranches at the

foot of the Rocky Mountains, the forests and fisheries of the different Provinces, the mineral wealth of coal, petroleum, gold, silver, lead, iron, nickel, asbestos, plumbago etc., etc., and their location, the exports of each of these, the markets to which they are sent and the amount of money they yield annually. This might also be accompanied with a graphic description of the lives of our fishermen and miners, lumbermen and farmers.

(8) *Our system of Government*—Early Colonial Government of each Province, the Parliament of Canada, how the Governor-General is appointed, the Constitution of the House of Commons, of the Senate, how elections are conducted, vote by ballot, how votes are polled, the Constitution of Provincial Parliaments, the duties of the Speaker and the heads of the various departments, how often elections occur, why Parliaments are required, pictures of distinguished members of Parliament and of the Parliament buildings of Canada, and the Provinces.

(9) *Our Municipal System*—County Councils and how they are elected and what are their functions, Municipal Councils, how elected and their functions, how and why taxes are imposed and the purposes to which they are applied, the duties of Assessor, Collector, Reeve, Warden, Mayor.

(10) *Our Judicial System*—The Supreme Court, the High Court of Justice, County Courts, Division Courts, Justices of the Peace, how judges are appointed, the kind of cases that come before them, the qualifications of Judges, the dignity of the office, the proceedings of a Court of Justice, trial by jury, giving evidence in a court.

(11) *Our Penal System*—Capital punishment, what it means, confinement in a penitentiary, at the Central prison for Ontario or in a county gaol or reformatory, necessity for such restraint, causes which lead to crime,—idleness, disobedience to parents, intemperance, etc.

(12) *Our School System*—Universities, high schools, public schools, industrial schools, kindergartens, how each of these is managed, who are admitted to them and how, qualifications of teachers, progress of our schools, school houses and their equipment, comparison between the past and present, school games, how school trustees, teachers and inspectors are appointed, their qualifications and duties, general benefits of education.

A programme for an entertainment could easily be prepared from the selections that follow.

THE PARLIAMENT OF CANADA.

If the young people of Canada are to be deeply impressed with the growth of our political privileges, the great facts connected with our early history should be placed graphically before them on every opportunity. Canada above all other countries should be uppermost in their thoughts. The heritage of civil and religious liberty which they enjoy and the almost perfect freedom from all disability which is now their happy condition should be pointed out. They should know, however, that this condition was not attained without effort—that freedom does not spring from the earth but that it can only be secured by courage, and often by the sacrifice of personal comfort and even life itself. If Canadians are now permitted to govern themselves, it was not till after many years of strife and contention that they obtained this privilege.

The advantages of the concessions made to the people of Canada should be clearly stated by the teacher, and the political development of the country from military rule, under the articles of capitulation in 1759 down to the priceless privilege of self-government which we now enjoy, duly emphasized. In this interval the most notable legislation was the Quebec Act of 1774, the Constitutional Act of 1791, the Union Act of 1841 and the British North America Act of 1867. Each Province has its own separate Acts of constitutional freedom and these should be specially considered; but as far as possible the minds of the pupils should be directed towards every movement which tended towards the greatest of all events in the history of Canada—the federation of all the Provinces under one Parliament.

Having fixed these points in the memory, the teacher might explain :—

(1) *The Federal System of Government*—One Parliament for Canada to consider Canadian matters; Parliaments for the Provinces to consider Provincial matters. Compare with the British system of government and with the United States system; what questions are within the jurisdiction of each; the importance of many of the questions to be considered.

(2) *The House of Commons*—Organized after the manner of the British House of Commons. The number of its members, the Provinces they represent; where they meet and how often; how elected and for how long; who elects them; why required. The Senate, how appointed and for how long. Description of the Parliament buildings, where situated. Why Ottawa was chosen for the capital.

(3) *The different Departments of the Government*—The Militia Department, its functions. The Post Office Department, rates of postage, how mails are carried, post office savings banks, registered letters, parcel post, mailing letters abroad. Public Works Department; Railways and Canals; Finance Department; Customs, why duties are imposed on imported goods; free goods, where our imports come from, what kind of goods we import, what export; Excise, etc

(4) *The Civil Service*—What it means; examinations for; superannuation; duties of civil servants. Responsibilities of, etc.

THE LEGISLATIVE ASSEMBLY OF ONTARIO.

By the Union Act of 1841 the old Parliament of Upper Canada was absorbed in the united Parliaments of Upper and Lower Canada, and in this form continued till 1867. The leading events of this period should be reviewed by the teacher, prominence being given always to such as extended the privileges of self-government. During this interval our school system was established, the self-governing character of which should be pointed out. Our municipal system had also its origin in the same interval, and it, too, is the ideal of self-government. The settlement of the country advanced rapidly. Upper Canada had become more populous than Lower Canada and wanted a corresponding ratio of influence in the Legislature. To settle differences and to unite the colonies in a confederation where the rights of all were guaranteed by a written constitution, the British North America Act of 1867 was passed. This Act gave to Upper Canada a new name—Ontario, and to Canada a birthday—the first of July. In connection with an historical sketch such as the preceding, the teacher might explain the following terms:—

1. Legislative Assembly, Electoral District, Riding, Election, Ballot, Open Voting, Voters' Lists, Ballot-Box, Polling-Booth, Polling subdivision.

2. The duties of a member of Parliament, returning-officer, deputy returning-officer, election clerk, scrutineer, clerk of the Crown in Chancery.

3. How elections are conducted, nomination of members, electioneering, canvassing, how votes are polled, who are entitled to vote, how election returns are made.

4. How Parliament is opened, the speech by the Lieutenant-Governor, the Speaker of the House and how appointed, the clerk of the House, the journals, the mace, the function of a Government, how business is conducted, Acts of Parliament or statutes, adjournment and prorogation of the House, etc.

The pupils should be encouraged to read the proceedings of Parliament as reported in the newspapers, and to become familiar with the questions on which the electors have to express an opinion at the polls. They should know that the responsibility of citizenship will soon be upon them, and that to discharge this duty intelligently should be the aim of every Canadian. In every term explained, there is bound up the history of heroic struggles for the privilege of self-government. To neglect any duty which under such a term they should discharge is to prove unworthy of the liberty which it represents, and to that extent unworthy of the country to which they belong.

The methods above suggested with regard to the Province of Ontario can be readily adapted by the teacher to the circumstances and history of any of the other Provinces.

THE FIRST PARLIAMENT OF UPPER CANADA.

The teachers should briefly sketch the circumstances which led to the passage of the Constitutional Act of 1791, and the purpose which that Act was intended to serve: namely, to give the people of Upper Canada a voice in the management of their own affairs. The meeting of the first Parliament at Newark in 1792 might then be described with its sixteen representatives appointed by the people, and its eight councillors appointed by the Crown for life. Previous to that time Canada was governed by the laws of England and Orders-in-Council. This first Parliament gave us regularly constituted courts and trial by jury, and abolished negro slavery. The teacher might give a brief sketch of some of the men who were conspicuous in those early times, of the Rebellion of 1837 and its causes, of the Union Act of 1841 which ended the Parliament of Upper Canada and the Act of 1867 which revived it under the name of the Legislative Assembly of Ontario.

In order to add greater interest to the study of the early history of the country, the teacher should explain the ceremony of opening Parliament, and for this purpose might designate pupils to represent the members composing the first Parliament. At the proper time a boy, representing Governor Simcoe, might enter the school room accompanied by his staff composed of boys selected for the purpose. The members of the Assembly and the Cabinet should stand near the dais; the Sergeant-at-arms with the mace and the Speaker should occupy a place to the right. After the Governor was seated his secretary might hand him his address which he would then read, as follows :—

*"Honorable Gentlemen of the Legislative Council and Gentlemen of the House of Assembly :—

"I have summoned you together under the authority of an Act of Parliament of Great Britain passed in the last year, which has established the British Constitution and all the forms which secure and maintain it in this distant country.

"The wisdom and beneficence of Our Most Gracious Sovereign and the British Parliament have been eminently proved, not only in imparting to us the same form of Government but in securing the many provisions which guard this memorable Act, so that the blessings of our invaluable Constitution thus protected and amplified, we hope, will be extended to the remotest posterity.

"The great and momentous trusts and duties which have been committed to the representatives of this Province, in a degree infinitely beyond whatever, till this period, have distinguished any other colony, have originated from the British Nation upon a just consideration of the energy and hazard with which the inhabitants have so conspicuously supported and defended the British Constitution.

* This is an exact copy of the address delivered by Gov. Simcoe at the opening of the first Parliament of Upper Canada and is therefore of historical interest.

"It is from the same patriotism now called upon to exercise, with due deliberation and foresight, by the various offices of the Civil administration, that your fellow subjects of the British Empire expect the foundation of the Union, of industry and wealth, of commerce and power, which may last through all succeeding ages.

"The natural advantages of the Province of Upper Canada are inferior to none on this side of the Atlantic; there can be no separate interest through its whole extent; the British form of Government has prepared the way for its speedy colonization, and I trust that your fostering care will improve the favorable situation, and that a numerous and agricultural people will speedily take possession of a soil and climate, which under the British laws and the munificence with which His Majesty has granted the lands of the Crown, offer such manifest and peculiar encouragements."

At the conclusion of his address the Governor rises, bows to the members of the House and retires.

This exercise can be adapted to any Province by substituting for Gov. Simcoe's address the speech delivered at the opening of the first parliament of the Province concerned.

SIR ISAAC BROCK'S ADDRESS TO THE PARLIAMENT OF UPPER CANADA IN 1812.

The opening of the Parliament of Upper Canada at the special session of 1812 is an event of great historical interest. For some time Canadians were greatly alarmed at the strained relations which existed between the British Government and the American Republic. They felt certain that no matter how promptly troops were sent to their defence, the country would suffer loss, both from incursions on the frontier and from the disturbances of trade. The great odds with which they had to contend were also to be considered. To allow the enemy to ravish the country unopposed would be cowardly in the extreme —to fight required more than ordinary pluck and courage. Fortunately for Canada, a British Officer, who felt himself the custodian of the honor of the British name, was acting Lieutenant-Governor, and, without losing one moment of time, he prepared to meet the enemy as a British soldier should.

His first duty was to summon Parliament and get the approval of the people's representatives for the line of action to be taken. For realizing the importance of this occasion the pupils should be asked to consider the circumstances which led to the declaration of war between Great Britain and the United States. Then might follow a few facts of great interest. Upper Canada had only a population of 75,000 ; Lower Canada 225,000. The population of the United States was about eight millions. The war was entered upon by the Americans with a view to the conquest of Canada, and was conducted along three different lines—in the east by an attack upon Montreal, in the centre by an attack on the Niagara Frontier and in the west by an attack by way of the Detroit Frontier. The Canadian forces consisted of a few battalions of regular troops not exceeding 5,000 in number. The main defence of the country rested upon the Canadian Militia and the loyal Indian tribes under Tecumseh.

General Brock was acting as Lieutenant-Governor in the absence of Lieutenant-Governor Gore. Immediately on the declaration of war, General Brock, who was at Kingston, issued a proclamation calling the members to an extra Session, which met at York on the 27th of July, 1812. His address is a memorable one and worthy of careful study. In order to give it effect it would be well to constitute a meeting of Parliament as was done at the delivery of Governor Simcoe's address, and with appropriate solemnity and ceremony the following speech should be delivered by a pupil representing Sir Isaac Brock:

"Honorable Gentlemen of the Legislative Council, and Gentlemen of the House of Assembly.

"The urgency of the present crisis is the only consideration which could have induced me to call you together at a time when public as well as private duties elsewhere demand your care and attention. But, gentlemen, when invaded by an enemy whose avowed object is the entire conquest of the Province, the voice of loyalty as well as of interest calls aloud to every person in the sphere in which he is placed, to defend his country.

"Our militia have heard that voice, and have obeyed it. They have evinced, by the promptitude and loyalty of their conduct, that they are worthy of the king whom they serve, and of the constitution which they enjoy; and it affords me particular satisfaction that, while I address you as legislators, I speak to men who, in the day of danger, will be ready to assist not only with their counsel but with their arms.

"We look, gentlemen, to our militia as well as to the regular forces for our protection; but I should be wanting to that important trust committed to my care if I attempted to conceal—what experience, the great instructor of mankind, and especially of legislators, has discovered—that amendment is necessary in our militia laws to render them efficient. It is for you to consider what further improvements they still may require.

"Honorable Gentlemen of the Legislative Council, and Gentlemen of the House of Assembly: From the history and experience of our Mother Country, we learn that in times of actual invasion or internal commotion the ordinary course of criminal law has been found inadequate to secure His Majesty's government from private treachery as well as from open disaffection; and that at such times its legislature has found it expedient to enact laws restraining, for a limited period, the liberty of individuals in many cases where it would be dangerous to expose the particulars of the charge; and although the actual invasion of the Province might justify me in the exercise of the full powers reposed in me on such an emergency, yet it will be more agreeable to me to receive the sanction of the two Houses.

"A few traitors have already joined the enemy, have been suffered to come into the country with impunity, and have been harbored and concealed in the interior, yet the general spirit of loyalty which appears to pervade the inhabitants of this Province, is such as to authorize a just expectation that their efforts to mislead and deceive will be unavailing. The disaffected, I am convinced, are few. To protect and defend the loyal inhabitants from their machinations is an object of your most serious deliberation.

"Gentlemen of the House of Assembly: I have directed the Public Accounts of the Province to be laid before you in as complete a state as this unusual period will admit. They will afford you the means of ascertaining to what extent you can aid in providing for the extraordinary demands occasioned by the employment of the militia, and I doubt not but to that extent you will cheerfully contribute.

"Honorable Gentlemen of the Legislative Council, and Gentlemen of the House of Assembly: We are engaged in an awful and eventful contest. By unanimity and dispatch in our councils, and by vigor in our operations, we may teach the enemy this lesson, that a country defended by *free men*, enthusiastically devoted to the cause of their King and Constitution, can never be conquered!"

At the conclusion of Sir Isaac Brock's address, the Speaker should take the Chair and the reply of the Assembly should be moved and seconded in stirring speeches by the pupils. In assisting the pupils in preparing such speeches an excellent opportunity would be afforded the teacher for impressing upon their minds the historical events of the period.

The reply was in the following words :—

"When invaded by an enemy whose avowed object is the entire conquest of this Province, we, laying aside all inferior considerations, do most willingly obey your Honor's commands by appearing in our Legislative capacity, for the purpose of using our utmost efforts for the protection and defence of everything that is dear to us as subjects and as men."

On the adoption of this reply some pupil should move the adjournment of the House.

THE ELECTION OF MUNICIPAL COUNCILLORS.

Next in importance to the election of Members of Parliament is the election of members of the Municipal Councils. To make these lessons on Constitutional Government more practical, the teacher might constitute his pupils into a meeting for the election of a Reeve or Mayor and Councillors for the Municipality. The duties and powers of such officers should be explained to the pupils, and as nearly as may be, the formalities of the Municipal Act complied with.

At the time appointed for the meeting a motion is made and seconded for the election of a Chairman, and a similar motion for the election of a Secretary. Candidates for the various positions are then nominated in short speeches. After the time for receiving nominations has closed, the candidates are called upon to state their views on Municipal matters to the meeting. Speeches for this purpose should be prepared by the boys who are to be candidates, material being easily found in the local questions which interest the people among whom they live, such as the improving of roads, the building of bridges, the appointment of health officers, the enforcement of such by-laws as the Municipal Council may pass, etc. On the conclusion of his speech each candidate signifies his intention of standing the contest or retiring, and proceedings may be varied by allowing one or more candidates to go by acclamation, leaving the contest simply for the chief offices of Mayor or Reeve. At the hour appointed the poll is opened by the returning-officer.

He has placed a table enclosed by a screen in the corner of the school-room so as to secure privacy. On this table there is a lead pencil with which the electors mark their ballots. He has furnished himself with a list of the persons qualified to vote, which in this case would be the pupils, or as many of them as might be considered qualified electors. Beside him is a ballot box. This one of the boys could make at home for the occasion, and should in all respects correspond to the one used in the elections. The ballots should also be written out in the form required by the Municipal Act. Scrutineers for the different candidates should be appointed. A constable should guard the door and keep order. At the time fixed the poll should be closed, the ballot box opened in the presence of the scrutineers and the ballots counted; ballots not properly marked should be rejected. The deputy returning-officer should sum up the votes and declare the result of the election.

In these exercises there is ample room for practice in speaking and in composition. Also, in following the statutory routine, the duties of the different officers concerned in the election are ascertained. As part of the instruction in Municipal Government the teacher should explain :—

1. What is meant by township, county, village, town, city, by-law, voter, debentures, minutes of meetings, corporation.

2. What are the duties of councillor, reeve, deputy-reeve, clerk, warden, mayor, constable, assessor, collector returning-officer, deputy-returning-officer, auditor, pound-keeper, fence-viewer, road commissioner, etc.

3. How taxes are levied, for what purpose they are levied, by whom they are collected, where deposited when collected, how they are paid out.

4. Who are voters in municipal elections; the legal age of voters; qualifications of voters; where votes are polled; who receives the votes; the mode of voting; illegal voting; a freeholder; a householder; an income voter; a farmer's son; blind or illiterate voters.

5. By-laws, how passed; for what purpose passed; raising money by debentures; for what purpose debentures are issued; by-laws regarding public morals; nuisances; cruelty to animals.

A very useful exercise in composition in connection with the points above mentioned for advanced pupils would be drawing up a by-law, or a notice calling a public meeting, or a petition to a municipal council asking for some amendments to a municipal by-law, or a resolution to a public meeting setting forth some grievance, or a letter to a reeve calling his attention to some nuisance, and so on. In all these cases attention should be paid to the form as well as to the matter of the composition.

PUBLIC SCHOOL ANNUAL MEETING.

For the purpose of illustrating a Public School Annual Meeting, the teacher may allow all pupils of a suitable age, both boys and girls, to consider themselves ratepayers within the meaning of the School Act. The Annual School Meeting is held in Ontario on the last Wednesday of December, at the hour of 10 o'clock in the forenoon. At the hour named a boy rises in his place and says:—

"Ladies and Gentlemen: I move that Mr. A. B. be appointed chairman of this meeting." Another boy immediately rises and says: "I beg leave to second that motion." If desired a third boy might be directed to rise in his place and say: "Ladies and Gentlemen: I beg leave to move as an amendment to the motion that Mr. B. C. be appointed chairman." This motion should also be seconded. If there are no other nominations the first boy rises and addresses the meeting as follows:—

"Moved by myself, seconded by Mr. ——, that Mr. A. B. be chairman, to which it is moved in amendment by Mr. ——, seconded by Mr. ——, that Mr. B. C. be chairman. I shall put the amendment first. All in favor of the amendment signify the same by the uplifted hand. (The votes are counted.) All opposed to the amendment will signify the same by the uplifted hand. (The votes are counted.) I declare the amendment lost." He then puts the original motion in the same way, declares Mr. A. B. elected; Mr. A. B. then takes the chair, and in a few remarks thanks the electors for the honor conferred upon him, and then asks them to appoint a secretary of the meeting. This is done by the ratepayers on motion in the same way as the chairman was appointed. The secretary takes his place at the teacher's desk and enters the minutes of the meeting.

The first business is to receive the annual report of the trustees. This report should contain a statement of the receipts and expenditure of the school section of the previous year, the form of which will be found in the Public School Register.

In addition to this the trustees may report on any matter affecting the school they desire. For instance, they may speak of the laying out of the school-grounds, the planting of trees, the repairs of the school-house in a general way, the necessity for a new school-house, the change of teacher, the progress of the school as ascertained by their own personal visits, the remarks made by the Inspector in his reports, the success of the pupils at examinations, etc., etc. When the report is read, it would be in order for any boy to rise and move the adoption of the report, and in doing so he might address the meeting as follows :—

Mr. Chairman and fellow-ratepayers: In moving the adoption of the report of the trustees it gives me great pleasure to notice the efficient manner in which they have discharged their duties during the past year. I can well remember the time when the trustees of this section, regardless of the comfort and convenience of our children, refused to expend a single dollar on necessary improvements on the schoolhouse and school-grounds. No longer than three years ago our children sat in a dingy house that for years had not been whitewashed, with here and there a broken window, in front of them a miserable, faded, little blackboard, and on the walls maps in bad repair, and worse still, twenty years behind the times. We all remember, too, the rusty stove with its jammed and broken pipes ready to tumble down on a moment's notice. We remember that the only chair in the school room was that which the teacher was supposed to occupy, and which from age and length of service had completely broken down. What was true of the inside of the school-room was equally true of its surroundings. The fence appeared as if struck by a cyclone; the gate swung on one hinge; the grounds without a shade tree; the fire-wood unprotected from the weather and scattered over the school-yard. Now all this is changed. Look at these finely-tinted walls and see if what I say is not true. Look at the blackboard, at the map, at the desk, at the teacher's chair and the chairs for visitors, and the globes, pointers, brushes and all other necessary equipment of the school and tell me if our Board of Trustees is not worthy of our confidence as well as of our sincere thanks. As one of the largest ratepayers of the section, I am delighted in having the pleasure of moving the adoption of this report, which I hope will pass unanimously."

On the conclusion of this speech another boy arises and says: Mr. Chairman and fellow-electors: It gives me much pleasure to second the motion just made by Mr. ——. I agree with the commendations given the Board of School Trustees. I believe every dollar expended by them has been a good investment. Not only have they made the schoolhouse comfortable, but they have in addition provided us with an excellent teacher, and by their frequent visits to the school-room have encouraged her to see that the school is kept properly ventilated, regularly swept and dusted by the caretaker and made comfortable for our children. A few years ago I had great difficulty in sending my children regularly to school, particularly in winter. Frequently in the mornings the fires were not made in time, and it was not until 10 o'clock that the schoolhouse was comfortable enough for them to settle down to their studies. I was told, too, that the school was sometimes so filled with dust in the morning because it was not swept out in time, that children could scarcely enter the door. The trustees never called to see whether any attention was paid to the ventilation; the snow was allowed to drift in heaps around the door, and no tracks were made to the closets; and then between the cold draughts at times and the excessive heat my children were troubled with colds and headaches and my doctor's bills would be three times the increased taxation of the last year. I am greatly pleased that all this has been remedied and that the trustees have so satisfactorily discharged their duties, and, with the permission of the mover, I desire to add the following words to the resolution: "and that the thanks of this meeting be tendered to the Board of Trustees for their efficient services during the past year."

The mover of the resolution rises and consents to this addition. The question is then put by the chairman: Moved by Mr. ——, seconded by Mr. ——, that the report of the trustees be adopted and that the thanks of this meeting be tendered them for the very efficient manner in which they discharged their duties during the past year. Shall the question be now put? A boy rises in the meeting and says:

"Mr. Chairman,—Before the question is put I desire to make a few observations. I do not propose to move an amendment to the motion so ably moved and seconded by the two gentlemen who preceded me, but I desire to say that although on the whole I like the way the school is managed and I have no fault to find with the teacher, I think the trustees have gone a little too fast. (No, no.) When I was a boy we had to go to school two or three miles—a great part of it through the woods. We had a log school house with an old-fashioned fireplace, long forms and desks against the walls; there were no chairs for visitors, and even the teacher had nothing better than a three-legged stool to sit upon. We were not required to spend any money on maps and blackboards and such fixings as appear to be required now, and yet we thought we got on pretty well. (Oh! oh!) We had our reading lessons and arithmetic and our geography, with plenty of flogging into the bargain. (You deserved it, too.) Now, although I like to see my children comfortable, still I think it costs us too much, and I would like to say to the trustees and to my fellow-ratepayers that a little old-fashioned economy would not come at all amiss these hard times. I may be an old fogy (so you are), but when taxes have to be paid I would like the trustees to remember that the old fogy's purse would like to be treated with greater consideration."

Other speeches might be made in answer to this showing that in school matters it is necessary to keep up with the times, and that the comforts which the ratepayers enjoy in their homes should be represented as far as possible in the school room, and that in either case these comforts cost something. The teacher might assist in the preparation of such additional speeches as might be considered necessary. When the speaking appears to be over the boys might call "Question, question." The chairman then rises and puts the motion, which is unanimously adopted. The Chairman of the Board of Trustees might then respond, acknowledging in suitable terms the vote of thanks tendered them by the meeting.

The Chairman then announces that the next order of business will be receiving the Annual Report of the Auditors of the School Section. That report might be as follows:

The undersigned Auditors of School Section No. — in the Township of ——— report that they have examined the books and vouchers and have found the same correct. The receipts for the year amounted to $526.82, and the expenditure to $480.30, leaving a balance in the treasury for next year of $46.52.

All of which is respectfully submitted.

(Signed) A. B., B. C., } Auditors.

Dated this 22nd day of December, 1893.

On the presentation of this report its adoption is moved and seconded and submitted to the meeting.

The chairman then announces that the next order of business will be the electing of an auditor for next year. This may be disposed of by a motion as in the appointment of a chairman. Miscellaneous business is now called for. Here an opportunity may be taken of instructing the trustees to make any needed improvements, such as the repair of the schoolhouse, obtaining a proper water supply, making arrangements for Arbor Day or Dominion Day, purchasing maps and globes, supplying the school with new furniture or whatever in the opinion of the meeting is most urgent.

The last order of business is the election of a school trustee. At this stage the Chairman announces that he is ready to receive nominations to fill the vacancy on the Board of Trustees occasioned by the retirement of Mr. A. B., who has served his full time of three years.. The teacher may arrange that the election shall be by show of hands as between the different candidates, or that a poll shall be taken. If a poll is taken the formalities of the Act should be followed out. When a ratepayer offers to vote, objection could be taken to him on account of his age, or that he was a non-resident, or that his name was not entered on the Assessment Roll. The time for closing the polls might be limited to twenty minutes, and when the result was declared, the trustee elected might be called upon for a speech.

Before the meeting was closed the Secretary should read the minutes. These minutes should be approved and then signed by the Secretary to be transmitted to the Inspector. With a little ingenuity on the part of the teacher and instruction beforehand, the proceedings of a mock school meeting could be made very instructive as an exercise in speaking and composition, and also as a real transaction of business.

The School Act of the Province to which this model exercise in civics is adapted should be strictly followed and its provisions regarding the statutory times and methods impressed upon the pupils.

MEETING OF A BOARD OF TRUSTEES FOR THE APPOINTMENT OF A TEACHER.

Three boys representing the trustees of a rural school section should enter the school-room, and after saluting each other pleasantly should seat themselves at a table, on which the secretary of the board places the minute book.

The chairman takes the chair and calls upon the secretary to read the minutes of the previous meeting. This the secretary does, giving from the minute book the various items of business transacted. The chairman then asks "Are the Minutes approved?" If no objection is made he signs the minute book and then announces that this meeting of the Board of Trustees was called for the purpose of appointing a teacher for the following year; that pursuant to instructions the secretary of the meeting advertised for a teacher, and that several applications have been received which they are now asked to consider, as follows:—

Application Number 1.—Male teacher, 25 years of age, 5 years' experience, holds a Second Class Certificate from Toronto Normal School, is recommended by several clergymen, the trustees of his former school, and asks to be engaged at a salary of $500.

Application Number 2.—Male teacher, 20 years of age, 1 year's experience, holds a Third Class Certificate, has several recommendations, salary $400.

Application Number 3.—Male teacher, age not mentioned, holds an extended Third Class Certificate, 15 years' experience, made personal application, salary $25 per month.

The chairman asks the secretary if these are all the applications, to which the secretary answers, they are. He then asks, what is your pleasure, gentlemen? Mr. Trustee Brown says:—

"I must confess that I like Application No. 1 very much. The applicant, judging from his age and standing, would, no doubt, make a very desirable teacher. He has taken a course at the County Model School and also at the Normal School, and there is much to be said in his favor on that account. I see also from his application that he has had his experience, or the greater part of it, in two schools, and this shows that his former trustees were reasonably well satisfied with him, but I see that he asks a very large salary. Now, we have not been accustomed to pay so large a salary in this section, and I am afraid the ratepayers would object to the payment of so much money for a teacher. Indeed, I cannot understand how a man can ask so large a salary to teach six hours a day when we consider the many holidays he has in the year and the comfortable, easy time he would have in our new school house with an average attendance of only 52. It seems to me, although I like this application very much, a man equally good could be obtained for $400. Perhaps he attaches some value to his Second Class Certificate. I cannot see that there is much in this, because we have had third class teachers who taught our school very well, and as our children are not very far advanced I think a third class teacher would serve every purpose. A good school is a very nice thing to have, but we must not pay too much for it. What do you think, Mr. Smith?" (Referring to his co-trustee.)

Mr. SMITH.—"Well, if you ask me, I think it is of the first importance to get the best teacher in the market. You see our children are growing up very fast. In a few years the large boys and girls will leave school, and if they are to have any education at all they must have it right away. Some of us cannot afford to send our children to a High School, and even if we could, unless a good foundation is laid in the Public School, much time will afterwards be lost in doing the work over again. Besides, a good teacher has a great deal of influence in forming the character of boys and girls. He can keep better order for one thing, and that is of great importance; then his work in the school-room is substantial and thorough, and this leads to the formation of habits which cling to pupils all their lives. I have seen teachers who knew a good deal, but who had no power of inspiring their pupils to love their studies, or to read outside of school hours, or to devote their spare moments to self improvement. Now, take the case of Application No. 3. There is a man who has wandered around a good deal, who has lost confidence in himself, apparently, for he is prepared to take a very low salary and has come to us almost as much as to plead with us to give him employment. I would be very much afraid to engage such a man because he knows that unless he holds himself cheap we would have no inducement to employ him at all. A cheap teacher is the worst investment we could make; even a cheap pair of boots, as a rule, does not pay, but perhaps the chairman has thought this matter over more carefully than any of us. I would like to hear what he has to say."

The CHAIRMAN.—" I have been chairman of this board now for twenty-two years, and the most of my children have been educated in this school. I have seen all sorts of teachers here, male and female, in my time, some at a salary of $20 a month and some at the salary of $40 a month. Sometimes a cheap teacher with a low certificate did pretty well. You know young men and women have to begin sometime, and in starting out in life they have to be contented with lower wages. In fact, it is right, perhaps, because it costs a teacher something to get experience, and until he has got it his services are not worth as much. If all the applications before us were from young teachers without experience, I would not care so much about the question of salary, although, as a rule, I like a person to place a fair value upon his services. I think it shows that he believes there is something in him, and he should be paid for giving it to those who employ him. The applicants we are considering, however, are all men of experience, and, strange to say, the man with the most experience is willing to take the lowest salary! Now, this to my mind is a very suspicious circumstance, and if I had my way I would rule out his application because he has condemned himself, first, by the estimate he has put on himself, and, secondly, because he thought it necessary to come round and canvass us for our support. I do not like teachers to canvass for a position. As to the other applicants, although they have experience, and although I do not despise their qualifications, still I believe the more enterprise a man has the better for others as well as himself. Applicant No. 1 has only taught five years and yet has been at the Normal School; he has shown an anxiety to fit himself for high class work. Now, should we not encourage this? What will $100 amount to a rich section like ours? It is scarcely $2 extra for every child attending school on the average attendance, or little more than $1 per child according to the number on the register. Now, do you think, even if times are hard, that the people of this section will object to an extra dollar for each child when they consider how much a well-trained teacher can do for them? I do not think they will. The closest man in the section, that I know of, is neighbor Jones; he has three big boys at school. I know if I could only see him for five minutes that I could convince him that there is no way he could spend $3 to better advantage than in paying for a good teacher for these boys. They are bright boys, and with proper education they will make bright men, and I know he thinks so, close as he is. My voice will be in favor of application No. 1."

Trustee BROWN.—"Well, I think there is a good deal in what our chairman says. I have two boys at school myself; the younger is fourteen years of age. I cannot send them to a High School, and I cannot buy a farm for them; they will have to learn a trade or become teachers themselves. You know I have a pretty large family and the older ones must make their way in the world, and a good education is perhaps all I can give them. Although a dollar is hard to make these times, still if I were buying a colt and wanted him I would not stick at a dollar or two in the price. I think after all, although I was afraid that the ratepayers would object to the payment of $500 for a teacher, I must agree with the chairman and vote for application No. 1."

The CHAIRMAN.—" If you are all agreed, I shall notify the applicant and ask him to meet us at a certain time and we will sign the agreement required by law. Will you make a minute of this, Mr. Secretary, in the book, that there may be no doubt as to the action taken.

" There being no other business, I declare the meeting adjourned until the 22nd day of December for the purpose of signing the agreement with the teacher." (Meeting adjourned.)

PART II.

CANADIAN PATRIOTISM.

PART II.

CANADIAN PATRIOTISM.

PRAYER.

O LORD our Heavenly Father, High and Mighty, King of Kings, Lord of Lords, the only Ruler of Princes, who dost from Thy Throne behold all the dwellers upon earth; Most heartily we beseech thee with Thy favor to behold our most gracious Sovereign Lady Queen Victoria, and so replenish her with the grace of Thy Holy Spirit that she may always incline to Thy will and walk in Thy way. Endue her plenteously with heavenly gifts; grant her in health and wealth long to live; strengthen her that she may vanquish and overcome all her enemies; and finally, after this life, may attain everlasting joy and felicity, through Jesus Christ our Lord.—Amen.

Almighty God, the Fountain of all Goodness, we humbly beseech Thee to bless Albert Edward, Prince of Wales, the Princess of Wales, and all the Royal Family. Endue them with Thy Holy Spirit; enrich them with Thy Heavenly Grace; prosper them with all happiness; and bring them to Thine everlasting Kingdom, through Jesus Christ our Lord.—Amen.

Most Gracious God, we humbly beseech Thee, as for the United Kingdom of Great Britain and Ireland, and Her Majesty's Dominions in general, so especially for this Dominion, and herein more particularly for the Governor-

General, the Senate, and the House of Commons, in their legislative capacity at this time assembled; that Thou wouldst be pleased to direct and prosper all their consultations, to the advancement of Thy glory, the safety, honor, and welfare of our Sovereign and her Dominion of Canada, that all things may be so ordered and settled by their endeavors, upon the best and surest foundations, that peace and happiness, truth and justice, religion and piety, may be established among us for all generations. These, and all other necessaries for them, and for us, we humbly beg in the name, and through the mediation of Jesus Christ, our Most blessed Lord and Saviour.—Amen.

Our Father which art in Heaven, Hallowed be Thy name. Thy Kingdom come. Thy will be done in earth, as it is in Heaven. Give us this day our daily bread. And forgive us our trespasses, as we forgive them who trespass against us. And lead us not into temptation; but deliver us from evil.—Amen.

NOTE.—The above is the form of prayer used at the opening of the Sessions of the House of Commons, and with slight changes also at the opening of the Sessions of the Legislative Assembly of Ontario. It would be very suitable for the opening of a Queen's Birthday or Dominion Day entertainment.

THE QUEEN.

Queen of the thousand isles! whose fragile form,
'Midst the proud structures of our Father Land,
Graces the Throne, that each subsiding storm
Which shakes the earth, assures us yet shall stand.
Thy gentle voice, of mild yet firm command,
Is heard in every clime; on every wave,
Thy dazzling sceptre, like a fairy wand,
Strikes off the shackles from the struggling slave,
And gathers, 'neath its rule, the great, the wise, the brave.

But yet, 'midst all the treasures that surround
Thy royal halls, one bliss is still denied,—
To know the true hearts at thy name that bound,
Which ocean from thy presence must divide,
Whose voices never swell the boisterous tide
Of hourly homage that salutes thy ear;
But yet who cherish with a Briton's pride,
And breathe to infant lips, from year to year,
The name thy many virtues taught them to revere.

How little deem'st thou of the scenes remote,
In which one word, all other words above,
Of earthly homage seems to gaily float
On every breeze, and sound through every grove—
A spell to cheer, to animate, to move—
To bid old age throw off the weight of years,
To cherish thoughts of loyalty and love,
To garner round the heart those hopes and fears
Which, in our western homes, Victoria's name endears.

'Tis not that, on our soil, the measured tread
Of armed legions speaks thy sovereign sway,
'Tis not the huge leviathans that spread
Thy meteor flag above each noble bay,
That bids the soul a forced obedience pay!
—The despot's tribute from a trembling thrall—
No! At our altars sturdy freemen pray
That blessings on Victoria's head may fall,
And happy household groups each pleasing trait recall.

JOSEPH HOWE.

AN ODE TO CANADA.

Awake, my country, the hour is great with change!
  Under this gloom which yet obscures the land,
From ice-blue strait and stern Laurentian range
  To where giant peaks our western bounds command,
A deep voice stirs, vibrating in men's ears
  As if their own hearts throbbed that thunder forth,
A sound wherein who hearkens wisely hears
  The voice of the desire of this strong North —
    This North whose heart of fire
    Yet knows not its desire
  Clearly, but dreams, and murmurs in the dream.
The hour of dreams is done. Lo, on the hills the gleam!

Awake, my country, the hour of dreams is done!
  Doubt not, nor dread the greatness of thy fate.
Tho' faint souls fear the keen, confronting sun,
  And fain would bid the morn of splendor wait;
Tho' dreamers, rapt in starry visions, cry,
  "Lo, yon thy future, yon thy faith, thy fame!"
And stretch vain hands to stars, thy fame is nigh,
  Here in Canadian hearth, and home, and name;
    This name which yet shall grow
    Till all the nations know
  Us for a patriot-people, heart and hand,
Loyal to our native earth,—our own Canadian land!

O strong hearts, guarding the birthright of our glory,
  Worth your best blood this heritage that ye guard!
Those mighty streams resplendent with our story,
  These iron coasts by rage of seas unjarred,—
What fields of peace these bulwarks will secure!
  What vales of plenty those calm floods supply!
Shall not our love this rough, sweet land make sure,
  Her bounds preserve inviolate, though we die?
    O strong hearts of the North,
    Let flame your loyalty forth,
  And put the craven and base to an open shame,
Till earth shall know the Child of Nations by her name!

CHARLES G. D. ROBERTS.

DOMINION DAY.

With loud huzzas and merry bells, and cannon's thundering peal,
And pennons fluttering on the breeze, and serried rows of steel,
We greet, again, the birthday morn of our young giant's land,
From the Atlantic stretching wide to far Pacific strand ;
With flashing rivers, ocean lakes, and prairies wide and free,
And waterfalls and forests dim, and mountains by the sea ;
A country on whose birth-hour smiled the genius of romance,
Above whose cradle brave hands waved the lily-cross of France ;
Whose infancy was grimly nursed in peril. pain, and woe ;
Whose gallant hearts found early graves beneath Canadian snow ;
When savage raid and ambuscade and famine's sore distress,
Combined their strength, in vain, to crush the dauntless French noblesse ;
When her dim, trackless forest lured, again and yet again,
From silken court of sunny France, her flower, the brave Champlain.
And now, her proud traditions boast four blazoned rolls of fame,—
Crecy's and Flodden's deadly foes our ancestors we claim ;
Past feud and battle buried far behind the peaceful years,
While Gaul and Celt and Briton turn to pruning-hooks their spears ;
Four nations welded into one,—with long historic past,
Have found in these our western wilds, one common life, at last ;
Through the young giant's mighty limbs, that stretch from sea to sea,
There runs a throb of conscious life—of waking energy.
From Nova Scotia's misty coast to far Columbia's shore,
She wakes,—a band of scattered homes and colonies no more,
But a young nation, with her life full beating in her breast,
A noble future in her eyes—the Britain of the West.

Hers be the noble task to fill the yet untrodden plains
With fruitful, many-sided life that courses through her veins ;
The English honor, nerve and pluck,—the Scotsman's love of right,—
The grace and courtesy of France,—the Irish fancy bright,—
The Saxon's faithful love of home, and home's affection blest ;
And, chief of all, our holy faith,—of all our treasures best.

A people poor in pomp and state, but rich in noble deeds,
Holding that righteousness exalts the people that it leads;
As yet the waxen mould is soft, the opening page is fair;
It rests with those who rule us now, to leave their impress there,—
The stamp of true nobility, high honor, stainless truth;
The earnest quest of noble ends; the generous heart of youth;
The love of country, soaring far above dull party strife;
The love of learning, art, and song,—the crowning grace of life;
The love of science, soaring far through Nature's hidden ways;
The love and fear of Nature's God,—a nation's highest praise.

So, in the long hereafter, this Canada shall be
The worthy heir of British power and British liberty;
Spreading the blessings of her sway to her remotest bounds,
While, with the fame of her fair name, a continent resounds.
True to her high traditions, to Britain's ancient glory
Of patient saint and martyr, alive in deathless story;
Strong in their liberty and truth, to shed from shore to shore
A light among the nations, till nations are no more.

AGNES MAULE MACHAR (Fidelis).

HURRAH FOR THE NEW DOMINION.

Let others raise the song, in praise
Of lands renown'd in story ;
The land for me, of the maple tree,
And the pine, in all his glory !

Hurrah ! for the grand old forest land,
Where Freedom spreads her pinion ;
Hurrah ! with me, for the maple tree,
Hurrah ! for the New Dominion !

Be her's the light, and her's the might,
Which Liberty engenders ;
Sons of the free, come join with me—
Hurrah ! for her defenders.

And be their fame in loud acclaim—
In grateful songs ascending ;
The fame of those, who met her foes,
And died, her soil defending.

Hurrah ! for the grand old forest land
Where freedom spreads her pinion ;
Hurrah ! with me, for the maple tree,
Hurrah ! for the New Dominion !

A. McLachlan.

THIS CANADA OF OURS.

We have made us a Dominion
  In this region of the west;
And this Canada of ours
  Is the land we love the best;
For our homes are halls of plenty,
  We have peace on every hand,
And our people are as noble
  As the lords of any land.

We have many little Edens
  Scattered up and down our dales;
We've a hundred pretty hamlets
  Nestling in our peaceful vales.
Here the sunlight loves to linger,
  And the summer winds to blow;
Here the rosy spring in April
  Leapeth laughing from the snow.

We have springs of healing waters;
  We have everduring rills
That encircle in their journey
  Half a thousand happy hills,
Tell the oppressed of every nation—
  Him that digs and him that delves—
If they'll cast their lot among us
  We will make them like ourselves.

For the west shall be a garden,
  And its glories be unfurled,
Till its beauty is a by-word
  With the peoples of the world;
And the east shall bring us shipping
  That shall whiten every sea;
And the boast of this Dominion
  Shall be British liberty.

And if foes too strong oppress us,
  On a little island shore
Dwells a lion that can shield us
  By the terror of his roar.
For its flag that rules the ocean
  Is the monarch of the shore—
It has braved a thousand battles,
  And can brave a thousand more.

'Neath its folds, in silent sorrow,
  We will wrap our fallen brave,
But we'll wave it high in triumph
  Over every coward's grave ;
Till in spite of foe and traitor
  By the world it shall be seen
That we pride in our Dominion,
  Love old England and her Queen.

And our fathers up in heaven,
  In the leal-land far away,
Looking down with pride upon us
  To each other there shall say :
" These our children emulate us,
  Tread the righteous path we trod,
Live in peace and honest plenty,
  Love their country and their God."

G. W. Johnson.

CANADA TO THE LAUREATE.

"And the true North, whereof we lately heard
A strain to shame us! Keep you to yourselves,
So loyal is so costly! Friends, your love
Is but a burden: loose the bond and go,
Is this the tone of Empire?"

—Tennyson's Ode to the Queen.

We thank thee, Laureate, for thy kindly words
Spoken for us to her to whom we look
With loyal love, across the misty sea;
Thy noble words, whose generous tone may shame
The cold and heartless strain that said "Begone;
We want your love no longer; all our aim
Is riches—*that* your love can *not* increase."
Fain would we tell them that we do not seek
To hang dependent, like a helpless brood
That, selfish, drag a weary mother down;
For we have British hearts and British blood
That leap up, eager, when the danger calls.
Once and again, our sons have sprung to arms
To fight in Britain's quarrel—*not our own*,—
And drive the covetous invader back,
Who would have let us, peaceful, keep our own,
So we had cast the British name away.
Canadian blood has dyed Canadian soil,
For Britain's honor, that we deemed our own,
Nor do we ask but for the right to keep
Unbroken, still, the cherished filial tie
That binds us to the distant sea-girt isle
Our fathers loved, and taught their sons to love,
As the dear home of freemen, brave and true,
And loving *honor* more than ease or gold.

Well do we love our own Canadian land,
Its breezy lakes, its rivers sweeping wide
Past stately towns and peaceful villages,
And banks, begirt with forests, to the sea;
Its tranquil homesteads and its lonely woods,
Where sighs the summer breeze through pine and fern!
But well we love, too, Britain's daisied meads,
Her primrose-bordered lanes, her hedgerows sweet,
Her purple mountains and her heathery braes,
Her towers and ruins, ivy-crowned and grey,
Glistening with song and story as with dew;
Dear to our childhood's dreaming fancy, since
We heard of them from those whose hearts were sore
For home and country left, and left for aye,
That they might found, in these our western wilds,
New Britains, not unworthy of the old!
We hope to *live* a history of our own,
One worthy of the lineage that we claim;
Yet, as our past is but of yesterday,
We claim as ours, too, that grand emblazoned roll
Of golden deeds that bind, with golden links,
The long dim centuries since King Arthur "passed."

AGNES MAULE MACHAR (Fidelis).

OUR CANADIAN DOMINION

Fair land of peace ! to Britain's rule and throne
Adherent still, yet happier than alone,
And free as happy, and as brave as free,
Proud are thy children,—justly proud, of thee ;—
Thou hast no streams renowned in classic lore,
No vales where fable heroes moved of yore,
No hills where Poesy enraptured stood,
No mythic fountains, no enchanted wood ;
But unadorned, rough, cold, and often stern,
The careless eye to other lands might turn,
And seek, where nature's bloom is more intense,
Softer delights to charm the eye of sense.

We cannot boast those skies of milder ray,
'Neath which the orange mellows day by day ;
Where the Magnolia spreads her snowy flowers,
And Nature revels in perennial bowers ;—
Here, Winter holds his long and solemn reign,
And madly sweeps the desolated plain ;—
But Health and Vigor hail the wintry strife,
With all the buoyant glow of happy life ;
And by the blazing chimney's cheerful hearth,
Smile at the blast 'mid songs and household mirth.

But we who know thee proudly point the hand
Where thy broad rivers roll serenely grand—
Where, in still beauty 'neath our northern sky,
Thy lordly lakes in solemn grandeur lie—
Where old Niagara's awful voice has given
The floods' deep anthem to the ear of heaven—
Through the long ages of the vanished past ;
Through Summer's bloom and Winter's angry blast,—
Nature's proud utterance of unwearied song,
Now, as at first, majestic, solemn, strong,

And ne'er to fail, till the archangel's cry
Shall still the million tones of earth and sky,
And send the shout to ocean's farthest shore :—
"Be hushed ye voices ! —time shall be no more !"

Here, Freedom looks o'er all these broad domains,
And hears no heavy clank of servile chains ;
Here man, no matter what his color be,
Can stand erect, and proudly say, "I'M FREE !"—
No crouching slaves cower in our busy marts,
With straining eyes and anguish-riven hearts.

The beam that gilds alike the palace walls
And lowly hut, with genial radiance falls
On peer and peasant,—and the humblest here
Walks in the sunshine, free as is the peer.
Proudly he stands with muscle strong and free,
The serf—the slave of no man doomed to be.
His own, the arm the heavy axe that wields ;
His own, the hands that till the summer fields ;
His own, the babes that prattle in the door ;
His own, the wife that treads the cottage floor ;
All the sweet ties of life to him are sure ;
All the proud rights of MANHOOD are secure.

Blest land of peace !—O may'st thou ever be
Even as now the land of LIBERTY !
Treading serenely thy bright upward road,
Honored of nations, and approved of God !
On thy fair front emblazoned clear and bright—
FREEDOM, FRATERNITY, AND EQUAL RIGHT !

Miss VINING.

GOD BLESS CANADA.

God bless our noble Canada !
  God bless the new Dominion !
Where law and liberty have sway,
Not one of all her sons, to-day,
  Is tyrant's serf, or minion.

Give joy a tongue, let peaceful mirth
  Dispel desponding fears—
We hail a youthful nation's birth,
Who, in the wondering eyes of Earth,
  Takes rank among her peers.

Fling out our banner to the breeze,
  And proudly greet the world
With words of amity and peace,
For never on more hopeful seas
  Was Freedom's flag unfurled.

We boast no charms of high degree
  In titles, rank, or blood—
No tales of knightly chivalry—
Long lines of lordly ancestry—
  Nor haunted stream or wood.

No proud historic names have we,
  Whose memory thrills the heart—
No scenes embalmed by Poesie—
No hoary castles grand to see—
  The pride of ancient art.

But though the Past has records few,
  In battle, song, or story,
The Future rises, fair to view,
Gleaming with morning's youthful dew,
  And bright with coming glory

O fair and fertile Canada!
 Where thought and speech are free,
Where'er my roaming feet may stray—
Whatever fate may come—I pray
 That God may shelter thee.

I love thy forests wet with dew,
 Where still the Red Men rove—
Thy trees, thy flowers of varied hue,
I love thy glorious lakes, as blue
 And vast as heaven above.

I love thy green and towering hills—
 Thy valleys rich and fair,
Where wealth in pearly dew distils—
Thy cool meandering forests rills,
 Hid from the Summer's glare.

I love thy rivers, broad and free—
 Thy cataracts sublime,
Where God unveils his majesty—
Whose hymns make grandest melody,
 That strikes the ear of Time.

I love thy homes, whose light retains
 Brave sons and daughters fair,
Where Liberty with Truth remains,
And every loyal heart disdains
 A servile yoke to wear.

And all that England boasts, we claim
 By right which none denies—
Her valor and undying fame—
Each noble deed and kingly name,
 That o'er oblivion rise.

The rich inheritance of thought,
 Which golden fruitage bears—
Achievements hero-hearts have wrought—
Freedom by bloody battles bought—
 Are ours as well as theirs.

Our fathers fought on gory plains,
  To vanquish Albion's foes :
And though between us ocean reigns,
We are no aliens—in our veins
  The blood of Britain flows.

If ever foeman's hostile tread
  Pollutes our sacred strand,
Our enemies will learn with dread,
How freely shall our blood be shed
  To guard our native land.

E. H. Dewart, D.D.

OUR BEAUTIFUL LAND.

What land more beautiful than ours?
What other land more blest?
The South with all its wealth of flowers?
The prairies of the West?

O no! there's not a fairer land
Beneath heaven's azure dome—
Where Peace holds Plenty by the hand,
And Freedom finds a home.

The slave who but her name hath heard,
Repeats it day and night;—
And envies every little bird
That takes its northward flight!

As to the Polar star they turn
Who brave a pathless sea,—
So the oppressed in secret yearn,
Dear native land for thee!

How many loving memories throng
Round Britain's stormy coast!
Renowned in story and in song,
Her glory is our boast!

With loyal hearts we still abide
Beneath her sheltering wing;—
While with true patriot love and pride
To Canada we cling!

We wear no haughty tyrant's chain,—
We bend no servile knee,
When to the mistress of the main
We pledge our fealty.

She binds us with the cords of love,—
All others we disown;
The rights we owe to God above
We yield to Him alone.

May He our future course direct
By His unerring hand;
Our laws and liberties protect,
And bless our native land!

HELEN M. JOHNSON.

HERE'S TO THE LAND.

Here's to the land of the rock and the pine ;
    Here's to the land of the raft and the river !
Here's to the land where the sunbeams shine,
    And the night that is bright with the North-light's quiver !

Here's to the land of the axe and the hoe !
    Here's to the stalwarts that give them their glory ;—
With stroke upon stroke, and with blow upon blow,
    The might of the forest has passed into story !

Here's to the land with its blanket of snow ;—
    To the hero and hunter the welcomest pillow !
Here's to the land where the stormy winds blow
    Three days, ere the mountains can talk to the billow !

Here's to the buckwheats that smoke on her board !
    Here's to the maple that sweetens their story ;
Here's to the scythe that we swing like a sword,
    And here's to the fields where we gather our glory !

Here's to her hills of the moose and the deer ;
    Here's to her forests, her fields and her flowers !
Here's to her homes of unchangeable cheer,
    And the maid 'neath the shade of her own native bowers !

WILLIAM WYE SMITH.

THE MAPLE AND SHAMROCK.

Let's sing of the Maple, the broad, gen'rous Maple,
A type of our country, fair, lovely and free,
And with it entwine in couplets the Shamrock,
An emblem of union, bright symbol of three ;
In joyous orison let each bounding river
Proclaim as it rolls its bright way to the sea,
That liberty, peace and patriotic devotion
Will flourish where Maple and Shamrock agree.

Hail, then, broad-leaf'd Maple, fair type of our country,
May Canada's sons grow as stalwart as thee,
And with the same vigor bud forth into manhood,
Bright forest of greatness, on one mighty tree ;
May virtue ennoble each deed of our country,
In letters of gold be emblazoned her name,
Towering up like the Maple, yet humble as Shamrock,
An ægis of safety, a triumph of fame.

Yes, this be the grandeur we seek for our country,
Let virtues be noble and toil be our king,
The axe of the woodman, while smiting the forest,
In bold proclamation our greatness shall ring ;—
Shall echo the accents of Canada's future,
In pæan of labor, in triumph of song,
And the grand notes of progress that greet our Dominion
Proclaim that the Maple and Shamrock are one.

Then weave in one garland the Maple and Shamrock,
A nation's sweet incense breathes fragrance around,
The pulse of our country shall quicken its paces,
As quicken the measures of freedom's bright sound.
May the dove of true peace wing it's way o'er the country,
Our people grow great in the sunshine of prayer,
And Maple and Shamrock, resplendent in beauty,
Embalm in sweet incense loved Canada fair !

THOS. O'HAGAN.

CANADIANS, AWAKE.

Ye sons of Canada, awake!
The star of morn has left the sky;
Your fathers' flag of victory,—
That glorious banner floats on high.
Earth is beneath and God above;
And human life is heavenly love;
Arise, young legions, onward move!

Ye sons of Canada, awake!
Protect the rights your sires have won!
The heritage of sire to son,—
The Crown of Peace,—Hope's rising sun.
'Tis valor to adore the light;
'Tis honor to make free with might;
'Tis glory to establish right.

Ye sons of Canada, awake!
Stretch forth the mighty arm of toil;
Embattle, beautify the soil
Your fathers won by brave turmoil;
And, while your glory swells, behold
Your virgin empire still unfold
Her halcyon hope, her wealth untold.

Ye sons of Canada, awake!
Let Christian mercy shrine your heart;
Let vice and vanity depart;
The poor may fight their country's part;—
Extend the hand of brotherhood
To honest hearts and loyal blood,—
The truly brave are truly good.

Ye sons of Canada, awake!
While in your loyal bosoms, burns
The patriot's fire, the heart that warns,
That victory loves, that thraldom spurns,—
Bid those, who would oppress you, know
You dread not death, you fear no foe;—
Your swords are sharp, your bosoms true.

Ye sons of Canada, awake!
Behold the grass on which ye tread,
Behold the white stars overhead,
All labor for a common need.
'Tis sacred dust beneath your feet;
Your fathers' graves in memory sweet,
Their patriot spirits ever beat.

 A. M. TAYLOR.

THE MEN OF THE NORTHERN ZONE.

Oh, we are men of the Northern Zone;
  Shall a bit be placed in our mouth?
If ever a Northman lost his throne,
  Did the conqueror come from the South?
    Nay, nay—and the answer blent
    In chorus is southward sent.
Since when has a Southern's conquering steel
  Hewed out in the North a throne?
Since when has a Southerner placed his heel
  On the men of the Northern Zone?

Our hearts are as free as the rivers that flow
  In the seas where the north star shines;
Our lives are as free as the breezes that blow
  Thro' the crests of our native pines.
    We never will bend the knee;
    We'll always and aye be free:
For liberty reigns in the land of the leal,
  Our brothers are round her throne;
A Southerner never shall place his heel
  On the men of the Northern Zone.

Oh, shall we shatter our ancient name,
  And lower our patriot crest;
And leave a heritage dark with shame
  To the infant upon the breast?
    Nay, nay—and the answer blent
    With a chorus is southward sent.
Ye claim to be free, and so are we;
  Let your fellow freemen alone;
For a Southerner never shall place his heel
  On the men of the Northern Zone.

Shall the mothers that bore us bow the head
  And blush for degenerate sons?
Are the patriot fires gone out and dead?
  Oh, brothers, stand to your guns!
    Let the flag be nailed to the mast
    Defying the coming blast,
For Canada's sons are true as steel;
  Their mettle is muscle and bone—
The Southerner never shall place his heel
  On the men of the Northern Zone.

Oh, we are men of the Northern Zone,
  Where the maples their branches toss.
The Great Bear rides in his state alone
  Afar from the Southern Cross.
    Our people shall aye be free;
    They never shall bend the knee,
For this is the land of the true and the leal,
  Where freedom is bred in the bone.
The Southerner never shall place his heel
  On the men of the Northern Zone.

ROBT. KERNIGAN.

SONG FOR CANADA.

Sons of the race whose sires
  Aroused the martial flame
That filled with smiles the triune isles,
  Through all their heights of fame.
With hearts as brave as theirs,
  With hopes as strong and high,
We'll ne'er disgrace the honored race
  Whose deeds can never die.
    Let but the rash intruder dare
      To touch our darling strand,
    The martial fires that thrilled our sires
      Would flame throughout the land.

Our lakes are deep and wide,
  Our fields and forests broad;
With cheerful air we'll speed the share,
  And break the fruitful sod;
Till blest with rural peace,
  Proud of our rustic toil,
On hill and plain true kings we'll reign
  The victors of the soil.
    But let the rash intruder dare
      To touch our darling strand,
    The martial fires that thrilled our sires
      Would light him from the land.

Health smiles with rosy face
  Amid our sunny dales,
And torrents strong fling hymn and song
  Through all the mossy vales;
Our sons are living men,
  Our daughters fond and fair;
A thousand isles where plenty smiles
  Make glad the brow of care.

But let the rash intruder dare
To touch our darling strand,
The martial fires that thrilled our sires
Would flame throughout the land.

And if in future years
One wretch should turn and fly,
Let weeping fame blot out his name
From freedom's hallowed sky;
Or should our sons e'er prove
A coward, traitor race—
Just Heaven frown in thunder down
T'avenge the foul disgrace.
But let the rash intruder dare
To touch our darling strand,
The martial fires that thrilled our sires
Would light him from the land.

CHARLES SANGSTER.

MADELEINE DE VERCHERES.

"Oh! my country, bowed in anguish 'neath a weight of bitter woe,
Who shall save thee from the vengeance of the desolating foe?
They have sworn a heathen oath, that every Christian soul must die,—
God of Heaven, in mercy shield us! Father, hear thy children's cry!"

Thus prayed Madeleine, the daughter of an old heroic line,—
Grecian poet, had he seen her, would have deemed her race divine;
But as the golden sun transcends the beauty of the brightest star,
Than all her charms of face or form her maiden heart was lovelier far.

We can see her now in fancy, through the dim years gazing back
To those stormy days of old, the days of valiant Frontenac,
When the thinly settled land was sadly wasted far and near,
And before the savage foe the people fled like stricken deer.

'Tis the season when the forest wears its many colored dress,
And a strange foreboding whisper answers back the wind's caress
As the swaying pines repeat the murmurs of the distant waves,
While the children of the summer flutter softly to their graves.

But—was that another whisper, warning her of ill to come,
As she stands beside the river, near her father's fortress home?
Hark! the sound of stealthy footsteps creeps upon the throbbing ear—
Maiden, fly! the foe approaches, and no human aid is near.

Surely He who decked with beauty this fair earth on which we dwell,
Never meant that men should change it by their madness into hell!
He who gave the trees their glory, gave the birds their gift of song,
Cannot smile from out yon heavens at the sight of human wrong.

But those savage hearts no beauty wins to thoughts of tender ruth—
Mother fond, or gentle maid, or smiling innocence of youth.
See! with fierce, exulting yells, the flying maiden they pursue—
Hear her prayer, O God, and save her from that wild vindictive crew.

Never ere that day or since was such a race by maiden run,
Never 'gainst such fearful odds was wished-for goal so swiftly won;
Fifty foes are on her track, the bullets graze her floating hair—
But worse than vain is all their rage, for God has heard her prayer.

Madeleine has reached the fort,—the gates are closed against the foe,
But now, a stricken throng sends up to heaven a wail of woe—
Feeble men and fainting women, without heart or hope or plan—
Then it was that God gave courage to a maid to act the man.

Then it was that Madeleine bethought her of her father's name
"Never shall a soldier's daughter die the coward's death of shame;
Never, in the days to come, when Canada is great and proud,
Be it said a Christian maiden by a heathen's threat was cowed.

"He is but a craven wretch would bid me yield in such an hour—
Never yet my country's sons in peril's face were known to cower.
No, my people! God is with us; 'tis our homes that we defend—
Let the savage do his worst, we will oppose him to the end.

"Women, I am but a girl, but heroes' blood is in my veins,
And I will shed it drop by drop before I see my land in chains;
Let them tear me limb from limb, or strew my ashes to the wind,
Ere I disgrace the name I bear, or leave a coward's fame behind

"Brothers mine, though young in years, you are old enough to know
That to shed your blood is noble, fighting with your country's foe!
Be the lesson unforgotten that our noble father gave,
Whether glory be its guerdon, or it wins us but a grave.

"Come, my people, take your places, every one as duty calls;
Death to every foe who ventures to approach these fortress walls;
Let no point be unprotected, leave the rest to God on high,
That we shall have done our duty, even if we have to die."

Thus she raised their drooping courage, matchless maiden, Madeleine;
And the cry, "To arms!" re echoed, till the roof-trees rang again;
Cannons thundered, muskets rattled, and the clank of steel was heard,
Till the baffled foe retreated, like a wolf untimely scared.

Seven days and seven nights, with sleepless eye and bated breath,
They held the fort against the foe that lurked around them plotting death.
At last a joyous challenge came, it was the brave La Monnerie,
And up to Heaven arose a shout, "The foe has fled, and we are free!"

JOHN READE.

THE CAPTURED FLAG.

Loudly roared the English cannon, loudly thundered back our own, *
Pouring down a hail of iron from their battlements of stone,
Giving Frontenac's proud message to the clustered British ships :
"I will answer your commander only by my cannons' lips."
Through the sulphurous smoke below us, on the Admiral's ship of war,
Faintly gleamed the British ensign, as through cloud-wrack gleams a star ;
And above our noble fortress, on Cape Diamond's rugged crest,—
Like a crown upon a monarch, like an eagle in its nest,—
Streamed our silken flag, emblazoned with the royal *fleur-de-lys*,
Flinging down a proud defiance to the rulers of the sea.
As we saw it waving proudly, and beheld the crest it bore,
Fiercely throbbed our hearts within us, and with bitter words we swore,
While the azure sky was reeling at the thunder of our guns,
We would strike that standard never, while Old France had gallant sons.
Loud and fiercely raged the struggle, oft our foes had sought to land,
But with shot and steel we met them, met and drove them from the strand ;
Though they owned them not defeated, and the stately Union Jack,
Streaming from the slender topmast, seemed to wave them proudly back,
Louder rose the din of combat, thicker rolled the battle smoke,
Through whose murky folds the crimson tongues of thundering cannon broke ;
And the ensign sank and floated in the smoke clouds on the breeze,
As a fluttering sea-bird floats upon the stormy seas.
While we looked upon it sinking, rising through a sea of smoke,
Lo ! it shook, and bending downwards, as a tree beneath a stroke,
Hung one moment o'er the river, then precipitously fell,

Like proud Lucifer descending from high heaven into hell.
As we saw it flutter downwards, till it reached the eager wave,
Not Cape Diamond's loudest echo could have matched the cheer we gave;
Yet the English, still undaunted, sent an answering echo back;
Though their flag had fallen conquered, still their fury did not slack,
And with louder voice their cannon to our cannonade replied,
As their tattered ensign drifted slowly shoreward with the tide.
There was one who saw it floating, and within his heart of fire,
Beating in a Frenchman's bosom, rose at once a fierce desire,
That the riven flag thus resting on the broad St. Lawrence tide
Should, for years to come, betoken how France humbled England's pride.
As the stag leaps down the mountain with the baying hounds in chase,
So the hero, swift descending, sought Cape Diamond's rugged base,
And within the water whitened by the bullet's deadly hail,
Springing, swam toward the ensign with a stroke that could not fail.
From the shore and from the fortress we looked on with bated breath,
For around him closer, closer, fell the messengers of death;
And as nearer, ever nearer, to the floating flag he drew,
Thicker round his head undaunted still the English bullets flew.
He has reached and seized the trophy! Ah! what cheering rent the skies,
Mingled with deep English curses, as he shoreward brought his prize!
Slowly, slowly, almost sinking, still he struggled to the land,
And we hurried down to meet him as he reached the welcome strand;
Proudly up the rock we bore him with the flag that he had won,
And that night the English vessels left us with the setting sun.

ARTHUR WEIR.

FREEDOM'S JOURNEY.

Freedom ! a nursling of the North,
Rocked in the arms of stormy pines,
On fond adventure wander'd forth
Where south the sun superbly shines ;
The prospect shone so bright and fair,
She dreamt her home was there, was there.

She lodged 'neath many a gilded roof,
They gave her praise in many a hall,
Their kindness checked the free reproof,
Her heart dictated to let fall ;
She heard the Negro's helpless prayer,
And felt her home could not be there.

She sought thro' rich Savannah's green,
And in the broad Palmetto grove,
But where her Altar should have been
She found nor liberty nor love ;
A cloud came o'er her forehead fair,
She found no shrine to freedom there.

Back to her nativ scenes she turn'd,
Back to the hardy, kindly North,
Where bright aloft the Pole-star burned,
Where stood her shrine by every hearth ;
"Back to the North I will repair,"
The Goddess cried, "my home is there."

THOS. D'ARCY MCGEE.

THE PLAINS OF ABRAHAM.

I stood upon the Plain,
That had trembled when the slain
Hurled their proud, defiant curses at the battle-heated foe,
When the steed dashed right and left.
Through the bloody gaps he cleft,
When the bridle-rein was broken, and the rider was laid low.

What busy feet had trod
Upon the very sod
Where I marshalled the battalions of my fancy to my aid!
And I saw the combat dire,
Heard the quick incessant fire,
And the cannons' echoes startling the reverberating glade.

I heard the chorus dire,
That jarred along the lyre
On which the hymn of battle rung, like surgings of the wave,
When the storm, at blackest night,
Wakes the ocean in affright,
As it shouts its mighty pibroch o'er some shipwrecked vessel's grave.

I saw the broad claymore
Flash from its scabbard o'er
The ranks that quailed and shuddered at the close and fierce attack;
When Victory gave the word,
Then Scotland drew the sword,
And with arm that never faltered drove the brave defenders back.

I saw two brave chiefs die,
Their last breaths like the sigh
Of the zephyr-sprite that wantons on the rosy lips of morn;
No envy-poisoned darts,
No rancor in their hearts,
To unfit them for their triumph over death's impending scorn.

And as I thought and gazed,
My soul, exultant, praised
The Power to whom each mighty act and victory are due,
For the saint-like Peace that smiled,
Like a heaven-gifted child,
And for the air of quietude that steeped the distant view.

Oh, rare, divinest life
Of Peace, compared with Strife !
Yours is the truest splendor, and the most enduring fame ;
All the glory ever reaped
Where the fiends of battle leaped,
Is harsh discord to the music of your undertoned acclaim.

CHARLES SANGSTER.

THE HEROES OF 1760.

O Ye who tread with heedless feet,
  This dust once laid with heroes' blood,
A moment turn your backward glance
  To years of dread inquietude :
When wars disturbed our peaceful fields;
  When mothers drew a sobbing breath ;
When the great river's hilly marge
  Resounded with the cry of death.

Then, full of fire, our heroes sprang
  To save our heritage and laws.
They conquered ! 'twas a holiday.
  Alas, the last in such a cause !
Bloody and shamed, the flag of France
  Perforce recrossed the widening seas ;
The sad Canadian mourned his hopes,
  And cherished bitter memories.

But noble he despite his woe !
  Before his lords he proudly bends,
Like some tall oak that storms may shake,
  And bow, but never, never rend.
And oft he dreams a happy dream,
  And sees a flag with lilies sown,
Come back whence comes the rising sun,
  To float o'er landscapes all his own.

Oh when the south wind on its wings
  Bears to his ear strange sounds afar,
To him they seem the solemn chant
  Of triumph after clam'rous war.
Those echoes weird of gallant strife
  E'en stir the coffined warrior-dead,
As stirs a nation's inmost heart
  At some proud pageant nobly led.

Hear ye, how in their ancient urns
  The ashes of our heroes wake?
Thus greet they ye, fair sons of morn,
  For this their solemn silence break.
They greet ye, whose renown has reached
  Past star on star to highest heaven!
Ye on whose brow their halo sits,
  To ye their altar shall be given!

And who shall dare our homesteads touch,
  That for our heritage ye gave:—
And who shall drive us from the shores
  To which your blood the verdure gave?
E'en they shall find the oppressed will rise
  More powerful for the foe withstood;
And ever for such heinous crime
  Shall pay the forfeit with their blood.

Ye, our defenders in the past,
  Your names are still a household word!
In childhood's ear old age recounts
  The toils your hardy youth endured.
And on the field of victory
  Hath gratitude your memory graved!
In during brass your story lives
A glory to the centuries saved!

Mrs. S. A. Curzon.

SIR ISAAC BROCK TO HIS SOLDIERS.

Ye men of Canada!
Subjects with me of that Imperial Power
Whose liberties are marching round the earth:
I need not urge you now to follow me,
Though what befalls will try your stubborn faith
In the fierce fire and crucible of war.
I need not urge you, you have heard the voice
Of loyalty, and answered to its call.
Who has not read the insults of the foe—
The manifesto of his purposed crimes?
That foe, whose poison-paint, false liberty,
Runs o'er his body politic and kills
Whilst seeming to adorn it, fronts us now!
Threats our poor Province to annihilate,
And should we find the red men by our side—
Poor injured souls, who but defend their own—
Calls back Extermination from its hell,
To stalk abroad, and stench your land with slaughter.
These are our weighty arguments of war,
Wherein armed Justice will enclasp its sword,
And sheath it in its bitter adversary;
Wherein we'll turn our bayonet-points to pens,
And write in blood:—*Here lies the poor invader;*
Or be ourselves struck down by hailing death:
Made stepping stones for foes to walk upon—
The lifeless gangways to our country's ruin.
For now we look not with the eye of fear;
We reck not if this strange mechanic frame—
Stop in an instant in the shock of war.
Our death may build into our country's life,
And failing this, 'twere better still to die
Than live the breathing spoils of infamy.
Then forward for our cause and Canada!
Forward for Britain's Empire—peerless arch
Of Freedom's raising, whose majestic span
Is axis to the world! On, on, my friends!
The task our country sets must we perform—
Wring peace from war, or perish in its storm!

CHAS. MAIR.

AROUSE YE, BRAVE CANADIANS.

Lines suggested by General Brock's stirring appeal to the people of Upper Canada at the opening of the war of 1812.

Canadian's arms are stout and strong,
  Canadian hearts are true;
Your homes were in the forest made,
  Where pine and maple grew.
A haughty foe is marching
  Your country to enthrall;
Arouse ye, brave Canadians,
  And answer to my call!

Let every man who swings an axe,
  Or follows at the plough,
Abandon farm and homestead,
  And grasp a rifle now!
We'll trust the God of Battles,
  Although our force be small;
Arouse ye, brave Canadians,
  And answer to my call!

Let mothers, though with breaking hearts,
  Give up their gallant sons;
Let maidens bid their lovers go,
  And wives their dearer ones!
Then rally to the frontier,
  And form a living wall;
Arouse ye, brave Canadians,
  And answer to my call!

J. D. EDGAR.

ON QUEENSTON HEIGHTS.

I stood on Queenston Heights ;
And as I gazed from tomb to cenotaph,
From cenotaph to tomb, adown and up,
My heart grew full, much moved with many thoughts.
At length I cried :
" O robed with honor and with glory crowned,
Tell me again the story of yon pile."
And straight the ancient, shuddering cedars wept,
The solemn junipers indued their pall,
The moaning wind crept through the trembling oaks
And, shrieking, fled. Strange clamor filled the air ;
The steepy hill shook with the rush of arms ;
Around me rolled the tide of sudden war.
The booming guns pealed forth their dreadful knell ;
Musketry rattled ; shouts, cries, groans, were heard ;
Men met as foes, and deadly strife ensued.
From side to side the surging combat rolled,
And as it rolled, passed from my ken.
But hark ! a ringing cheer peals up the height,
Once more the battle's tide bursts on my view.
Brock to the rescue ! Down goes the alien flag !
Back, back the dark battalions fall. On, on
The " Tigers " come. Down pours the rattling shot
From out the verdant grove, like sheets of hail.
Up, up they press, York volunteers and all.
Aha ! the day is ours ! See, where the hero comes
In conquering might, quick driving all before him !
O brave ensample ! O beloved chief !
Who follows thee keeps ever pace with honor.
Such tale the hill-side told me, and I wept.
Nay ! I wept not ! The hot, indignant thoughts
That filled my breast burned up the welling tears
Ere they had chance to flow, and forward Hate
Spake rashly. But calm reflection
Laid her cool hand upon my throbbing brow
And whispered, " As up the misty stream
The Norseman crept to-day, and signals white
Waved kind salutes from yon opposing shore ;
And as ye peered the dusky vista through,
To catch first glimpse of yonder glorious plinth,
Yet saw it not till I your glance directed,—
So high it towered above the common plane ;—
So towering over Time, shall Brock e'er stand.—
So, from those banks, shall white-robed Peace e'er smile."

MRS. S. A. CURZON.

ALONG THE LINE.

A.D. 1812.

Steady be your beacon's blaze
  Along the line! along the line!
Freely sing dear Freedom's praise
  Along the line! along the line!
Let the only sword you draw
Bear the legend of the law,
Wield it less to strike than awe,
  Along the line! along the line!

Let them rail against the North,
  Beyond the line! beyond the line!
When it sends its heroes forth.
  Along the line! along the line!
On the field or in the camp
They shall tremble at your tramp,
Men of the old Norman stamp,
  Along the line! along the line!

Wealth and pride may rear their crests,
  Beyond the line! beyond the line!
They bring no terror to our breasts,
  Along the line! along the line!
We have never bought or sold
Afric's sons with Mexic's gold,
Conscience arms the free and bold,
  Along the line! along the line!

Steadfast stand, and sleepless ward,
  Along the line! along the line!
Great the treasures that you guard
  Along the line! along the line!
By the babes whose sons shall be
Crowned in far futurity,
With the laurels of the free,
  Stand your guard along the line!

THOS. D'ARCY MCGEE.

THE VETERANS OF 1812.

Forget not, Canada, the men who gave,
In fierce and bloody fray, their lives for thine.
Pause thou, Ontario, in thy forward march,
And give a tear to those who, long ago,
On this day fell upon those Heights where now
Their ashes rest beneath memorial pile.
And while those names, Brock and Macdonell wake,
A throb of emulative gratitude
And patriotic fervor in thy breast,
Forget not those—"the boys," the nameless ones,—
Who also fought and fell on that October day;
Nameless their ashes, but their mem'ries dear!
Remember, too,
Those grandsires at thy hearths who linger still;
Whose youthful arms then helped to guard thy peace,—
Thy peace their own. And ere they go to join
Their ancient comrades of the hard-won fight,
Glad their brave hearts with one applauding cheer
In memory of the day. Comfort their age
With plenty. Let them find that sturdy youth,
Whose heritage they saved, bows rev'rent head,
And lends a strong arm to ancient men,
Whose deeds of patriot prowess deck the silk
That waves so proudly from the nation's towers.

Mrs. S. A. Curzon.

CAPTURE OF DETROIT, 1812.

The summons spread throughout the land, the summons to the brave;
It speeded west to far St. Clair, and north to Huron's wave.
And fast into the forest wild its thrilling notes did float;
It called the woodman from his toil, the fisher from his boat.
And high upon the mountain, lone and deep within the dell,
The red man heard its stirring notes and answered to them well.
In haste they came responsive to their country's call for aid,—
The young, the old, the white, the red, for Truth and Right arrayed;
Their arms were strong, their mettle true, but few in numbers they—
To cope in arms upon the field against the great array.

On marched the force invading, looking at their foe in scorn,
And sure that they would vanish like the mist before the morn;
But hearts of giant might were there that knew not how to fear,
And willing hands were waiting to provide a bloody bier;
And warmly did they welcome th' approach of that proud band
That came to conquer and subdue their fair, free, noble land.
And then in haste and terror, back unto their native shore,
The boastful host went surging,—their advance was quickly o'er;
Behind them thronged the heroes, while a bright chivalric glow
Went flashing o'er their faces as they chased the beaten foe.
"No time to rest!" cried Brock the Brave; "Let's conquer now or die!"
And swarth Tecumseh at his side re-echoed back the cry.
And fast and far, from rank to rank, the thrilling orders came,
That they must cross the river in the face of shot and flame,
And on they went undaunted, they, the bravest of the brave,
And thought then but of honor, and they thought not of the grave.
The leader's towering figure stood erect in his canoe,
And o'er him England's banner out upon the breezes blew.
Ah! who at such a moment, and with such a leader there,

With such a flag above him, would of victory despair ?
Not one I ween who followed, through the midst of shot and shell,
The grand heroic figure they knew and loved so well.
They reached the shore, they scaled the beach, and from a favored post,
They hurled like chaff before the wind, the huge opposing host;
These fled for shelter to the fort, where shelter there was none,
The flashing fire on ev'ry side boomed from each leaguer's gun.
"Advance ! advance," rang out the cry along the line of red ;
"Advance ! advance," in trumpet tones their fearless leader said.
With answering cheers upon their lips obeyed the willing men,
While far and wide, on every side, upstarting from the glen,
The painted Indians whooping came, amid the battles din,
And rushed along with bounding step the carnage to begin.
But oh ! what now ? the charge is checked, and all along the line
The men in wonder see, and stop in answer to the sign
That by their leader's hand is made. My country can it be
That he is craven-hearted turned ? No craven heart is he !
See high above yon bastioned wall that flutt'ring flag of white,
Where Stripes and Stars a moment since were glittering on the sight !
And list, adown the joyous ranks the thrilling tidings go,
"The fort has fallen into our hands, and with it all the foe !"
A cheer triumphant rang aloud o'er forest, field, and plain,
And distant echoes caught its notes and pealed them forth again.
Right proudly beat the hearts, I trow, of all the gallant few,
As flaunting o'er the battlements the flag of England flew,
And from the ramparts of the fort they made the welkin ring
With plaudits loud for Brock the Brave, and cheers for England's King.

CHARLES EDWIN JAKEWAY.

A BALLAD FOR BRAVE WOMEN.

A STORY worth telling, our annals afford,
'Tis the wonderful journey of Laura Secord!
Her poor crippled spouse hobbled home
With the news
That Boerstler was nigh! "Not a minute to lose,
Not an instant," said Laura, "for stoppage or pause—
I must hurry and warn our brave troops at Decaws."
"What! you!" said her husband "to famish and tire!"
"Yes, me!" said brave Laura, her bosom on fire.
"And how will you pass the gruff sentry?" said he,
"Who is posted so near us?"
"Just wait till you see;
The foe is approaching, and means to surprise
Our troops, as you tell me. Oh, husband, there flies
No dove with a message so needful as this—
I'll take it, I'll bear it, good bye, with a kiss."
Then a biscuit she ate, tucked her skirts well about,
And a bucket she slung on each arm, and went out
'Twas the bright blush of dawn, when the stars melt from sight,
Dissolved by its breath like a dream of the night;
When heaven seems opening on man and his pain,
Ere the rude day strengthens, and shuts it again.
But Laura had eyes for her duty alone—
She marked not the glow and the gloom that were thrown
By the nurslings of morn, by the cloud-lands at rest,
By the spells of the East, and the weirds of the West.
Behind was the foe, full of craft and of guile;
Before her, a long day of travel and toil.
"No time this for gazing," said Laura, as near
To the sentry she drew.
"Halt! you cannot pass here."
"I cannot pass here! Why, sirrah, you drowse,
Are you blind? Don't you see I am off to my cows."

"Well, well you can go." So she wended her way
To the pasture's lone side, where the farthest cow lay,
Got her up from her bed, and with pail at her knees,
Made her budge, inch by inch, till she drew by degrees
To the edge of the forest. "I've hoaxed, on my word,
Both you and the sentry," said Laura Secord.

With a lingering look at her home, then away
She sped through the wild woods—a wilderness gray
And denser and deeper the solitude grew,
The underwood thickened, and drenched her with dew;
She tripped over moss covered logs, and fell, arose,
Sped, and stumbled again by the hour, till her clothes
Were rent by the branches and torn, and her feet
Grew tender and way-worn and blistered with heat.
And on, ever on, through the forest she passed,
Her soul in her task, and each pulse beating fast,
For shadowy forms seemed to flit from the glades
And beckon her into their limitless shades:
And mystical sounds—in the forest alone,
Ah! who has not heard them?—the voices, the moan,
Or the sigh of mute nature, which sinks on the ear,
And fills us with sadness or thrills us with fear?
And who, lone and lost, in the wilderness deep,
Has not felt the strange fancies, the tremors which creep,
And assemble within, till the heart 'gins to fail,
The courage to flinch, and the cheeks to grow pale,
'Midst the shadows which mantle the spirit that broods
In the sombre, the deep haunted heart of the woods?

Once more on the pathway, through swamp and through mire,
Through covert and thicket, through bramble and brier,
She toiled to the highway, then over the hill,
And down the deep valley, and past the new mill,
And through the next woods, till, at sunset, she came
To the first British picket and murmured her name;
Thence, guarded by Indians, all footsore and pale
She was led to Fitzgibbon, and told him her tale.

For a moment her reason forsook her ; she raved,
She laughed, and she cried—"They are saved, they are saved !"
Then her senses returned, and with thanks loud and deep
Sounding sweetly around her she sank into sleep.
And Bœrstler came up, but his movements were known,
His force was surrounded, his scheme was o'erthrown
By a woman's devotion—on stone be't engraved—
The foeman was beaten and Burlington saved.

Ah ! faithful to death were our women of yore !
Have they fled with the past to be heard of no more ?
No, no ! Though this laurelled one sleeps in the grave,
We have maidens as true, we have matrons as brave ;
And should Canada ever be forced to the test—
To spend for our country the blood of her best !
When her sons lift the linstock and brandish the sword,
Her daughters will think of brave Laura Secord !

CHAS. MAIR.

LUNDY'S LANE.

July it was, and the sun's fierce heat
On road and meadow glistened and beat.

Glistened and beat till the hillside brown
Shrivelled and parched in its angry frown.

Till the dust lay white 'neath the creaking wain,
And never a zephyr to promise the rain

Backward from Queenston, backward for aye,
The hostile invaders had passed on their way.

While hot on their rear like a hound on the track,
By the way he retreated brave Riall came back.

By the way he retreated from Chippewa fight,
Outnumbered and beaten that terrible night.

And now where the ground softly slopes from the plain,
And the fragrance of orchards breathes o'er Lundy's Lane,

At the point where it joins with the old Portage road,
His scanty battalions defiantly stood.

In front lay the foe ; to his challenge they come,
But behind hear the beat of the patriot drum !

For Drummond is marching that pitiless day,
And the feet of his soldiers are swift for the fray.

Undaunted by numbers, by odds undismayed,
"Form the line with the guns in the centre," he said.

Six o'clock, and the sun as it sunk to its rest,
Like a circle of blood shot its glow from the West.

One instant its gleam on their battle ranks broke ;
The next it was lost in the batteries' smoke.

And they grappled, they struggled, they fought and they fell,
'Mid the flash of the bayonet, the hiss of the shell.

One to four! they are Britons in blood and in bone,
And the land that they fight for they know is their own.

One to four! shall they perish when wisdom says "Fly?"
On! Forward like heroes! for valor says "Die."

One to four! and the twilight in horror shrinks down,
And over the dead casts her mantle of brown.

One to four! and there fades the last glimmer of light,
And they fought hand to hand for the guns in the night.

And the flashes of flame shot their glare o'er the gloom,
And the cannons re-echoed the cataract's boom.

And the smoke of their volleys strewn far o'er the plain
Seemed the ghosts of the fallen contending again.

Rose the moon, pallid orbed, her pale course to pursue,
Belated, reluctant, aghast at the view!

So their hands from the slaughter a moment they stay,
A moment they stand statue-like in its ray.

A moment of breathing—a moment—no more,
Then bellowed the cannons their grape as before.

Till the foe, horror-smitten at blood so out-poured,
Withdrew with the bayonet, withdrew with the sword.

So, baffled and vanquished, they sullenly fled,
And night and the victors kept watch with the dead.

W. THOMAS WHITE.

THE U. E. LOYALISTS.

THE war was over. Seven red years of blood
Had scourged the land from mountain top to sea ;
(So long it took to rend the mighty frame
Of England's empire in the western world)
Rebellion won at last, and they who loved
The cause that had been lost, and kept their faith
To England's crown, and scorned an alien name,
Passed into exile, leaving all behind
Except their honor, and the conscious pride
Of duty done to Country and to King.

Broad lands, ancestral homes, and gathered wealth
Of patient toil and self-denying years
Were confiscate and lost ; for they had been
The salt and savor of the land ; trained up
In honor, loyalty and fear of God.

Not drooping like poor fugitives they came
In exodus to our Canadian wilds,
But full of heart and hope, with heads erect
And fearless eyes victorious in defeat.
With thousand toils they forced their devious way
Through the great wilderness of silent woods,
That gloomed o'er lake and stream, till higher rose
The northern star above the broad domain
Of half a continent, still theirs to hold,
Defence and keep for ever as their own,
Their own and England's, to the end of time.

The virgin forests, carpeted with leaves
Of many autumns fallen, crisp and sear,
Put on their woodland state ; while overhead
Green seas of foliage roared a welcome home
To the proud exiles, who for empire fought

And kept, though losing much, this northern land
A refuge and defence for all who love
The broader freedon of a commonwealth
That wears upon its head a kingly crown.

Our great Canadian woods of mighty trees,
Proud oaks and pines that grew for centuries,
King's gifts upon the exiles were bestowed.
Ten thousand homes were planted ; and each one
With axe, and fire, and mutual help made war
Against the wilderness and smote it down.
Into the open glades, unlit before,
Since forests grew and rivers ran, there leaped
The sun's bright rays, creative light and heat,
Waking to life the buried seeds that slept
Since time's beginning in the earth's dark womb.

The tender grass sprang up, no man knew how,
The daisies' eyes unclosed, wild strawberries
Lay white as hoar frost on the slopes, and sweet
The violets perfumed the evening air ;
The nodding clover grew up everywhere ;
The trailing rasp, the trefoil's yellow cup
Sparkled with dew drops, while the humming bees
And birds and butterflies, unseen before,
Found out the sunny spots and came in throngs.

But long and arduous were their labors ere
The rugged fields produced enough for all,
For thousands came ere hundreds could be fed ;
The scanty harvests gleaned to their last ear
Sufficed not yet, men hungered for their bread
Before it grew, yet cheerful bore the hard,
Coarse fare and russet garb of pioneers,
In these great woods, content to build a home
And commonwealth where they could live secure,
A life of honor, loyalty and peace.
Amid the quaking of a continent
Torn by the passions of an evil time,

THE U. E. LOYALISTS.

They counted neither cost nor danger, spurned
Defections, treasons, spoils ; but feared their God,
Nor shamed of their allegiance to the king.

Oh ! keep the empire one in unity,
The vast dominion stretched from sea to sea ;
A land of labor but of sure reward,
A land of corn to feed the world withal,
A land of life's best treasures, plenty, peace,
Content and freedom, both to speak and do ;
A land of men to rule, with sober law,
A Christian commonwealth, God's gift ; oh keep
This part of Britain's empire next the heart,
Loyal as were our fathers, and as free.

WILLIAM KIRBY.

THE BATTLE OF RIDGEWAY.

So fall the brave of every age and clime,
  Where'er true valor burns or foemen meet ;
So fall the brave, dying their deaths sublime
  At their dear country's feet.

Gems in her crown, and landmarks of her youth
  In years to come, when might and strength are hers ;
Martyrs of Freedom, Liberty and Truth,
  And Fame's true worshippers.

So fell the brave on Queenston's Heights, when Brock
  Rolled back aggression and repelled the foe ;
So fell the brave where Wolfe sustained the shock
  That laid his young heart low.

So fell the brave when Tecumseh fell ;
  So fell the brave at Chateauguay's proud field ;
Yet there are lying lips that dare to tell
  We would not die, but yield !

Nor did they fall in vain ; each drop of blood
  Was as the dragon's teeth from which armed men
Have sprung, brave and invincible of mood
  As those who perished then.

Sprung up by tens of thousands, ripe for war ;
  Ready to tread the fiery path that leads
Too oft to death ; disdaining scathe and scar
  To serve their country's needs.

CHAS. SANGSTER.

IN MEMORY OF THE "QUEEN'S OWN."

Toll for the dead, the gallant dead!
Who calmly sleep in glory's bed,
With victory's laurels o'er each head
　In never fading bloom!
They fought for home and fireside
By Erin's old historic tide
For Canada's renown they died,
　Come with me to their tomb.

Come stand around the honor'd graves,
Where slumber now our fallen braves
Who battled with the miscreant knaves
　Whose touch defiled our land;
Give first one hearty British cheer;
And then draw closer, fondly near;
And drop a Brother's farewell tear
　O'er that devoted band.

Roused by the bugle's warning sound
The old red cross they rallied round
With every other feeling drowned
　In honor's sacred call;
And fearless as the steel they wore
Down on the ruffian foe they bore,
A Spartan spirit blazed once more
　Around them in their fall.

Peace to each gallant spirit fled,
Peace to our noble Brothers dead,
Whose bold intrepid souls were fed
　With patriotic fire!
Oh! for one burst of living flame
To wreath around each hero's name
A chaplet of eternal Fame,
　That never could expire!

WILLIAM PITTMAN LETT.

BRAVO! STAIRS.

Lieut. Stairs was a graduate of the Royal Military College, Kingston, Ontario, and acted under H. M. Stanley in his famous Congo expedition.

Up the gleaming river stretches of the Congo's widening tide,
Where the revelled grass and sedges teem with monsters Argus-eyed;
Through the fever-laden forests, where the craven heart despairs,
Onward pressing, never faltering, Bravo! Stairs.

Thoughts of cool Ontario's waters, rippling on Fort Frederick's strand
Or the white-maned ocean horses, scouring Nova Scotia's sand,
Come, like dreams, to weary toiler, as 'neath Afric's sun he fares,
But the strong will never wavers—Bravo! Stairs.

Marshalling his dark battalions, all impatient of control
With a firmness and a patience earnest of a noble soul;
First in danger, never laggard, Alma Mater's crest he wears,
Thrilling with "Truth, Valor, Duty"—Bravo! Stairs.

Bearing Britain's torch of freedom to the darkness of the grave,
Striking chains and riving shackles from the scarred limbs of the slave;
Loosing captives where they languish, braving lions in their lairs,
While the world looks on in wonder—Bravo! Stairs.

Weave the maple with the laurel, though its veins are tinged with red,
Place the chaplet in its freshness, proudly on our hero's head;
Canada grows grander, nobler, from the glory that he bears,
Shouts from all her lakes and forests, Bravo! Stairs.

K. L. JONES.

MANITOBA.

Softly the shadows of prairie-land wheat
Ripple and riot adown to her feet ;
Murmurs all Nature with joyous acclaim,
Fragrance of summer and shimmer of flame :
Heedless she hears while the centuries slip :
Chalice of poppy is laid on her lip.

Hark ! From the East comes a ravishing note,—
Sweeter was never in nightingale's throat,—
Silence of centuries thrills to the song,
Singing their coming awaited so long ;
Low, yet it swells to the heaven's blue dome,
Child-lips have called the wild meadow-land, Home !

Deep, as she listens, a dewy surprise
Dawns in the languor that darkens her eyes ;
Swift the red blood through her veins, in its flow,
Kindles to rapture her bosom aglow ;
Voices are calling, where silence has been,—
Look to thy future, thou Mother of Men !"

Onward and onward ! Her fertile expanse
Shakes as the tide of her children advance ;
Onward and onward ! Her blossoming floor
Yields her an opium potion no more ;
Onward ! and soon on her welcoming soil
Cities shall palpitate, myriads toil.

EMILY MCMANUS

MY PRAIRIE HOME.

Come back, O Friend, to your prairie home,
  To the plains that are wide like the sea,
To the brown foot-hills where the cattle roam,
  Where the wind, the wind blows free!

The wind blows free and the cattle graze,
  And the eagle sails on high,—
While the land lies asleep in the smoky haze,
  And faint comes the ground-bird's cry.

The ground-bird's cry and the plover's call,
  And the whistle of hawk I hear,
While the blackbird flock, like a sable pall,
  On the sedgy bank appear.

On the sedgy bank of the ruffled pool
  Where the sportful wind careers,
You may joy in the plash of its waters cool,
  And drown in their depths your fears.

You may drown the fears that oppress you sore,
  And the cares so wearily rife,
And blessed peace shall be yours once more
  As in spring-time years of life

Come then from the City's din and roar,
  From breathing its heavy air,
From dim-eyed search of that wondrous lore
  That the strifes of men prepare.

You can 'scape from the strife of tongues away,
  And be here alone with God,
While all about you the stars of day
  Shine bright in the prairie-sod.

WILLIAM P. MCKENZIE.

THE NORTH-WEST REBELLION.

"Forward!"
The captain said,
Out of the morning's red
Brave and noble and dread,
With hero and martial tread,
Into the North and the Westward.

Over dim forest and lake,
Over lone prairie and brake,
The clamor of battle to wake,
For kindred and country's sake,
Into the North and the Westward.

"Forward!"
'Neath northern sky,
Ready to fight and die.
Where the shadowy marshbirds fly
With their weird and lonely cry,
Far to the North and the Westward.

Only the rifle's crack,
And answer of rifle back;
Heavy each haversack,
Dreary the prairie's track
Far to the North and the Westward.

"Forward!"
Seeking the foe,
Starving and bleeding they go,
Into the sleet and the snow,
Over bleak rivers that flow
Far to the North and Westward.

Falling on frozen strands;
Falling, devoted bands,
Sleeping with folded hands!
Dead, for home and for lands—
Dead in the North and the Westward!

William Wilfred Campbell.

OUR CANADIAN FATHERLAND.

What is our young Canadian land?
Is it far Norembega's* strand?
Or wild Cape Breton by the sea?
Quebec? Ontario? Acadie?
Or Manitoba's flower-decked plain,
Or fair Columbia's mountain chain?
Can any part—from strand to strand—
Be a Canadian's fatherland?
Nay! for our young Canadian land
Is greater, grander far, than these;
It stretches wide on either hand
Between the world's two mighty seas!
So let no hostile lands divide
The fields our feet should freely roam;
Gael, Norman, Saxon,—side by side,
And Canada our nation's Home;
From sea to sea, from strand to strand,
Spreads our Canadian fatherland!

Where'er our country's banner spreads
Above Canadian free-born heads,
Where'er the story of our land
Enshrines the memory of the band
Of heroes, who, with blood and toil,
Laid, deep in our Canadian soil,
Foundations for the future age,
And wrote their names on history's page,
—*Our* history:—From strand to strand
Spreads our Canadian fatherland?
So each to each is firmly bound
By ties each generous heart should own,
We cannot spare a foot of ground,
No part can, selfish, stand alone!

* The old name for a great part of the Maritime Provinces and eastern coast of the New England States.

So Nova Scotia and Quebec
Shall meet in kinship leal and true,—
New Brunswick's hills be mirrored back
In fair Ontario's waters blue!
From sea to sea, from strand to strand,
Spreads our Canadian fatherland!

Where'er Canadian thought breathes free,
Or wakes the lyre of poesy,—
Where'er Canadian hearts awake
To sing a song for her dear sake,
Or catch the echoes, spreading far,
That wake us to the noblest war
Against each lurking ill and strife
That weakens, now, our growing life,
No line keeps hand from grasping hand,
—*One* is our young Canadian land!
McGee and Howe she claims her own
Hers all her eastern singers bays,
Fréchette is hers, and in her crown,
Ontario every laurel lays;—
Let CANADA our watchword be,
While lesser names we know no more,
One nation, spread from sea to sea,
And fused by love, from shore to shore;
—From sea to sea, from strand to strand,
Spreads our Canadian fatherland!

AGNES MAULE MACHAR (Fidelis).

LEAVING SCOTLAND FOR CANADA.

Adieu my native land—adieu
The banks of fair Lochfyne,
Where the first breath of life I drew,
And would my last resign!
Swift sails the bark that wafteth me
This night from thy loved strand:
O must it be my last of thee,
My dear, dear Fatherland?

O Scotland! o'er the Atlantic roar,
Though fated to depart,
Nor time nor space can e'er efface
Thine image from my heart.
Come weal, come woe—till life's last thore,
My Highland home shall seem
An Eden bright in Fancy's light,
A Heaven in Memory's dream!

Land of the maids of matchless grace,
The bards of matchless song,
Land of the bold heroic race
That never brook'd a wrong!
Long in the front of nations free
May Scotland proudly stand:
Farewell to thee—farewell to thee,
My dear, dear Fatherland!

EVAN M'COLL.

MY NATIVE LAND.

My native land, how dear to me
The sunshine of your glory!
How dear to me your deeds of fame,
Embalm'd in verse and story!
From east to west, from north to south,
In accents pure and tender,
Let's sing in lays of joyous praise
Your happy homes of splendor.

Across the centuries of the past,
With hearts of fond devotion,
We trace the white sails of your line
Through crest'd wave of ocean;
And every man of every race
Whose heart has shaped your glory
Shall win from us a homage true
In gift of song and story.

O let not petty strife e'er mar
The bright dawn of your morning,
Nor bigot word of demagogue
Create untimely warning!
Deep in our hearts let justice reign—
A justice broad and holy—
That knows no creed, nor race, nor tongue,
But our Dominion solely.

Dear native land, we are but one
From ocean unto ocean;
The sun that tints the Maple Leaf
Smiles with a like devotion
On Stadacona's fortress height,
On Grand Pré's storied valley,
And that famed tide whose peaceful shore
Was rock'd in battle sally.

Here we will plant each virtue rare,
And watch it bud and flourish—
From sunny France and Scotia's hills
Kind dews will feed and nourish ;
And Erin's heart of throbbing love,
So warm, so true and tender,
Will cheer our hearths and cheer our homes
With wealth of lyric splendor.

Dear native land, on this New Year,
We pray you ne'er may falter,
That patriot sons may feed the flames
That burn upon your altar !
May heaven stoop down upon each home,
And bless in love our people,
And ring through hearts—both rich and poor—
Sweet peace from heav'nly steeple.

THOMAS O'HAGAN.

THE QUEEN'S JUBILEE.

Twice twenty years and ten have fields been green,
And forests bare, and flowers have decked the lea,
And summer suns have burned, and winter keen
Has hushed the vocal throngs in bower and tree;
While round thy Island Throne the restless sea
Still flings his thundering anthems to the skies,
And joins with mighty bass our Jubilee,
And shouts defiance when the wild winds rise,
And guards thy rock-bound coast, confounds thy enemies.

From all thy wave-washed shores, thy turrets gray,
Thy sea-beat cliffs, thy rocks and beetling towers,
Of man's and nature's build; and far away
Beyond Old Ocean's marge, where Asian bowers
Awake with melting song the morning hours;
From lands that stem the Atlantic's fearful surge,
And where the fierce sirocco hotly scours
Australian plains; from earth's remotest verge,
To thee all loyalty, and love, and joy, converge.

One wish, one thought intense, one impulse strong,
Hath governed all thy long eventful reign;
Imbued thy days of sadness and of song,
With sweetest sympathy for all thy train;
And strengthen'd thy strong heart, and nerved thy brain,
To do the work an empire lays on thee:
'Tis love for thine own people doth sustain
The pillars of thy throne. Love makes them free,
And guides thy ship of state o'er Time's tempestuous sea.

God bless our Queen! and guard her lest she fall;
And may her reign be long, her life be true:
God bless her children, bless them one and all,
Those golden heads that were, and eyes of blue.

O bless their course in life the whole way through!
May all her mother-prayers answered be—
And all her children's children, bless them too,
Those near and those that dwell beyond the sea,
Make all their hearts be glad in this her Jubilee.

God bless her many peoples, and protect
Their every step, and lead them to the light,
Subdue their stubborn passions and correct
Their wayward hearts, impatient of the right;
And guard them from the moonless, starless night
Of selfish, thoughtless, hard, unhallowed ways.
The cleanest life among us, is not white;
The holiest saint laments his evil days;
And Conscience, strictly just, must mingle blame with praise.

God save the Queen! God save our Queen and bless
Her when she riseth up and lieth down;
And when he calleth, be her answer, "yes,
I come O Lord! A handmaid of Thine own."
And may she never merit Thy just frown,
But truly dutiful to Thee alway,
Receive as just reward, a saintly crown;
And through the cycles of eternal day,
Shall join the happy throngs in Thy triumphal lay.

DR. MASSIE.

AS REDMEN DIE.

Captive! Is there a hell to him like this?
A taunt more galling than the Huron's hiss?
He, proud and scornful, he, who laughed at law,
He, scion of the deadly Iroquois,
He, the bloodthirsty, he, the Mohawk chief,
He, who despises pain and sneers at grief,
Here in the hated Huron's vicious clutch,
That even captive, he disdains to touch.

Captive! But *never* conquered! Mohawk brave
Stoop not to be to *any* man a slave;
Least, to the puny tribe his soul abhors,
The tribe whose wigwams sprinkle Simcoe's shores.
With scowling brow he stoically stands by,
Watching, with haughty and defiant eye,
His captors, as they counsel o'er his fate,
Or strive his boldness to intimidate.
Then fling they unto him the choice.

"Wilt thou
Walk o'er the bed of fire that waits thee now—
Walk with uncovered feet upon the coals
Till thou doest reach the ghostly Land of Souls,
And with thy Mohawk death-song please our ear?
Or wilt thou with the women rest thee here?"
His eyes flash like the eagle's, and his hands
Clash at the insult. Like a god he stands.
"Prepare the fire!" he scornfully demands.

He knoweth not that soon this jeering band
Will bite the dust—will lick the Mohawk's hand;
Will kneel and cower at the Mohawk's feet;
Will shrink when Mohawk war-drums wildly beat.
His death will be avenged with hideous hate

By Iroquois swift to annihilate
His vile, detested captors that now flaunt
Their war-clubs in his face with sneer and taunt,
Nor thinking soon that reeking, red and raw,
Their scalps will deck the belts of Iroquois.

The path of coals outstretches, white with heat,
A forest fir's length—ready for his feet.
Unflinching as a rock he steps along
The burning mass—and sings his fierce war-song—
Sings as he sang when once he used to roam
Throughout the forests of his southern home,
Where down the Genesee the water roars,
Where gentle Mohawk purls between its shores,—
Songs that of exploits and of prowess tell,—
Songs of the Iroquois invincible.
Up the long trail of fire he boasting goes,
Dancing a war-dance to defy his foes.
His flesh is scorched, his muscles burn and shrink,
But still he dances to death's awful brink.
The eagle plume that crests his haughty head
Will *never* droop until his heart be dead.
Slower and slower yet his footstep swings,
Wilder and wilder still his death-song rings,
Fiercer and fiercer thro' the forest sounds
His voice, that leaps to Happier Hunting Grounds.
One savage yell—
Then, loyal to his race,
He bends to death—but *never* to disgrace.

E. PAULINE JOHNSON.

ON THE FRONTIER WAY.

As I went up the frontier way,
I heard the wondering people say:
"Our land is wide and richer far
"Than all the golden Indies are,
"Our fathers' lives are passed and spanned,
"Our fathers' glorious swords are sheathed,
"Then shall we fling away the land
"The God of Hosts to them bequeathed?"
From sea to sea, in sun and snow,
The answer thundered southward "No."

As I stood on the frontier way,
I heard the indignant people say:
"Who fought and bled to save our rights
"At Chateauguay and Queenston Heights?
"Who is it fills each silent grave
"That marks the hill or dots the plain?
"The dust of patriots true and brave,
"Who, if they lived, would cry again,
"You're welcome as the flowers of May,
"To Queenston Heights and Chateauguay."

As I went up the frontier way,
I heard the patriot people say:
"No alien flag shall ever wave
"Above the hero's honored grave,
"No alien heel shall e'er defile,
"Each green and grassy diadem,
"No cunning tongue shall wean or wile,
"The shelter of our swords from them,
"Their name shall never pass away,
"From Queenston Heights and Chateauguay."

As I stood on the frontier way,
I heard the dauntless people say :
"God loves a patriot people—He
"Despises those who won't be free ;
"Shall traitors our proud ensign drag ?
"Shall we submit in fear and frown ?
"If they would have the grand old flag
"They'd better come and pull it down,
"They're welcome as the flowers of May,"
Roar Queenston Heights and Chateauguay.

ROBT. KERNIGAN.

WHAT CANADA WANTS.

Canada wants men—not walking effigies,
Who smirk and smile with art polite, and sport
The borrowed vesture of their richer friends ;
But men of souls capacious who can plant
The standard of their worth on noble deeds,
And dare respect their conscience and their God.

Canada wants Honest Men—men who shall lay
Her empire's corner stone secure upon
The solid granite of eternal truth,
And build her towers and all her columns hew
From the deep quarry of a nation's love.

Canada wants Progressive Men—men who
The stirrings of ambition feel, to join
The glorious ranks of those who lead the van
In Freedom's sacred cause and pour the wealth
Of Heaven born genius at their country's shrine.

Canada wants Independent Men—men who
Regardless of applause will speak the truth—
Men who will spurn a bribe and scorn to bend
In cringing self-abasement at the feet
Of titled villany. Men who have drunk
From Freedom's sacred fount, and who their necks
Will never bend to wear the bondsman's yoke—
Men from deceit who'd tear the mask and show
The knave in all his nakedness and guilt.

Canada wants Virtuous Men—men with their hearts
Attuned to holiness—men who will take
The Bible as the Charter of their faith—
Adore the God whom it reveals and learn
ith gratitude sincere to sound His praise.

Canada wants Heroic Men—men who shall dare
To struggle in the solid ranks of truth;
To clutch the monster error by the throat;
Hurl base oppression from her seat, break down
Her walls and let the world with pæans
Of universal rapture usher Freedom in.

Canada wants Noble Men—not those who trace
Nobility through tortuous channels of
Hereditary blood and boasting of
Ancestral worth, swell with profound conceit,
At every mention of their little selves—
But men of noble souls—men tested well
In life's great struggle, tempered in the forge
Of hard experience, and fortified against
Temptation's wiles by purity of heart—
Men who will dare assert their rights and do
What duty bids though all the world should sneer.

Canada wants Patriotic Men—men who
Can feel their bosoms throb at mention of
Their country's name—men whose allegiance is
Not based on selfishness; whose honesty of soul
Would scorn promotion's highest seat,
If treason were the price—men who will guard
Her soil with sacred care and when she sounds
The trumpet of alarm, will grasp their swords,
Rush to the battle field with martial tread,
And fearless hurl destruction on her foes.

These be the men, Oh Canada, to spring
From out thy virgin soil. These be the men
To wield the sceptre of thy power, extend
Dominion o'er thy vast estate and write
In history the glory of thy name.

1879. GEO. W. ROSS.

CANADA TO ENGLAND.

The lark at dawn, the nightingale at eve
Conspire to make it beautiful. I had dreamed
Of some such beauty—Lo! it rose around me
More exquisite than any dream, more fair,
Than even the favorite dreams of cherished children,
And what those are—how strange how sweet, how rare,
We all remember—when a touch, a sound,
Startles us, and we look
Backwards—ten, twenty, thirty, forty years.
Yet fairer even than those
Cloud-visions capped with rose,
My England—with her abbeys framed in green;
Gray Tintern set not too far from the sea
By subtle monks, safe in its rim of hills,
And gayer Furness, clad in mellow reds
That glimmer warm through many an ivy-mat,
And tall cathedrals tipped with shimmering spires,
That hang over hut and hall,
And satin poppies, scarlet, wild,
Clasped in the hands of the laborer's child,
And tangled cottage gardens gaily drest
In all their rustic Sunday summer best.
O blame them not who evermore
Upon a cold colonial shore
Feel their hearts burn within them at the thought
Of all that beauty! Let it be said of such—
Not that they loved their Canada the less
But only England the more. Let it be said
Of them them that nature did so feed their souls
With all that was grand, illimitable, potent, fresh,
That poesy failed them. Nature was all in all;
Too self-sufficing, strong, relentless, masterful,
To aid the human spirit. Then there stole
From English valleys, leafy lanes, high hills,
From sloping uplands, farms and lichened towers,
From roofless ruins gracious in decay—
Something—a sentiment, aspiration, wish—
That soothed, inspired at once, that gave for wild
Dissatisfaction, peace. Dear England! I—
I have not—yet I fain had been—thy child!

MRS. HARRISON (Seranus).

THE FLAG OF OLD ENGLAND.

(*A Centenary Song, written for the one hundredth anniversary of the landing of Lord Cornwallis at Halifax.*)

All hail to the day when the Britons came over,
And planted their standard, with sea-foam still wet,
Around and above us their spirits will hover,
Rejoicing to mark how we honor it yet.
Beneath it the emblems they cherished are waving,
The Rose of Old England the roadside perfumes;
The Shamrock and Thistle the north winds are braving,
Securely the Mayflower blushes and blooms.

In the temples they founded, their faith is maintained,
Every foot of the soil they bequeathed is still ours,
The graves where they moulder, no foe has profaned,
But we wreath them with verdure, and strew them with flowers
The blood of no brother, in civil strife pour'd,
In this hour of rejoicing encumbers our souls!
The frontier's the field for the Patriot's sword,
And cursed be the weapon that Faction controls!

Then hail to the day! 'tis with memories crowded,
Delightful to trace 'midst the mists of the past,
Like the features of Beauty, bewitchingly shrouded,
They shine through the shadows Time o'er them has cast.
As travellers track to its source in the mountains,
The stream, which far swelling extends o'er the plains,
Our hearts, on this day fondly turn to the fountains
Whence flow the warm currents that bound in our veins.

And proudly we trace them: No warrior flying
From city assaulted, and fanes overthrown,
With the last of his race on the battlements dying,
And weary with wandering, founded our own.
From the Queen of the Islands, then famous in story,

A century since, our brave forefathers came,
And our kindred yet fill the wide world with her glory,
Enlarging her Empire, and spreading her name.

Every flash of her genius our pathway enlightens—
Ev'ry field she explores we are beckoned to tread,
Each laurel she gathers, our future day brightens—
We joy with her living, and mourn for her dead.
Then hail to the day when the Britons came over,
And planted their standard, with sea-foam still wet,
Above and around us their spirits shall hover,
Rejoicing to mark how we honor it yet.

JOSEPH HOWE.

CANADIAN PIONEERS.

Toll the bell, and toll it slowly; let the echoes mournful rise.
Sound the dead march of the battle, while the swelling requiem dies.
From the homes so fondly cherished, from the dear ones, fair and bright.
From the scenes and recollections that have filled them with delight;
Lo! our fathers, martyrs, heroes, daily passing from our view,
From the world of false and fleeting, to the realms of bright and true.

From the deep, unbroken forest, they have hewn our happy homes;
From the giants of the forests, they have reared our glittering domes.
Still we see the axe uplifted; still we hear the woodland ring;
See the thundering hemlocks falling prostrate to their sturdy king;
Still we hear their native chorus ling'ring, dying in the grove;
See the sickles strongly wielded; see the brawny muscles move.

As we ponder to contemplate all their nobleness of soul,
Daring courage, pious patience, honest reason and control;
When we think them persevering, sacrificing all for us,
Toiling, battling, hoping, praying; how in gratitude we bless.
How we wonder if we ever shall accomplish deeds so grand,
If our loyalty and valor will protect our father's land.

Noble was their cause and country; nobly was their cause maintained;
They have bravely fought and conquered; and immortal glory gained.
For, upon broad History's pages, there's no record more sublime,—
Art and Science have no patrons worthier on their book of time—
Than the genial independence, social joy, and love sincere,
Strength of courage, faith and reason, that our fathers held so dear.

On the earth no calling higher, than the hand that holds the plough ;
Not the soldier's palm of triumph ; not the poet's laurelled brow.
Genius may enroll her children on the golden scroll of fame ;
But the monument of glory, Industry must ever claim.
Onward ! Onward ! ever onward, speed the cause of honest worth.
May the stained hand of labor, honored be, while rolls the earth.

They have left, with all its grandeur, Caledonia's heathered hills,
Land of scholars, nurse of poets, where the shepherd's pibroch thrills.
They have left the gentle valleys, flowing hills, and rippling streams
That make England's mild expanses earnest of unending dreams.
They have left the land of beauty, isle of warmth and wit and worth.
Clime of eloquence and passion, home of chivalry and mirth.

Chose the music of the forest for the murmur of the wave ;
Left on shore their friends forsaken, dear ones sleeping in the grave ;
Chained their beauty and their laughter, in the bondage of their strength ;
Fought with hardships, dangers, trials ; conquered all, and won, at length.
Where the blue smoke of their shanties curled above the western wood,
There the smiling fields and pastures bask in evening's purple flood.

They are going, ever going ; but their mem'ry, beaming bright,
Will reanimate our bosoms, actuating to the right ;
We, by honor, shall endeavor, with strong ever-grateful hearts,
To be brave in every battle ; in each scene to take our parts ;
For their noble blood is in us, and their patriot spirit high ;
They have won for us and perished, we shall fight for them or die.
Toll the bell, and toll it slowly ; let its throbbings softly rise.
Sweetly, sadly keep it ringing, at each knell a hero dies.

A. M. TAYLOR.

LAKE HURON.

We cannot boast of high green hills,
Of proud bold cliffs where eagles gather—
Of moorland glen and mountain rills,
That echo to the red-bell'd heather.
We cannot boast of mouldering towers,
Where ivy clasps the hoary turret—
Of chivalry in ladies' bowers—
Of warlike fame, and knights who won it—
But had we Minstrel's Harp to wake,
We well might boast our own broad lake.

And we have streams that run as clear,
O'er shelvy rocks and pebbles rushing—
And meads as green, and nymphs as dear,
In rosy beauty sweetly blushing—
And we have trees as tall as towers,
And older than the feudal mansion—
And banks besprent with gorgeous flowers,
And glens and woods with fire-flies glancing,—
But prouder, loftier boast we make,
The beauties of our own broad lake.

The lochs and lakes of other lands,
Like gems may grace a landscape painting ;
Or where the lordly castle stands,
May lend a charm when charms are wanting ;
But ours is deep and broad and wide,
With steamships through its waves careering ;
And far upon its ample tide,
The barque its devious course is steering ;
While hoarse and loud the billows break
On islands of our own broad lake.

Immense, bright lake, I trace in thee
An emblem of the mighty ocean;
And in thy restless waves I see
Nature's eternal law of motion;
And fancy sees the Huron Chief
Of the dim past kneel to implore thee—
With Indian awe he seeks relief,
In pouring homage out before thee;
And I, too, feel my reverence wake,
As gazing on our own broad lake.

I cannot feel as I have felt,
When life with hope and fire was teeming;
Nor kneel as I have often knelt
At beauty's shrine, devoutly dreaming.
Some younger hand must strike the string,
To tell of Huron's awful grandeur.
Her smooth and moonlight slumbering,
Her tempest voices loud as thunder;
Some loftier lyre than mine must wake,
To sing our own broad gleaming lake.

THOMAS MCQUEEN

A SONG FOR OUR INLAND SEA.

A song for the glorious Hudson Bay,
For the fathomless ice-bound sheet,
Where the waters lap through the six months day,
'Gainst the ice-floes dimmed by the frozen spray,
And the wild gull wheels with its mate at play
O'er the vast deep, speeding fleet.

A song for the restless heaving mass
Imprisoned by ice-fields grim,
With never a vessel to come, alas!
And spread its white wings and slowly pass
With nothing afloat save the icy glass
Of the bergs that careen and trim.

A song for the source of a nation's wealth
Awaiting the master mind,
For the vasty deep that is teeming with wealth,
Albeit locked in a slumbering stealth
That awaits a nation with thews and health,
And a people no longer blind.

A song for the route to fair England's shore,
Whence came Hudson in years gone by,
And thrilled with pride to his stern heart's core,
Then trembled anon with a mighty awe
As he gazed where man had ne'er gazed before,
And harked to the wind's wild sigh.

A song for the sea that is all our own,
For this jewel in Canada's robe,
For this uncut diamond, this regal stone,
Flashing cold light from its setting lone,
And guarding, despite the wind's whispering moan,
Its secrets for us to probe.

ELLEN M. BOULTON.

A SONG OF CANADIAN RIVERS.

Flow on, noble rivers ! flow on ! flow on !
  In your beauteous course to the sea ;
Sweep on, noble rivers ! sweep on ! sweep on !
  Bright emblems of true liberty !
Roll noiselessly on a tide of bright song,
  Roll happily, grandly and free ;
Sweep over each plain in silv'ry tongued strain,
  Sweep down to the deep-sounding sea !

Flow on, noble rivers ! flow on ! flow on ?
  Flow swiftly and smoothly and free ;
Chant loudly and grand, the notes of our land—
  Fair Canada's true minstrelsy ;
Roll joyously on, sweep proudly along,
  In mirthfullest accents of glee !
Flow on, noble rivers ! flow on ! flow on !
  Flow down to the deep-sounding sea !

Flow on ! sweep on ! sweep on ! flow on !
  In a measureless, mystical key ;
Each note that you wake on streamlet and lake
  Will blend with the song of the sea ;
Through labyrinth-clad dell, in dreamy-like spell,
  Where slumbers each sentinel tree !
Flow on, noble rivers ! flow on ! flow on !
  Flow down to the deep-sounding sea !

THOMAS O'HAGAN.

THE SISTER PROVINCES.

[For this exercise the teacher should select seven girls, one to represent each of the Provinces. Beginning with Prince Edward Island, each girl should recite the part assigned to her. The girl representing Ontario should refer to the map with pointer in hand when describing its boundaries. The last few lines are to be recited in concert, all the girls joining hands and forming a circle.]

PRINCE EDWARD ISLAND.

I come from where the Atlantic wave beats back
The rushing waters which St. Lawrence pours
Into the sea. My cheeks are fanned by winds
As fresh and sweet, as ever kissed the brow
Of beauty. I have spent my life in fields
Where daisies smile, and though I cannot boast
Of rolling prairies, and of forests wild
And grand, yet fair as Eden are my bowers,
And in my thousand homes are nurtured men
Of royal worth, who from my eastern shores,
Like sentinels, keep watch lest traitor's foot
Should stain my sacred soil. My very name
A royal lineage bears, and every wave
That murmurs at my feet, in ceaseless strains
The praises sing of my Canadian home.

NOVA SCOTIA.

Have you heard of Acadia and the lovely Evangeline who dwelt on
The shores of the basin of Minas in the little village of Grand Pré?
Well there was I born, and there was the home of my father.
How I love to think of her broad sloping valleys of verdure,
And her long winding rivers that shimmer and dance in the sunlight,

And her orchards as white with the blossoms of Spring as if angels
Had dropped their long mantles upon them, and the song of the robin,
And the humming of bees, and the cottages under the pine trees,
Filled with the perfume of flowers, as lovely as that wherein dwelt
The son of Basil the blacksmith in the olden Norman time.

But that is not all of Acadia. Have you heard of her seamen?
Well come with me to Cape Breton and the harbors of Canso,
And look where the restless sea gulls near the horizon are flying
And there you will see, rocking fearless on whitecap and billow,
Men as brave as the sea kings who ravaged the coast of old England
More than a thousand years ago.

Have you heard of her statesmen?
No. Then read her annals and learn, how after many a struggle,
And in spite of the babble and strife of ambitious leaders,
The bondage of arrogant placemen was broken forever,
And the rulers, who rejected the voice of the people were taught
That Acadian freemen would never submit to oppression.

Oh loveliest land! As the doves to their windows go flying,
So to Acadia turns my heart with never dying devotion.

NEW BRUNSWICK.—

My sisters have many pleasant things to say of Prince Edward Island and Nova Scotia. I would like to see these beautiful valleys of which they have spoken, and I would like to read the story of Evangeline, of the little village of Grand Prè. I am not jealous of my sisters because their fathers were good and brave men or because their native land was so lovely, but who that has seen New Brunswick will not say that she too is equally fair? Have you ever stood on some eminence overlooking one of her magnificent harbors with its islands and lighthouses and its waters dancing in the moonlight, or have you sailed up the St. John river and seen the great expanse of field and orchard, with here and there shady bowers of maple and herds of cattle luxuriating in the meadows? Have you traversed her grand forests of pine and fir and seen there the busy woodman hewing down great spars for the navies of the world?

Have you ever thought of her people, happy, contented, prosperous and loyal? If you have thought of these things as I have, then you would love New Brunswick as I do—love her because her people are happy and free—love her as I do because she made my childhood happy with her scenes of beauty and I expect, even in old age, to find all that can make life comfortable within her borders.

QUEBEC.—

You don't seem to know me! Not know me?
I'm a litttle Norman girl. *Parlez-vous Français?*
Do you see this ribbon tied round my neck?
Look! my name is on it and it spells—Quebec.
You are all my sisters, so I am told,
And such a pretty lot of girls, all as good as gold.
They say I'm the eldest, well that may be true,
But my cheeks are still rosy and my eyes bright too.
You are all English and perhaps would like to know
How I became your sister. It was many years ago.
Just sit down awhile, I'll do my very best
To tell you. If I don't, you can think out the rest.
My people came from France. They were the first to see
This country, now so dear to you and me,
They cleared away the forests and built them pretty homes
Round which the wild rose clusters when the robin comes.
And little hamlets everywhere the travellers eye to meet,
With their whitewashed cottages lining every street;
And their pointed gables so very quaint and white,
And their groups of children laughing with delight.
Well, after a while (it was about two hundred years)
The British came and my people were in tears,
For they loved their homes and they could not see
What General Wolfe had to do with them. But he
Was a fighting man and so were his soldiers and they
Climbed up the steeps below Quebec, just at the break of day,
And although Montcalm resisted (no braver man than he)
He was beaten and slain, and the *fleur-de-lys*

Of old France was pulled down, and over their heads
The flag of old England fluttered instead.
Then we all became British and ever since then
We fought for her flag again and again ;
And some way at that time, just how I don't know,
I became your sister (it was some time ago,
We forget little points), but don't let us bother,
We are one family now and we all love each other.
We love the dear country that gave us our birth,
And I love Quebec as the dearest spot on earth.
The French and the English are united as friends,
And now dearest sisters my simple story ends.

ONTARIO.—

Come with me to this map which hangs
Upon the wall that you may see how large
The bounds of my dear home. There on the south
The ocean channel for the mighty lakes
Which westward lie—the blue St. Lawrence—marks
The limits of my farms and fields.

See you
That lake with islands gemmed ? There holidays
Glide past mid bowers of birch and maple where
The trailing vine shuts out all sounds of life
Save the cool murmur of the flowing stream.
And now in mood serenest spreads before
Our eyes the lake from which I get my name.
And next Niagara, with a rush that fills
The mind with awe, leaps from its rocky heights
Into the mist below, lashing its banks
With many strange contortions in its rage,
Then sinks into a stolid calm.

Here next
Still westward, pass Lake Erie's ragged shores,
Then for a moment pause as mem'ry lifts
Her silken curtain from the past and fills
These fields and streets with hosts of armed men.

There, see the kingly form of him who fell
On Queenston Heights, with sword in hand, as die
The brave. And there Tecumseh, noblest of
His race, leads forth his dusky knights,
That we to day this land might call our own.
That mighty river now so calm was then
Stirred by the oars of daring men, and where
These lofty spires speak to the clouds, was seen
The smoke of battle darkening all the sky.
Hark ! o'er the waters comes a British cheer.
There ! See the flag of England flies, Hurrah !
Detroit is ours, the gallant Brock has won
The day and rash invasion's foiled once more.

But let us hence, and on the wings of peace
My northern lakes explore.—St. Clair we pass
With hurried glance, and through Lake Huron rush
To where the King of Lakes holds royal court.
How vast his realm ! Shoreless to human eye.
How grand his empire ! Walled on every side
With granite strangely carved to mock the skill
Of puny man, and richly stored with gold
And many ores of strangest alchemy.
But haste ye now, nor tempt the forest long.
With swift canoe, with portages that test
Your strength of limb, with here and there a halt
By flick'ring fires from which the hungry wolf
Slinks howling to his lair, we push our way,
And sweeping through my northern bounds we pass
St. James' Bay, nor cease our circuit till
With hastening breath we've circumscribed my vast
Domain.

See where the shaded lines define
The northern watershed. From east to west o'er all
That region stand majestic pines and firs ;
Its very rocks are iron, waiting the call
Of commerce to be turned to gold. Look south

Where dwell the freemen of the soil, and fields
Waving with grain stretch far as eye can see.
Cities I have where busy heads trade with
The world, and opulence and pleasure find
A home. Whate'er that strong resolve can do,
Whate'er the cunning brain devise or courage dare
My sons are equal to and full of hope,
And, trusting in their father's God, perform
They will. So shall my country be in wealth
And worth the pride of all Canadian sons.

MANITOBA.—

I have found a home—a home at last,
　　Where the sky is blue and clear,
And I want no forest its shadows to cast
　　On the land I love so dear.
For the choice I make is the rolling plain,
　　Where the wind sweeps fresh and free,
And the youthful bloom of my new domain
　　Still crimsons my cheek as you see.

The wild rose blossoms beneath my eaves,
　　Where the swallow builds her nest,
And the prairie flowers peep atween the sheaves
　　Which the reaper clasps to his breast.
The water-fowl lingers among my lakes.
　　Where else can she happier be?
And when she at last a farewell takes,
　　'Tis to return in the spring to me.

Do you want a home for those who sigh
　　Where the busy shuttle plays;
For a breath of air and a clearer sky
　　And for brighter and better days?
Do you want a home for the men you reared
　　To honor the sweating brow,
By whom country and Queen are always revered,
　　Whether guiding the state or the plough?

Then send them to me—to my home in the West;
My prairies have waited long
For the plough share to cleave their grassy breast
And the reaper's merry song.
With bounteous fields of waving grain
And a sky that is blue and clear
I'll reward the labor of hand and brain
In the home I love so dear.

BRITISH COLUMBIA.—
Come, get your Alpen-stocks, you've halted long
On plain and prairie. I would bid you seek
The summit of yon mountain, where, refreshed
By scenes of grandeur which no other land
Can rival, you may know Columbia's worth.
See you the ocean break on yonder shore?
There, lulled by soft and soothing winds which from
The Orient blow, Vancouver lies fair as
The fabled groves, where Grecian nymphs in days
Of old their vigils kept.
See you that bay
Far reaching inland, where majestic ships
Loom up and from their mast the meteor flag
Of England floats? That is the trysting place
Of commerce. There the wealth of many climes
Halts on its journey to the East. See now
Yon river, where the fluttering wheel and clouds
Of densest smoke tell of an age of fire
And steam. Look down the misty canyon where
The pent up waters struggle to be free
And in a voice which makes the mountains shake
Demand a pathway to their ocean home.
Look through that mountain gorge and mark the streams
Which trickle down the hills on either side.
'Tis there the miner, stout of heart and limb,
Sets up his tent and lives on scanty fare

That from the sand beneath his naked feet
Imperial coffers might be filled with gold.
Here, where the forest spreads on every side
And 'mid the mountains capped by God himself
With snow on which no summer shines, I rear
My home. Strength from these hills I take,
And freedom from the sea that rolls beyond
The setting sun. And when, in years to come,
The story of my land is told, I know
My sisters to the farthest east shall sing
With loud acclaim the praises of Columbia's sons.

(The seven sisters join hands, form a circle and recite in concert :)

Then let us all as one united band
Make Canada the praise of every land
Though far apart our several homes may be,
Some on the Eastern, some the Western sea,
We all are sisters and no feud shall sever
The loving ties that bind our hearts together.

GEO. W. ROSS.

THE LOYAL BRIGADE.

[The teacher should direct a company of boys under the command of a leader to march to the platform and arrange themselves in proper order. As called upon each boy would step out and recite a patriotic quotation, previously prepared, and then step back into the ranks.]

The leader might introduce himself and his company to the school as follows :—

"LADIES AND GENTLEMEN,—With your permission I shall introduce to you a number of young gentlemen who will give you a few quotations from some of our most eminent poets and orators containing expressions of loyalty which I hope you will consider befitting such an occasion as this. The language of these quotations expresses the patriotic sentiments of the greatest nations of the world. They are the sentiments of men who loved their country with a devotion which Canadians might well imitate; they are the sentiments of men whose genius reflects glory on the race, and I am glad to believe that every member of my company, which I call the Loyal Brigade, will endeavor to illustrate in his future life by his devotion to his country and by his manliness of character that spirit of loyalty which pervades the words to which he gives utterance. It gives me great pleasure to ask you to listen to the language of Sir Walter Scott, from the lips of Master A. B. *(The pupil's full name should be used.)*

Master A. B. advances and says :—

Breathes there a man, with soul so dead,
Who never to himself hath said,
This is my own, my native land ?
Whose heart hath ne'er within him burned,
As home his footsteps he hath turned,
From wandering on a foreign strand ?
If such there breathe, go, mark him well ;
For him no minstrel raptures swell ;
High though his titles, proud his name,
Boundless his wealth as wish can claim ;
Despite those titles power, and pelf,
The wretch concentered all in self,
Living, shall forfeit fair renown,
And doubly dying, shall go down
To the vile dust, from whence he sprung,
Unwept, unhonored, and unsung

LADIES AND GENTLEMEN,—Master B. C. has given a good deal of attention to the study of history, and in the course of his reading has become impressed with the idea that neither wealth, nor commerce, nor great armies and navies alone can make a nation great. His views are very tersely summarized by Sir William Jones in answering the question "What Constitutes a State ?" I shall ask him to speak for himself :

Master B. C. :—

What constitutes a state ?
Not high-raised battlements or labored mound,
Thick wall or moated gate ;
Not cities proud with spires and turrets crowned ;
Not bays and broad-armed ports,
Where, laughing at the storm, proud navies ride ;
Not starred and spangled courts,
Where low-browed baseness wafts perfume to pride.

No :—men, high-minded men,
With powers as far above dull brutes endued
In forest, brake, or den,
As beasts excel cold rocks and brambles rude,—
Men who their duties know,
But know their rights, and, knowing, dare maintain,
Prevent the long-aimed blow,
And crush the tyrant while they rend the chain :
These constitute a state ;
And sovereign Law, that state's collected will,
O'er thrones and globes elate,
Sits empress, crowning good, repressing ill.

LADIES AND GENTLEMEN,—I shall now introduce to you a young gentleman who takes great pride in reading of the British navy. He becomes quite enthusiastic over the biography of such navigators as Cook and Drake, and had he lived in the time of Nelson I have no doubt he would have been on board the flagship if he had the opportunity. His recitation is from the poems of Thomas Campbell, and is entitled "Ye Mariners of England" :—

Master C. D. :—

Ye mariners of England !
Who guard our native seas,
Whose flag has braved a thousand years
The battle and the breeze,
Your glorious standard launch again,
To match another foe,
And sweep through the deep
While the stormy tempests blow ;
While the battle rages long and loud,
And the stormy tempests blow.

The spirits of your fathers
  Shall start from every wave!
For the deck it was their field of fame,
  And ocean was their grave:
Where Blake and mighty Nelson fell
  Your manly hearts shall glow,
As ye sweep through the deep
  While the stormy tempests blow;
While the battle rages long and loud.
  And the stormy tempests blow

Britannia needs no bulwarks,
  No towers along the steep;
Her march is o'er the mountain waves
  Her home is on the deep:
With thunders from her native oak
  She quells the floods below,
As they roar on the shore
  When the stormy tempests blow;
When the battle rages long and loud,
  And the stormy tempests blow.

The meteor flag of England
  Shall yet terrific burn,
Till danger's troubled night depart,
  And the star of peace return.
Then, then, ye ocean-warriors!
  Our song and feast shall flow
To the fame of your name,
  When the storm has ceased to blow;
When the fiery fight is heard no more,
  And the storm has ceased to blow.

LADIES AND GENTLEMEN,—The next man in the ranks has a recitation from Shakespeare, in which we have an admirable description of that heroic daring with which the British soldier is expected to fight for his Queen and country. It is taken from the speech of Henry V. at the Siege of Harfleur:

Master D. E. :—

Once more unto the breach, dear friends, once more ;
Or close the wall up with our English dead !
In peace, there's nothing so becomes a man
As modest stillness and humility ;
But when the blast of war blows in our ears,
Then imitate the action of the tiger—
Stiffen the sinews, summon up the blood,
Disguise fair nature with hard-favored rage
Then lend the eye a terrible aspect ;
Let it pry through the portage of the head,
Like the brass cannon ; let the brow o'erwhelm it,
As fearfully as doth a galled rock
O'erhang and jutty his confounded base,
Swilled with the wild and wasteful ocean.
Now set the teeth, and stretch the nostril wide ;
Hold hard the breath, and bend up every spirit
To his full height !—On ! on, you noblest English,
Whose blood is fetched from fathers of war-proof !
Fathers, that, like so many Alexanders,
Have, in these parts, from morn till even fought,
And sheathed their swords for lack of argument.—
Dishonor not your mothers : now attest
That those whom you called fathers did beget you !
Be copy now to men of grosser blood,
And teach them how to war !—And you, good yeomen,
Whose limbs were made in England, show us here
The mettle of your pasture ; let us swear
That you are worth your breeding : which I doubt not ;

For there is none of you so mean and base,
That hath not noble lustre in your eyes.
I see you stand like greyhounds in the slips,
Straining upon the start. The game's afoot;
Follow your spirit: and, upon this charge,
Cry—"Heaven for Harry! England! and St. George!"

LADIES' AND GENTLEMEN,—You have now heard fervent expressions of patriotism for lands which no matter how important they may be, are not so dear to some of us as the land which gave to us our birth, and which we are proud to call our own Canadian home. We all admire the graphic descriptions which poets give of English scenery, and of Scotland's hills and glens, and of Irish lakes. These countries have given to the world many great men—men who served their country with a devotion worthy of the most exalted character, but beautiful as are these distant and sacred lands, great as were the men who shaped their history, I believe Canada is just as beautiful, and that with the growth of our schools and universities we will show that genius, and refinement, and manliness, and statesmanship, are not confined to one country, nor are they the exclusive property of any nationality. I now call upon Master E. F. to speak for Canada:

Master E. F. says:—

Look over this beauteous land from east to west, and what do we behold? In a panoply of green, sheltered from burning suns by the warm mists of the Atlantic, and laved by waters which no tyrant hand has yet subdued, mark the fair form of the youngest province of our great Dominion. Westward follow the march of empire, and whether it be where the Bay of Fundy breaks with incessant roar on two Provinces; or where the St. Lawrence sweeps with imperial majesty past the frowning bastions of Quebec; or where four lakes woo like jealous lovers the fair Province of Ontario; or where, bowing beneath the luxuriance of nodding corn-fields, Manitoba invites the halting emigrant; or where, looking towards the Orient, Columbia smiles amid her golden sands; is this not a land of wealth and beauty and glorious fruition? Has Scotland its sylvan lochs that shimmer in the sunshine and mirror the richness of heather and gorse and fir tree? And have we not lakes as beautiful as artist ever painted, or poet longed to see? Have Britons made their land glorious by heroic deeds? Then why should not we, who are the heirs to all the ages, and with British blood in our veins to boot, make this land the home of independence, the very Valhalla of heroes? Has England shown that out of an admixture of alien races—Danish, Scandinavian, Saxon and Norman—with all their various dialects and tribal jealousies, she could form a nation so firmly knit together as to defy the wear of centuries, and the opposition of her most determined foes; and shall not we, whether of Saxon, Celtic or Norman blood, whether speaking the language of Northumbria or of Gaul, laying aside all jealousies of race and creed, work out a Canadian nationality equally strong, and self reliant. We are the descendants of the same British stock. We are heirs to her vast Canadian estates and a still vaster history of conquest and renown. The heritage won for us by the courage of the British soldier has been committed to our keeping. Shall we make this a land where the history of British prowess, valor and honor shall be perpetuated, or shall we supinely fold our arms, and regardless of the past—regardless of the traditions of our race, transfer this great heritage to a foreign flag? Surely this shall not be done. The heroes who fell on the plains of Abraham say it must not be; the loyalists who preferred the freedom of our forests to the restraints of an alien civilization, say it must not be. The pioneers, who made the solitary places blossom as the rose, say it must not be. Citizen and soldier, sower and reaper of every nationality and creed, say it must not be. Let us then seize the inspiration of these mighty spirits, "who, though dead, still speak to us from their urns," and by a law of succession stronger than Norman feudalism, bind our children to transmit this beautiful land with all its records of chivalry and its glorious traditions of connection with the British Empire, unimpaired to the keeping of a free, loyal and God-fearing posterity.

Long may our land of Maple green,
  Our land of lake and river,
The brightest gem in Britain's crown
  Be British blue forever.

Long may our sons and sires rejoice,
  Each heart leap at the story
Of British right, of British might,
  Of British power and glory.

LADIES AND GENTLEMEN,—I fear I have detained you too long. The other members of my company could entertain you as well as those who addressed you. I trust what you have heard has interested you. Depend upon it we all love Canada, and we assure you it is our earnest desire to prove ourselves worthy of the great advantages which it is our happy privilege to enjoy, and for which we are greatly indebted to the wisdom, honor and energy of those great and good men who laid the foundation of our liberties. We will close this exercise by singing "The Maple Leaf." (The teacher can substitute any other song or dispense with singing altogether.)

OUR CONNECTION WITH BRITAIN.

An extract from the Speech of Sir John A. Macdonald, in the Canadian Parliament, on the Confederation of the Provinces of British North America.

One argument, but not a strong one, has been used against this Confederation, that it is an advance towards independence. Some are apprehensive that the very fact of our forming this union shall hasten the time when we shall be severed from the Mother Country. I have no apprehension of that kind. I believe it will have a contrary effect. I believe that as we grow stronger, that as it is felt in England that we have become a people, able from our union, our strength, our population, and the development of our resources, to take our position among the nations of the world, she will be less willing to part with us than she would be now, when we are broken up into a number of insignificant colonies, subject to attack piece-meal, without any concerted action or common organization of defence. I am strongly of opinion, that year by year, as we grow in population and strength, England will see more clearly the advantages of maintaining the alliance between British North America and herself. Does any one imagine that when our population, instead of three and a half, will be seven millions, as it will be ere many years pass, we would be one whit more willing than now, to sever the connection with England? Would not those seven millions be just as anxious to maintain their allegiance to the Queen, and their connection with the Mother

Country, as we are now? I believe the people of Canada, east and west, to be truly loyal. But if they can, by possibility, be exceeded in loyalty, it is by the inhabitants of the Maritime Provinces. Loyalty, with them, is an overruling passion. In all parts of the Lower Provinces there is a rivalry between the opposing political parties, as to which shall most strongly express, and most effectively carry out the principle of loyalty to Her Majesty and to the British Crown.

When this union takes place, we will at the outset be no inconsiderable people. We find ourselves with a population approaching four millions of souls. Such a population in Europe would make a second, or at least, a third-rate power. And with a rapidly increasing population—for I am satisfied that under this union our population will increase in a still greater ratio than before—with increased credit—with a higher position in the eyes of Europe—with the increased security we can offer to immigrants, who would naturally prefer to seek a new home in what was known to them as a great country than in one little colony or another—with all this I am satisfied that, great as has been our increase in the last twenty-five years, since the union between Upper and Lower Canada, our future progress, during the next quarter of a century will be vastly greater. And when, by means of this rapid increase, we become a nation of eight or nine millions of inhabitants, our alliance will be worthy of being sought by the great nations of the earth. I am proud to believe that our desire of alliance will be reciprocated in England.

I know that there is a party in England—but it is inconsiderable in numbers, though strong in intellect and power—which speaks of the desirability of getting rid of the colonies; but I believe such is not the feelings of the statesmen and people of England. I believe it will never be the deliberately expressed determination of the Government of Great Britain. The colonies are now in a transition state, gradually a different colonial system is being developed—and it will become, year by year, less a case of dependence on our part, and of overruling protection on the part of the Mother Country, and more a case of healthy and cordial alliance. Instead of looking on us as a merely dependent colony, England will have in us a friendly nation—a subordinate, but still a powerful people—to stand by her in North America, in peace as in war. The people of Australia will be such another subordinate nation; and England will have this advantage, if her colonies progress under the new colonial system, as I believe they will, that though at war with all the rest of the world, she will be able to look to the subordinate nations in alliance with her, and owing allegiance to the same Sovereign, who will assist in enabling her again to meet the whole world in arms, as she has done before. And if in the great Napoleonic War, with every port in Europe closed against her commerce, she was yet able to hold her own, how much more will that be the case when she has a colonial empire increasing in power, in wealth, in influence, and in position.

It is true that we stand in danger, as we have stood in danger again and again in Canada, of being plunged into war, and all its consequences, as the result of causes over which we have no control, by reason of this connection. This, however, need not intimidate us. At the very mention of the prospect of war some time ago, how were the feelings of the people aroused from one extremity of British America to the other, and preparations made for meeting its worst consequences. Although the people of this country are fully aware of the horrors of war, should a war arise, unfortunately, between the United States and England, and we pray it never may—they are still ready to encounter all ills of this kind, for the sake of the connection with England. So long as that alliance is maintained, we enjoy, under her protection, the privileges of constitutional liberty according to the British system. We will enjoy here that which is the great test of constitutional freedom—we will have the rights of the minority respected. In all countries the rights of the majority take care of themselves, but it is only in countries like England, enjoying constitutional liberty, and safe from the tyranny of a single despot or of an unbridled democracy, that the rights of minorities are regarded. So long, too, as we form a portion of the British Empire, we shall have the example of her free institutions, of the high standard of the character of her statesmen and public men, of the purity of her legislation, and the upright administration of her laws. In this younger country one great advantage of our connection with Great Britain will be, that under her auspices, inspired by her example, in a portion of her empire, our public men will be actuated by principles similar to those which actuate the statesmen at home. These, although not material physical benefits, of which you can make an arithmetical calculation, are of such overwhelming advantage to our future interests and standing as a nation, that to obtain them is well worthy of any sacrifices we may be called upon to make, and the people of this country are ready to make them.

We should feel, also, sincerely grateful to a beneficent Providence, that we have had the opportunity vouchsafed to us, of calmly considering this great constitutional change—this peaceful revolution, that we have not been hurried into it, like the United States, by the exigencies of war—that we have not had a violent revolutionary period forced on us, as in other nations, by hostile action from without, or by domestic dissensions within. Here we are in peace and prosperity, under the fostering care of Great Britain—a dependent people—with a government having only a limited and delegated authority, and yet allowed without restriction, and without jealousy on the part of the Mother Country, to legislate for ourselves, and peacefully and deliberately to consider and determine the future of Canada and British North America. It is our happiness to know the expression of the will of our Gracious Sovereign, through her Ministers, that we have her full sanction for our deliberations, and her only solicitude is, that we shall adopt a system really for our advantage, and that she promises to sanction whatever conclusion, after full deliberation, we may arrive at, as to the best mode of securing the well-being—the present and future prosperity of British America. It is our privilege and happiness to be in such a position, and we cannot be too grateful for the blessings thus conferred upon us.

In conclusion, I would again implore the House not to let this opportunity pass. It is an opportunity that may never recur. It was only by a happy concurrence of circumstances that we were enabled to bring this question to its present position. If we do not take advantage of the time, if we show ourselves unequal to the occasion, it may never return, and we shall hereafter bitterly and unavailingly regret, having failed to embrace the happy opportunity now offered, of founding a great nation under the fostering care of Great Britain, and our Sovereign Lady, Queen Victoria.

CONFEDERATION.

An extract from the Speech of the Hon. George Brown, in the Canadian Parliament, on the Confederation of the Provinces of British North America.

One hundred years have passed away since the conquest of Quebec, but here we sit, the children of the victor and the vanquished, all avowing hearty attachment to the British Crown, all earnestly deliberating how we shall best extend the blessings of British institutions; how a great people may be established on this continent, in close and hearty connection with Great Britain. Where, Sir, in the page of history, shall we find a parallel to this? Will it not stand as an imperishable monument to the generosity of British rule? And it is not in Canada alone that this scene has been witnessed. Four other colonies are at this moment occupied as we are—declaring their hearty love for the parent State, and deliberating with us, how they may best discharge the great duty entrusted to their hands, and give their aid in developing the teeming resources of these vast possessions.

And well, Mr. Speaker, may the work we have unitedly proposed rouse the ambition and energy of every true man in British America. Look, Sir, at the map of the continent of America. Newfoundland, commanding the mouth of the noble river that almost cuts our continent in twain, is equal in extent to the Kingdom of Portugal. Cross the straits to the mainland, and you touch the hospitable shores of Nova Scotia, a country as large as the Kingdom of Greece. Then mark the sister Province of New Brunswick—equal in extent to Denmark and Switzerland combined. Pass up the St. Lawrence to Lower Canada—a country as large as France. Pass on to Upper Canada—twenty thousand square miles larger than Great Britain and Ireland put together. Cross over the continent to the shores of the Pacific, and you are in British Columbia, the land of golden promise—equal in extent to the Austrian Empire. I speak not now of the vast Indian Territories that lie between, greater in extent than the whole soil of Russia—and that will, ere long, I trust, be opened up to civilization, under the auspices of the British American Confederation. Well, Sir, the bold scheme in your hands is nothing less than to gather all these countries into one; to organize them under one government, with the protection of the British flag, and in heartiest sympathy and affection with our fellow-subjects in the land that gave us birth. Our scheme is to establish a government that will seek to turn the tide of emigration into this northern half of the American continent; that will strive to develop its great national resources, and that will endeavor to maintain liberty, and justice, and Christianity throughout the land.

What we propose now is but to lay the foundations of the structure, to set in motion the governmental machinery that will, one day, we trust, extend from the Atlantic to the Pacific. And we take especial credit to ourselves, that the system we have devised, while admirably adapted to our present situation, is capable of gradual and efficient expansion in future years to meet all the purposes contemplated by our scheme. But, if honorable gentlemen will recall to mind, that when the United States seceded from the Mother Country, and for many years afterwards, their population was not nearly equal to ours at the present moment, that their internal improvements did not then approach to what we have already attained; and that their trade and commerce was not a third of what ours has already reached, I think they will see that the fulfilment of our hopes may not be so very remote, as at first sight might be imagined. And they will be strengthened in that conviction, if they remember that what we propose to do is to be done with the cordial sympathy and assistance of that great Power, of which it is our happiness to form a part.

And, said I not rightly, Mr. Speaker, that such a scheme is well fitted to fire the ambition and rouse the energy of every member of this House? Does it not lift us above the petty politics of the past, and present to us high purposes and great interests, that may well call forth all the intellectual ability, and all the energy and enterprise to be found amongst us? I readily admit all the gravity of the question; and that it ought to be considered cautiously and thoroughly before adoption. Far be it from me to deprecate the closest criticisms, or to doubt for a moment the sincerity or patriotism of those who feel it their duty to oppose the measure. But in considering a question on which hangs the future destiny of half a continent, ought not the spirit of mere fault-finding to be hushed? Ought not the spirit of mere partisanship to be banished from our debates? Ought we not to sit down and discuss the arguments presented, in the earnest and candid spirit of men, bound by the same interest, seeking a common end, and loving the same country ?

Some honorable gentlemen seem to imagine that the members of the Government have a deeper interest in this scheme than others ; but what possible interest can any of us have, except that which we share with every citizen of the land ? What risk does any one run from this measure, in which all of us do not fully participate ? What possible inducement could we have to urge this scheme, except our earnest and heartfelt conviction that it will conduce to the solid and lasting advantages of our country ? There is one consideration, Mr Speaker, which cannot be banished from this discussion, and that ought, I think, to be remembered in every word we utter ; it is that the constitutional system of Canada cannot remain as it is now. Something must be done. We cannot stand still. We cannot go back to chronic sectional hostility and discord—to a state of perpetual ministerial crisis. The events of the last eight months cannot be obliterated ; the solemn admissions of men of all parties can never be erased. The claims of Upper Canada must be met, and met now. I say, then, that every one who raises his voice in hostility to this measure is bound to keep before him, when he speaks, all the perilous consequences of its rejection. I say, then, that no man who has a true regard for the well-being of Canada can give a vote against this scheme, unless he is prepared to offer, in amendment, some better remedy for the evils and injustice that have so long threatened the peace of our country.

Sir, the future destiny of these great Provinces may be affected, by the decision we are about to give, to an extent, which at this moment we may be unable to estimate. But, assuredly the welfare, for many years, of four millions of people hangs on our decision. Shall we then rise equal to the occasion ? Shall we approach this discussion without partisanship, and free from every personal feeling, but the earnest resolution to discharge, conscientiously, the duty which an overruling Providence has placed upon us ? Sir, it may be that some among us may live to see the day when, as the result of this measure, a great and powerful people shall have grown up in these lands : when the boundless forest all around us shall have given way to smiling fields and thriving towns, and when one united government, under the British flag, shall extend from shore to shore ; but who could desire to see that day, if he could not recall with satisfaction the part he took in this discussion ? Mr. Speaker, I have done. I leave the subject to the conscientious judgment of the House, in the confident expectation and belief that the decision it will render will be worthy of the Parliament of Canada.

THE CONSTITUTIONAL SYSTEM OF CANADA.

I take the British constitutional system as the great original system upon which are founded the institutions of all free States. I take it as one of a family born of Christian civilization. I take it as combining in itself permanence and liberty; liberty in its best form—not in theory alone, but in practice; liberty which is enjoyed in fact by all the people of Canada, of every origin and of every creed.

Can any one pretend to say that a chapter of accidents which we can trace for eight hundred years, and which some antiquarians may even trace for a much longer period, will account for the permanence of these institutions? If you say that they have not in themselves the elements of permanence which preserve the foundations of a free State from one generation to another, how do you account for their continued and prosperous existence? How do you account for it, that of all the ancient constitutions of Europe this alone remains; and remains not only with all its ancient outlines, but with great modern improvements,—improvements, however, made in harmony with the design of its first architects? Here is a form of government that has lasted, with modifications to suit the spirit of successive ages, for a period of eight hundred years. How is it that I account for the permanence of its institutions? By asserting that, in their outline plan, they combined all the good of material importance that has ever been discovered.

The wisdom of the middle ages, and the political writers of the present time, have all laid down one maxim of government. That no unmixed form of government can satisfy the wants of a free and intelligent people; that an unmixed democracy, for instance, must result in anarchy or military despotism; but that the form of government which combines in itself an inviolable monarchy, popular representation, and the incitements of an aristocracy—a working aristocracy—an aristocracy that takes its share of toil and danger in the day of battle, of care and anxiety in the time of peace—an aristocracy of talent open to any of the people who make themselves worthy to enter it—that three-fold combination in the system of government is the highest conception of political science.

Let us see if the British form, apart from any details of its practice, combines in itself these three qualities. The leading principle of the British system is, that the head of the State is inviolable. It is necessary to the stability of any state that there should be an inviolable authority or tribunal; and under the British system this is recognized in the maxim that "the king can do no wrong." Having placed the principle of inviolability in the Crown, and the principle of privilege in the Peerage, the founders of the State took care at the same time that the peerage should not stagnate into a small and exclusive caste. They left the House of Lords open to any of the people who might distinguish themselves in war or in peace, although they might be the children of paupers (and some have been ennobled who were unable to tell who their parents were), to enter in and take their place on an equality with the proudest there, who trace back their descent for centuries.

It was for the people of Canada, with the precedent of England and the example of the American republic before them, to decide which should be the prevailing character of their government—British constitutional, or republican constitutional. For my part, I prefer the British constitutional government, because it is the best; and I reject the republican constitutional government, because it is not the best. We are now witnessing a great epoch in the world's history; and the events daily transpiring around us teach us not to rely too much upon our present position of secure independence, but rather to apprehend and be prepared for attempts against our liberties, and against that system of government which, I am convinced, is heartily cherished by the inhabitants of this province.

T. D'Arcy McGee.

THE CLAIMS OF OUR COUNTRY.

The love of country is a noble and laudable sentiment. It has inspired many of the most heroic deeds that sparkle in the history of the world. Like attachments to party or sect, it may degenerate into bigotry and exclusiveness; but a liberal and enlightened patriotism ennobles its possessor. The man who cannot rise above selfish and personal interests, to an intelligent sympathy with the prosperity of his country, is not worthy to share the blessings of citizenship, in a civilized community.

This attachment to our country, is not the result of its superiority to other lands. It does not depend on fertility of soil, or salubrity of climate. Countries of stern climate and unproductive soil have given some of the highest examples of unselfish patriotism. It is like a mother's love, instinctive and spontaneous. It is planted in the human breast, by the Creator, that it may prompt us to labor for the welfare of our country. All forms of selfishness, are antagonistic to the growth of patriotism. A man may be very noisy in his profession of loyalty, yet if his own character be wanting in integrity and industry, he will, to the extent of his influence, prevent the prosperity of his country.

At the present crisis in our history, it is of the first importance that we realize our obligations as patriots, and the extent to which the present has the character and interests of the future in its keeping. It is an inspiring spectacle, to behold our beloved Canada rising majestically to assume her place among the nations, which are in the vanguard of the world's progress. The light of hope is on her brow. The vigor of youth throbs in her veins. Her undazzled eye is on the future, where the star of a lofty destiny beams before her.

We enter upon a race for an honorable position among the kingdoms of the earth, under circumstances of the highest promise. We possess a country, vast in extent, and rich in agricultural, commercial, and manufacturing resources. We are also profundly indebted to the past. We eat the fruit of the trees, which past generations have planted. While many of the older countries of Europe are enslaved by ignorance and crushed by despotic power, we have a birthright of free constitutional government—of civil and religious liberty—the noblest ever bequeathed to any youthful nation. We are heirs to a heritage of literature, rich in every department of intellectual wealth—a heritage of deathless memories of noble and heroic lives, which should inspire us to émulate the faith and fortitude by which they vanquished every foe, and won their imperishable renown. And better than all, we inherit the priceless legacy of an unsealed Bible, with its holy lessons of truth and love, teaching us how this life may be redeemed from the slavery of selfishness, and bringing life and immortality to light in the gospel.

It is not surprising that statesmen should regard such a remarkable combination of advantages, as an earnest of a prosperous and glorious future. But we should not forget, that it is not material prosperity, but "righteousness," that "exalteth a nation." No combination of propitious circumstances—no fertility of soil, extent of dominion, legacies of thought, commercial prosperity, nor bannered armies in their conquering might, can give any sure pledge to futurity of true greatness without the improvement and moral elevation of the people. The moral and intellectual condition of the population will reflect itself in every department of national life, and determine our position in the scale of civilization. Material progress and intellectual activity will not save us from national degeneracy, unless the foundations of nationhood be laid in truth and righteousness.

The history of the past is full of instructive lessons.—Nations, which once ranked high and swayed the sceptre of imperial power over vast dominion, as the result of internal corruption, have crumbled into decay, and passed away, leaving only their name and fate as a warning to future ages. And at the present hour, some of the fairest countries beneath the sun, fertile in soil, and genial in climate, are the high places of ignorance, tyranny, and moral degradation.

It becomes us to lay these lessons deeply to heart. Without that inner moral life, which alone gives a permanent and elevating influence to the social and political institutions of a country, all our advantages may be sacrificed on the altar of selfish ambition and sordid gratification, and only accelerate our national decay. We may boast of our freedom and yet be the most abject slaves. We may have the rights and privileges of British freemen, and yet be destitute of the independence without which they will not be exercised for the true welfare of our country. We may have wise laws, and yet want the incorruptible integrity essential to their just administration. We may have wealth—but it will be the instrument of intemperance, avarice, and vanity. We may have a literature, full of genius, but it will be "of the earth, earthy." We may have intellectual energy —but it will leave the spiritual and nobler capacities of our being, paralyzed by low selfish activities.

Let us rise to the dignity and responsibility of our position. We are launching the ship of state on a voyage towards a glorious destiny. We are sowing the seeds of national character, the fruits of which future generations shall reap. We are watching over the infancy of our country. To us it is given to stamp our moral likeness on its future history. By the lives we live, and the work we do, we shall determine whether posterity shall bless our memory, or whether our selfish indolence and recreancy to our high trust will bequeath them a heritage of ignorance, lax political morality, and religious indifference, that shall darken their history through all coming time.

E. H. DEWART, D.D.

THE GREATNESS OF OUR HERITAGE.

From an address by the Hon. John Schultz, Lieutenant-Governor, Manitoba, Dominion Day, 1891

A single glance at an ordinary school geography shows Canada to be one of the most favored portions of the globe; and as if Providence had kept in reserve its best gifts for this latest born of nations, we have, wafted into our spacious western harbors and along our picturesque Pacific coast, the balmy winds of the Western Ocean, and with them that ocean stream which makes flowers bloom and trees bud near the Arctic circle, as early as on the Mississippi or the St. Lawrence, just as the great stream poured out by the Mexican Gulf foils the Ice King's blockade of the magnificent harbors of our Eastern coasts, and nourishes those deep-sea pastures of which Canada possesses the richest in the world. As a means of access to the interior of this favored land, Nature has cleft our rugged Eastern coast with mighty rivers and great lakes which bear the home hunter to the verge of our great Cereal Table-land, where, through future wheat fields, turn and wind the rivers of the great plain, the Red, Assiniboine, Souris, Qu'Appelle and Saskatchewan.

This great country bounded by three oceans has the greatest extent of coast line; the greatest number of miles of river and lake navigation; the greatest extent of coniferous forest; the greatest coal measures; the most varied distribution of precious and economic minerals; the most extensive salt and fresh water fisheries; and the greatest extent of arable and pastoral land of any country in the world.

This great northern heritage so vast in area and resources and which we call our own country, is possessed by a northern race and ruled by a northern Queen. Its national characteristics are northern, it is the Norland of this continent ; to the northern races of the old world whence we sprang we look for our national characteristics.

We have in this Dominion more Celts than had Brian when he placed his heel upon the neck of Odin, more Saxons than had Alfred when he founded his kingdom, more Normans than had William when he drew from them the armed host with which he invaded England, more of Norse blood then there were Norsemen when their kings ruled Britain and their galleys swept the sea. We are the descendants of all the northern kingdom-founders of Western Europe. We have the laws of Edward, the Magna Charta and the Roman Code; we have copied the constitution which English statesmen, legislators, patriots and martyrs lived or died to secure and save. We have resources by sea and land, civil and religious liberty ; we are heirs, equally with those who live in the British Isles, to the glory and traditions of the British Empire. Canadians have fought side by side with the Englishman, Irishman and Scot on the burning sands of India and Africa, and on the bleak battle fields of the Crimean Peninsula, and they have died as bravely, too, as any of them.

But while, with just pride, we remember the deeds of our ancestors for the past thousand years, and know that when necessary the blood of the sea-kings, the sturdy

Saxon, the gallant Norman and the fiery Celt, which is in our veins, will assert itself again, yet thanks be to Almighty God, our national life began and has continued in peace; and as we chose for our national emblems the Canadian beaver and the maple leaf, so have we sought to build up, harmonize and beautify our splendid heritage by the arts of peace and not by the arts of war. During the short period, less than a quarter of a century, of our national life, we have girded the continent with bands of steel, piercing mountains, spanning torrents; and crossing the snow-capped giants of the Rocky and Selkirk chains we have linked our young Canadian empire to Japan and China, the oldest empires of the Orient. We have justified our traditions on the sea, in making Canada third in rank of the maritime nations of the world; and at this moment the sails of Canadian ships whiten every sea, commanded by Canadian descendants of Drake and Hawkins, Frobisher and Richard Grenville, Nelson and Collingwood, Cartier and D'Iberville. Better still than even this material progress is the fact that our nationality is founded upon the mutual respect and confidence of the people, surrounded by the sanctity of Religion, and crowned with its only appropriate capital, Lawful Constitutional Authority.

On the youth of Canada rests the future of this great country, the exemplification of the attributes of our great race Recreant to this trust they may possibly be, but I see nothing to disturb my deep-seated conviction that they will continue as we have begun; and building this nation in the fear of Him who gave us this Great Heritage, with love for Her who gave us national life, endeavoring, as we have done, to dissolve all differences and melt away all jealousies in the crucible of moderation and justice, they will be strong enough to preserve its unity and successful enough to cause the day we now celebrate to be even more deeply honored, and to rejoice in that birthright, which to my mind is even now the highest and best the world contains.

You will prosper so long as you are worthy of this great trust; you will be blessed in preserving it and strengthening it, so long as you seek divine aid to maintain it as the most precious of your birthrights, and you will rise to that place as a people in the great Empire, of which we form a part, in proportion as you follow His precepts and obey his Divine Law. Great as you are now, greater you will become, and as citizens of Canada, citizens of the Great British Empire you will fulfil the prophecy of the Druid priest to Boadicea, the first British Queen,

"Regions Cæsar never knew
Your posterity shall sway,
Where his eagles never flew,
None invincible as they."

THE FUTURE OF CANADA.

From a Speech delivered by Lord Dufferin in Toronto, a few days before the close of his term as Governor-General.

What, then, is to be my valediction—my parting counsel to the citizens of the Dominion before I turn my face to the wall. A very few words will convey them. Love your country, believe in her, honor her, work for her, live for her, die for her. Never has any people been endowed with a nobler birthright, or blessed with prospects of a fairer future. Whatever gift God has given to man is to be found within the borders of your ample territories. It is true, the zone within which your lines are cast is characterized by ruder features than those displayed in lower latitudes and within more sunward-stretching lands, but the north has ever been the home of liberty, industry and valor; it is also true you are not so rich as many other communities, but the happiness of a people does not so much depend upon the accumulation of wealth, as upon its equable distribution. In many of the wealthiest nations of Europe thousands can scarcely obtain their daily bread, and though Canada is by no means at present a nation of millionaires, there is not amongst us an agricultural homestead, between the Atlantic and the Pacific, where content and a rude plenty do not reign, and in a thousand localities the earth is bursting with the mineral wealth which only requires improved transportation to develop.

Moreover, you possess the best form of Government with which any historical nation has ever been blessed. The excellency of the British Constitution, with the self-expanding energies it embodies, is an ancient story which I need not insist upon, but as there are always external forces which disturb the working of the most perfect mechanism, so in an old country like England, many influences exist to trouble the harmonious operations of the political machine; but here our constitution has been set agoing entirely disencumbered of those entanglements which traditional prejudices and social complications have given birth to at home. My advice to you, then, would be to guard and cherish the characteristics of your constitution with a sleepless vigilance.

Almost every modern constitution has been the child of violence, and remains indelibly impressed with the scars of the struggle which ushered in its birth. A written constitution is of necessity an artificial invention —a contrivance, a formula as inelastic as the parchment on which it is written—instead of being a living, primeval, heaven-engendered growth, whereas the foundations of the polity under which you live are of secular antiquity. No revolutionary convulsion has severed the continuity of your history or disinherited you of your past—your annals are not comprised within the lifetime of a centenarian, but reach back through a thousand years of matchless achievement in every field of exertion open to mankind. Nor do even the confines of two oceans suffice to hedge you in; but you share an Empire whose flag floats, whose jurisdiction asserts itself in every quarter of the globe, whose ships whiten every sea, whose language is destined to spread further than any European tongue, whose institutions every nation aspiring to freedom is endeavoring to imitate, and whose vast and widespread colonies are vying with each other in their affectionate love for the Mother Country in their efforts to add lustre to the British name, in their longing to see cemented still more closely the bonds of that sacred and majestic union within which they have been born.

SOURCES OF CANADIAN POWER.

The country you call Canada, and which your sons and your children's children will be proud to know by that name, is a land which will be a land of power among the nations. Mistress of a zone of territory favorable for the maintenance of a numerous and homogeneous white population, Canada must, to judge from the increase in her strength during the past, and from the many and vast opportunities for the growth of that strength in her new Provinces in the future, be great and worthy her position on the earth. Affording the best and safest highway between Asia and Europe, she will see traffic from both directed to her coasts. With a hand upon either ocean she will gather from each for the benefit of her hardy millions a large share of the commerce of the world. To the east and to the west she will pour fourth of her abundance, her treasures of food and the riches of her mines and of her forests, demanded of her by the less fortunate of mankind. In no other land have the last seventeen years, the space of time which has elapsed since your Federation, witnessed such progress. Other countries have seen their territories enlarged and their destinies determined by trouble and war, but no blood has stained the bonds which have knit together your free and order-loving populations, and yet in this brief period, so brief in the life of a nation, you have attained to a union whose characteristics from sea to sea are the same. A judicature above suspicion, a strong central government to direct all national interests, the toleration of all faiths with favor to none, a franchise recognizing the rights of labor by the exclusion only of the idler, a government ever susceptible to the change of public opinion and ever open, through a responsible ministry, to the scrutiny of the people—these are the features of your rising power. Truly, you present the spectacle of a nation already possessing the means to make its position respected by sea or by land. I esteem those men favored indeed, who, in however slight a degree, have had the honor to take part in the councils of the statesmen, who, in this early era of her history, are moulding a nation's laws. For me, I feel that I can be ambitious of no higher title than to be known as one who administered its government in thorough sympathy with the hopes and aspirations of its founders, and in perfect consonance with the will of its free parliament.

LORD LORNE.

ADVANTAGES OF CANADA.

Canada has rare and exceptional advantages. As a people, we share in all the grand historic past of the mother-land; while we enjoy an immunity from impediments, involved in some of time's bequests to her. We inherit what it scarce seems hyperbole to speak of as a boundless territory, unencumbered, and ours to make of it what we will. The training of those who ere long must be called upon to take part in the carrying out of this transformation, is the work of our schools and colleges. It is for us as teachers, not only to guide the student through a course of instruction; but to animate him with the resolve to turn the knowledge acquired to wise account; to stimulate him with the ardor of proud hopes and noble endeavors;

> "To arouse the deeper heart,
> Confirm the spirit glorying to pursue
> Some path of steep ascent and lofty aim."

Never was there a time when the responsibilities were greater or more urgent. Our young Dominion throbs with eager, undefined longings and aspirations: "yearning for the large excitement that the coming years will yield." It is of vital importance that such aspirations be wisely directed, and the true goal be kept in view. There is a tempting hallucination in the acquisition of a domain that stretches from ocean to ocean. The rhetoricians of the neighboring Republic have yielded only too freely to its seductions. But however just the pride with which we enter on the task of fashioning out of the savage wilderness of half a continent, the provinces and states of the future, history teaches us other lessons. If breadth of mind is coincident with amplitude of territory Russia ought to be the centre of Europe's intellectual life; and England the narrow sphere of bigotry and ignorance. The lamented historian John Richard Greene, charmed all readers with his "Making of England;" but his fascinating volume sufficies to show that it is men not acres that go to the making up of great nations. From a little speck on the world's map, lying between the mountains of Moab and the sea have come the melodies of sacred song, and the inspired lessons that still glow with living power for the regeneration of the world. The land of Hellas and the islands of the Ægean sea were the nurseries of letters, arts, and science; and a still smaller republic in the valley ot the Arno stepped into her place, as the Athens of the Middle Ages, and the cradle of the Renaissance. And as for England, the land of Shakespeare and Milton, of Newton, Locke, Adam Smith, Darwin and other epoch-makers of the past and present: America's genial poet, Oliver Wendell Holmes, looking on the insular cradle of our common race from his own ample domain, exclaims with kindly irony:—

"His home! The Western giant smiles,
And twirls the spotty globe to find it;
This little speck the British Isles?
'Tis but a freckle,—never mind it!"

But it is only to recall the words:—

"For Memory blushes at the sneer;
And Honor turns with frown defiant;'
And Freedom, leaning on her spear,
Laughs louder than the laughing giant.

'An islet is a world,' she said,
'Where glory with its dust has blended;'
And Britain keeps her noble dead
Till earth, and sea, and sky are rended."

We inherit the energy of the race that has made of England what she is; and with it the heritage of her example, and the lessons which her history teaches. The capacity is ours; let it find wise guidance, as it has ample scope; and what may it not accomplish? Our faith in the life that lies beyond earth's narrow span finds confirmation from the very insignificance of man's highest achievements here, compared with his capacities and aspirations. Yet here is your present field of action, in which you are called to play your part manfully; ever keeping before you that higher life, of which this is but the probationary stage. Let it be vital with deeds, and not with boastful words. Science has come to your aid with appliances undreamt of till now. Philosophy turns aside from abstract speculation to solve the vexed problems of social and political life. With advantages rarely, if ever equalled, you enter on the inheritance of a virgin soil, with all the grand possibilities of a new era. But the willing hand of the industrious toiler will need the help of the keen intellect and the no less busy brain, if we would not be mere gleaners, loitering in the rear of a progressive age, "Reaping where we have not sown, and gathering where we have not strawed."

SIR DANIEL WILSON.

CANADA AND THE UNITED STATES.

We are here to determine how best we can draw together, in the bonds of peace, friendship and commercial prosperity, the three great branches of the British family, In the presence of this great theme all petty interests should stand rebuked. We are not dealing with the concerns of a city, a province or a state, but with the future of our race in all time to come.

Why should not these three great branches of the family flourish, under different systems of government, it may be, but forming one grand whole, proud of a common origin and of their advanced civilization? The clover lifts its trefoil leaves to the evening dew, yet they draw their nourishment from a single stem. Thus distinct, and yet united, let us live and flourish. Why should we not? For nearly two thousand years we were one family. Our fathers fought side by side at Hastings, and heard the curfew toll. They fought in the same ranks for the sepulchre of our Saviour. In the earlier and later civil wars, we can wear our white and red roses without a blush, and glory in the principles those conflicts established. Our common ancestors won the great Charter and the Bill of Rights—established free Parliaments, the Habeas Corpus, and Trial by Jury. Our Jurisprudence comes down from Coke and Mansfield to Marshall and Story, rich in knowledge and experience which no man can divide. From Chaucer to Shakespeare our literature is a common inheritance. Tennyson and Longfellow write in one language, which is enriched by the genius developed on either side of the Atlantic. In the great navigators from Cortereal to Hudson, and in all their "moving accidents by flood and field" we have a common interest.

On this side of the sea we have been largely reinforced both by the Germans and French, there is strength in both elements. The Germans gave to us the sovereigns who established our freedom, and they give to you industry, intelligence and thrift; and the French, who have distinguished themselves in arts and arms for centuries, now strengthen the Provinces which the fortune of war decided they could not control.

But it may be said we have been divided by two wars. What then? The noble St. Lawrence is split in two places—by Goat Island and Anticosti—but it comes down to us from the same springs in the same mountain sides; its waters sweep together past the pictured rocks of Lake Superior, and encircle in their loving embrace the shores of Huron and Michigan. They are divided at Niagara Falls as we were at the Revolutionary War, but they come together again on the peaceful bosom of Ontario. Again they are divided on their passage to the sea; but who thinks of divisions when they lift the keels of commerce, or when, drawn up to heaven, they form the rainbow or the cloud?

It is true that in eighty-five years we have had two wars—but what then? Since the last we have had fifty years of peace, and there have been more people killed in a single campaign in the late civil war than there were in the two national wars between this country and Great

Britain. The people of the United States hope to draw together the two conflicting elements and make them one people. In that task I wish them God-speed! And in the same way I feel that we ought to rule out everything disagreeable in the recollection of our old wars, and unite together as one people for all time to come. I see around the door the flags of the two countries. United as they are there, I would have them draped together, fold within fold, and let

> "Their varying tints unite,
> And form in Heaven's light,
> One arch of peace."

JOSEPH HOWE.

CANADIAN ORATORY.

[For this exercise, the teacher might select a number of boys, each of whom should commit to memory the part assigned to him. The leader of the boys selected might address the visitors present as follows:—]

LADIES AND GENTLEMEN,—I shall have the pleasure, to day, of presenting to you a number of young gentlemen who have made selections from the speeches and writings of some of our most prominent Canadians. You will be gratified to observe that in the case of speeches delivered long ago, as well as in those of later date, there prevails a sentiment of loyalty to Canada and of confidence in its future prosperity and development. The first speaker represents Sir Wm. Young, late Chief Justice of Nova Scotia, who has expressed in language, which I think you will not soon forget, his *attachment to the Sovereign* who reigns over us and the constitution under which the British Empire has been so firmly established.

First Speaker:—

Our attachment to the Queen, our own Victoria, is mingled with a tenderness not inconsistent with the sterner sentiment which it softens and embellishes without enervating. Let her legitimate authority as a constitutional Monarch; let her reputation as a woman be assailed, and notwithstanding the lamentation of Burke, that the age of chivalry was past, thousands of swords would leap from their scabbards to avenge her. Ay, and they would be drawn as freely, and wielded as vigorously and bravely in Canada—in Nova Scotia—as in England. Loyalty! love of British Institutions! They are engrafted in our very nature; they are part and parcel of ourselves; and I can no more tear them from my heart even if I would, and lacerate all its fibres, than I would sever a limb from my body. And what are those institutions? A distinguished American statesman recently answered this question. He said: "The proudest Government that exists upon the face of the earth is that of Great Britain, and the great Pitt her proudest statesman, when he would tell of Britain's crowning glory, did not speak as he might have done, of her widespread Dominion, upon which the sun never sets. He did not speak of martial achievements, of glorious battlefields, and of splendid naval conflicts; but he said, with swelling breast, and kindling eye, that the poorest man of Great Britain in his cottage might bid defiance to all the forces of the Crown. It might be frail, its roof might shake, the wind might blow through it, the storm might enter, the rain might enter; but the King of England could not enter it. In all his power he dare not cross the threshold of that ruined tenement."

LADIES AND GENTLEMEN,—I shall next introduce to you a young gentleman who represents Sir John Beverley Robinson, a Chief Justice of Upper Canada and the father of one of our most esteemed Lieutenant-Governors. Sir J. B. Robinson shews that *a monarchical system of government* supplies all the advantages of the most liberal democracy, combined with greater stability, and more substantial guarantees for the security of life and property. Will you kindly listen to what he has to say on the monarchical system as it exists in Canada?

Second Speaker:—

It is common for us to hear of that great experiment in government in which the vast republic near us is engaged. But in the Provinces of British North America we have an experiment going on, of no light interest to our glorious mother country, or to mankind. We occupy a particular and somewhat critical position on this continent, and more than we can foresee may probably depend upon the manner in which our descendants may be able to sustain themselves in it. It will be their part, as it is now ours, to demonstrate that all such freedom of action as is consistent with rational liberty, with public peace, and with individual security, can be enjoyed under a constitutional monarchy as fully as under the purest democracy on earth; to prove that, in proportion as intelligence increases, what is meant by liberty is better understood, and what is soundest and most stable in government is better appreciated and more firmly supported. The glorious career of Britain among the nations of the world, demands of us this tribute to the tried excellence of her admirable constitution; it should be our pride to show that, far removed as we are from the splendors of Royalty and the influences of the Court, monarchy is not blindly preferred among us from a senseless attachment to antiquated prejudices, nor reluctantly tolerated from a sense of duty or a dread of change; but that, on the contrary, it is cherished in the affections, and supported by the free and firm will of an intelligent people, whose love of order has been strengthened as their knowledge has increased—a people who regard with loyal pleasure the obligations of duty which bind them to the Crown, and who value their kingly form of government not only because they believe it to be the most favorable to stability and peace, but especially for the security it affords to life and property, the steady support which it gives to the laws, and the certainty with which it ensures the actual enjoyment of all that deserves to be dignified with the name "Freedom."

LADIES AND GENTLEMEN,—The next speaker will discuss the *advantages of Education* as set forth by the late Dr. Ryerson, the founder of our school system, and a man to whom we are largely indebted for the intelligence which now is so happily diffused throughout the whole of Canada.

Third Speaker :—

It is my earnest prayer that the "internal guard" of a truly Christian education may be planted in the heart-citadel of every youth of our land. It is the union of moral and intellectual qualities which adorn and elevate the individual man; and it is their united development which constitutes the life and strength, the happiness and progress of society. If, then, we wish to see our country accomplish its high destiny—our unbroken forests converted into waving wheat fields—single manufactories growing into prosperous towns, and towns swelling into cities—canals and railroads intersecting the various counties, and commerce covering the rivers and lakes; if we wish to see our institutions settled and perfected, and our government fulfilling its noblest function—our schools and colleges radiating centres of intellectual light and moral warmth to the youthful population—the poor as well as the rich properly educated, and a rich and varied home literature created—the experience of past ages giving lessons in all our domestic dwellings, by means of books and libraries; in a word, if we wish to see the people of Canada united, intelligent, prosperous and happy—great in all that constitutes the real grandeur of a people—let us feel that the eventful issues of that anticipated futurity are in our hands, and that it is for each individual of our grown-up generation to say how far these hopes of patriotism and philanthropy shall be realized or disappointed. Above all, let us never forget that there is a moral as well as a physical universe, and as it is in the harmony of the two that the perfections of the divine character and government are fully displayed, so it is in the harmonious development of the moral with the intellectual man that the perfection of his nature consists. What God has joined together we must never put asunder in any of our plans and efforts for the social advancement of Canada. Our motto should be the words of the inspired Isaiah—"Wisdom and knowledge shall be the stability of thy times; the fear of Jehovah, this shall be thy treasure."

LADIES AND GENTLEMEN,—Many of you are, no doubt, familiar with the name of Dr. McCaul, the first president of the University of Toronto, a gentleman of great culture and wide experience. It will be interesting for you to learn the effect which, in his opinion, the *general diffusion of education* would produce upon the people of Canada, and upon their attachment to the British Crown. Allow me to present to you a young gentleman who will give you Dr. McCaul's words on this point.

Fourth Speaker:—

I have said that the diffusion of the blessings of education throughout the land is the ultimate end of the work which is to be pursued in this university,—a work second in importance to none in the Province, for it is destined to perpetuate its benign influences throughout successive generations. Yes, the stamp which education impresses, however faint at first, or difficult of recognition, remains permanent and enduring, and continues indelible from age to age,—so that whatever be the national characteristics of the population of Canada, the influence of that system of instruction now established will be perceptible in its distinctive features. What mind can justly estimate—what tongue can adequately express—the benefits which must flow from such a diffusion? What influence will it have in strengthening the intellect, elevating the taste, and curbing the passions? And oh! how many are there who, if they but had the avenues of enjoyment thrown open to them which education presents, would have never fallen into the grovelling habits which have ruined both themselves and their families.

But in another respect, too, the diffusion of education must exercise a most important influence throughout the country. We live in times when the tendency is to diffusion throughout the masses of a greater amount of political privilege than they have hitherto enjoyed. The times exist when the majority of the people must exercise political privileges, and if so, of what immense importance is it that the masses should be educated—that they should know their rights and understand their obligations—that they should possess that power, which education gives, of protecting themselves against political or religious impostors—that they should discharge those duties, which our free constitution assigns to them, with that independence and discrimination which knowledge bestows and fosters. Of what consequence is it that our people should understand and be prepared to show that they maintain their allegiance to the British Crown and their adherence to the limited monarchy under which they live, not through any antiquated prejudices, nor yet through any traditionary veneration, but because they prefer that which they have, entertaining the well grounded conviction, that under a government such as that of Great Britain, they and their children can enjoy all real liberty, and under it have happiness here, and the means and opportunity of preparing themselves for happiness hereafter.

Ladies and Gentlemen,—The union of the different provinces of British North America, under the Confederation Act of 1867, was regarded by many Canadians as the founding of a new empire, and so I believe it was. There was some division of opinion, however, as to the effect of this Act upon the future of Canada. Of those who took the hopeful view of the situation and, as I believe the correct view, the Honorable D'Arcy McGee is worthy of notice, partly because of the polished language in which he expressed himself and partly because of his wide range of knowledge as a historian and a man of letters.

The young gentleman who will next address you will give you a quotation from one of Mr. McGee's speeches.

Fifth Speaker :—

The reason why we have not hitherto attracted and retained more people in Canada from the other side of the Atlantic, is because we have not made our country attractive to them; because we are not known as a nation abroad; because those isolated Provinces have not impressed the imagination of the emigrating classes. Who in the byeways of Germany, or even of Britain, knew anything of Canada, until the other day? In those hives of human labor, they knew only one country—America—and only one seaport—New York. But once give our united Provinces the aspect of empire, make them a power and a name, and the reputation and credit of the Dominion will be our best emigration agent abroad. . . . I cannot, for one, agree that the best way to make ourselves respected abroad, and to secure impunity from attack, is to depreciate the sources of our strength; but rather to make the most of what Lord Bacon, in his "True Greatness of Britain," considers the main element of a nation's strength, its "breed of men." By the breed of men, that brings a nation safely through its destinies, Lord Bacon meant—not only the muscle of men, their bodily hardihood, but also their *morale*—their courage, docility, and capacity for combination—the wisdom of the few to command, and the wisdom of the many to co-operate. I do not disparage the power of numbers; I do not underrate the power of wealth; but above both I place the safety of any State, great or small, in the spirit and unity of its inhabitants.

The policy of self-abasement I cannot see in the light of policy at all. View it how we may; turn it round and round; hang it in any light you like, it will not wear the lineaments of prudence, or fortitude or patriotism. While we should, on the one hand, avoid all bravado as unbecoming our position, we should, on the other hand, endeavor to elevate and not depress the public spirit of the country. We should strengthen the faith of our people in their own future, the faith of every Canadian in Canada, and of every Province in its sister Province. This faith wrongs no one; burthens no one; menaces no one; dishonors no one; and, as it was said of old, faith moves mountains, so I venture reverently to express my own belief, that if the difficulties of our future as a Dominion were as high as the peaks of the Alps or Andes, yet that the pure patriotic Faith of a united people would be all sufficient to overcome and, ultimately, to triumph over all such difficulties.

LADIES AND GENTLEMEN,—The next speaker represents a Canadian to the manner born, the Reverend Dr. Ormiston. The stirring speech which you are about to hear was delivered some years ago—the subject being, "*The Young Men of Canada.*" Hear what he says.

Sixth Speaker:—

What a large, wide, happy home is the land we live in! We have found it a goodly land, and have no sympathy with those who love it not! There is no piety, no genuine Christianity, in the heart of him who does not love his country, native or adopted! He cannot be a true, large, leal-hearted man, who, looking through the vista of coming years, does not hope to see his own country grow greater and more glorious; and he is not a true Canadian who does not say, "Peace and Prosperity to Canada."

It matters not on what line of longitude or latitude it may be, but one's native land should be the dearest, sweetest, and most hallowed spot on this side of heaven. Canada, our country, we love it; and because we love, we wish its young men to be worthy of it. Our fathers have done much. They came from almost every country beneath the sun. They were a varied people; and we are, to some extent, varied still. Their national, educational, and ecclesiastical prejudices were varied. They had but two things to bind them together,—the deep fertile soil beneath their feet, and the clear canopy of the bright blue sky above their heads. Pioneers in this goodly land, some have found a home—many only a grave, and on the resting-place of these we should tread lightly, doing reverence to their ashes, and living so as to honor them. With the young men of Canada we should arm for the conflict, and gird ourselves for the coming struggle. We are the strength of the country. Upon us it depends whether, in twenty years, this country shall be progressive, and rise to assume its own just place in the heraldry of nations, and have the proud boast of possessing a God-fearing people; whether it shall become a dark spot in the geography of the world, and, by and by vanish altogether; or whether intelligence and industry shall place Canada in the vanguard of nations.

The following selections might be used in lieu of those given, or in addition, if deemed desirable.

Future of Manitōba.

From its geographical position, and its peculiar characteristics, Manitoba may be regarded as the keystone of that mighty arch of sister Provinces which spans the continent from the Atlantic to the Pacific. It was here that Canada, emerging from her woods and forests, first gazed upon her rolling prairies and unexplored North-West, and learnt as by an unexpected revelation that her historical territories of the Canadas, her eastern seaboards of New Brunswick, Labrador and Nova Scotia, her Laurentian lakes and valleys, corn lands and pastures, though themselves more extensive than half a dozen European kingdoms—were but the vestibules and ante-chambers to that till then undreamt-of Dominion, whose illimitable dimensions alike confound the arithmetic of the surveyor and the verification of the explorer. It was here that counting her past achievements as but the preface and prelude to her future exertions and extending destinies, she took a fresh departure, received the afflatus of a more imperial inspiration, and felt herself no longer a mere settler along the banks of a single river, but the owner of half a continent, and in the magnitude of her possessions, in the wealth of her resources, in the sinews of her material might, the peer of any power on the earth. And so, secluded from all extraneous influences, nestling at the feet of her majestic mother, Canada will, with confidence and hope, dream her dream and forebode her destiny—a dream of ever broadening harvests, multiplying towns and villages and expanding pastures; of constitutional self-government and a confederated Empire; of page after page of honorable history, added as her contribution to the annals of the Mother Country and to the glories of the British race; of a perpetuation for all time upon this continent of that temperate and well-balanced system of Government which combines in one mighty whole as the eternal possession of all Britons, the brilliant history and traditions of the past with the freest and most untrammelled liberty of action in the future.

DUFFERIN.

CANADIAN LOYALTY.

Canadian loyalty is the perpetuation of that British national life which has constituted the strength and glory of Great Britain since the morning of the Protestant Reformation, and placed her at the head of the freedom and civilization of mankind. This loyalty maintains the characteristic traditions of the nation—the mysterious links of connection between grandfather and grandson—traditions of strength and glory for a people, and the violations of which are a source of weakness and disorganization. Canadian loyalty, therefore, is not a mere sentiment, or mere affection for the representative or person of the Sovereign; it is a reverence for, and attachment to, the laws, order, institutions and freedom of the country. As Christianity is not a mere attachment to a bishop, or ecclesiastic, or form of church policy, but a deep love of divine truth; so Canadian loyalty is a firm attachment to that British constitution and those British laws, adopted or enacted by ourselves, which best secure life, liberty and prosperity, and which prompt us to Christian and patriotic deeds by linking us with all that is grand and noble in the traditions of our national history.

DR. RYERSON.

ADVANTAGES OF CANADA.

Let us now consider what are the advantages, natural or acquired, which we enjoy here. A fertile soil, amply rewarding labor in the abundance and diversity of its produce; a salubrious climate, calculated to rear a hardy and vigorous race; water communication by noble rivers and vast lakes (or rather Mediterranean seas), unequalled in the world; and millions of acres of unoccupied land, able to support millions of additional immigrants. Let us add to these natural blessings, the results of the energy and enterprise of an active and intelligent population; our cities, with all the conveniences and comforts of European towns of twice their population, and of twenty times their age; our villages springing up where lately were but dismal swamps or tangled forests; the remotest points of this extensive country soon to be connected by railroads, now either drawing to completion, in progress, or guaranteed; the facilities afforded for the education of our children by our public schools, our grammar schools, our private seminaries, our colleges and our universities; the progress of knowledge, advanced by the scientific and literary societies and institutes established in our cities and towns; the solemn duties of religion inculcated by fixed ministrations or by the occasional visits of the missionary; the voice of prayer and praise rising each Sabbath alike from the stately piles in our towns, which rear their spires towards heaven, and the lowly shanty, which scarce lifts its humble head under the leafy arches of our backwoods; and all this with the full and free enjoyment of the blessings of civil and religious liberty. In his opinion, the language of dissatisfaction or complaint but little becomes those who enjoy such advantages. Thanksgiving was rather their duty—thanksgiving to Him from whom all blessings flow, for what in His abundant mercy He had given to them, and prayer to the same Almighty Being for contentment with what they had—for peace, wherein they might use and enjoy what His bountiful hand had provided for them. By peace, he meant not freedom from war—he meant not tranquillity undisturbed by aggression from without—of that he had no fears; but he did mean freedom from internal strife, from civil commotion, from the injurious influences of bickerings and contentions with each other. He did mean that peace which is produced by mutual forbearance—by laying aside national feuds and party differences, and by the union of all, casting aside their distinctions—whilst they still held fast to their principles—for the advancement of the welfare of their common country, the land of the Maple Leaf. He knew no more appropriate words in which this supplication could be offered than those, which must be familiar to many whom he addressed, and in which he doubted not all would cordially join—that "they might live in fear of God, in dutiful allegiance to the Queen, and in brotherly love and Christian charity each towards the other." DR. McCAUL.

THE FUTURE OF CANADA.

What can we say as to our future? What of our destiny? Our destiny under a kind Providence will be just what we will make it. It rests in our own hands. We may in the face of all our advantages, mar it if we will. As it is with individual destiny, so is it with national destiny; we are largely the architects of our own fortunes. We have laid, as I have shown, deep and safe and broad the foundations for a bright future. What country can show legislation more advanced or leading up to better results than ours? In what land do we find a people enjoying more fully than we do the rights of self-government, or where is there a people more fitted to be entrusted with that precious right? Our laws have been well administered. Our courts of justice have won the unlimited confidence of the people. Imbued with the healthy sentiment which has prevailed in the mother land for centuries, attached to her forms of government, cherishing her precedents and traditions, we have passed from childhood to youth. We are approaching manhood, and its strength and vigor must depend upon ourselves. What is needed, then? We must appease inter-provincial jealousies; we must modify mere local patriotism; we must cultivate an increased national feeling and show in every way we can that we have crossed the line of youth and pupilage. If our public men will be true to themselves and govern us with wisdom and foresight and high statesmanship, and if our people will be intelligent, honest and vigilant, then we will enjoy a degree of success to which no limit can be fixed.

RICHARD HARCOURT.

GENERAL WOLFE AND OLD QUEBEC.

A problem of singular interest is being solved here. Two races, the foremost in the ranks of humanity, long rivals in arts and arms: the stolid, slow, but long-enduring Saxon; the lively, impressible, gallant Frank, are here invited to share a common destiny, and work out a future of their own. The Norman and Saxon of elder centuries have united with the Celt to make England what she is. Saxon, Norman and Celt meet here anew, under other fortunes, to make of our common Dominion what future generations will know how to prize. Men of the old French monarchy before the era of revolutions, have been succeeded by those who here, under the ægis of Great Britain, have been admitted and trained to all the rights and privileges of a free people.

It is a privilege not to be lightly thrown away, that we share the destinies of an Empire where the Rajah of a British Province on the Indian Ocean—beyond the farthest footprint of the Macedonian Alexander—sends as his loyal gift to the Olympian Games of our common nationality, the prize cup which victors from our young Dominion have twice brought in triumph to our shores.

Our living present, as well as the sacred memories which we inherit, as a member of that great British Confederacy which embraces in one united Empire, India and Canada; New Zealand and Newfoundland; the Bahamas; the Antilles; Australia and the Cape; are too precious to be lightly cast away. But if the time is ever to come—

"Far on in summers that we shall not see,"

when this young Dominion shall stretch across the continent, a nation, with duties and interests all its own; it will be for its interest as well as its honor that it can then look back only with loving memories on the common mother of the Anglo-Saxon race, while it emulates her example, and aspires to her worth.

SIR DANIEL WILSON.

NATIONAL UNITY NECESSARY.

I am not ignorant of, nor will I minimize, the danger which arises to Canada from the fact that we have here a duality of language and a duality of race. But the fact exists, and ostracism of any kind, instead of removing the danger, would simply intensify it, by forcing a section of our population to hate the institutions under which they live—intensify it, because it would bring a section of our population into conflict with the majority which would thus abuse the brute power of number. Any policy which appeals to a class, to a creed, to a race, or which does not appeal to the better instincts to be found in all classes, in all creeds, and in all races, is stamped with the stamp of inferiority. The French-Canadian who appeals to his fellow-countrymen to stand by themselves, aloof from the rest of this continent; the English-Canadian who appeals to his fellow-countrymen on grounds affecting them alone, may, perhaps, win the applause of those whom they may be addressing, but impartial history will pronounce their work as vicious in conception as it is mischievous and wicked in its tendency. We are here a nation, composed of the most heterogeneous elements—Protestants and Catholics, English, French, German, Irish, Scotch, every one, let it be remembered, with his traditions, with his prejudices. In each of these conflicting antagonistic elements, however, there is a common spot of patriotism, and the only true policy is that which reaches that common patriotism and makes it vibrate in all towards common ends and common aspirations.

WILFRID LAURIER.

BRITAIN'S OVERSHADOWING POWER.

The proudest position Great Britain could occupy is that the overshadowing power and influence which she has so long possessed in giving shape to the destinies and relations of nations has always been exercised with a view to the amelioration of the condition of mankind; that she has the will as well as the power to maintain, in a great measure, the peace of the rest of the world, and that prosperity, peace and contentment have followed her flag all over the earth, upon whatever soil it has ever been planted. I hope its march of triumph will never be interrupted until it shall become the one absorbing and powerful instrumentality in the hands of Providence for the prevention of war, the extension of commerce, and the promotion of the arts of peace. To the full extent of their power Her Majesty's government in Canada would contribute to the development and maintenance of this sentiment. At the same time let us remember that Canada is our home; that while we think with gratitude of the land of our birth, while our hearts are filled with the warmest patriotism when its history and its heroes are recalled to mind, we should not forget that we have great duties and responsibilities, not of a sectional, but of a national, character to discharge and that we ought to devote ourselves faithfully and honestly to the task of creating and upholding a Canadian spirit Canadian sentiment and Canadian enthusiasm; in a word, a spirit of nationality always British, but still Canadian. The patriotism of the British people and government will ever be with us, and we in turn hope always to reside under the shadow of the grand old flag of Britain, at once the symbol of power and civilization. These sentiments I believe to be an expression of the aspirations which animate the great body—may I not say the whole of the Canadian people.

ALEXANDER MACKENZIE.

A Public Spirit Necessary for Canada.

We have to contend with political difficulties consequent upon our singular semi-dependent position as a small state between two very great ones, with both of which we have very close relations; with geographical difficulties caused by the great stretches of barren wilderness interposed between the three great divisions of our territory—which have often caused me to wish we lived rather in three islands, with the sea as a means of connection and communication; with national or race difficulties, arising from the circumstances of our early settlement, and lastly with economical difficulties, partly natural and partly of our own making, but none the less real, notwithstanding. What we need, and we need it very badly, is more public spirit—a larger share of the true instinct of patriotism—and to become thoroughly impregnated with the feelings which inspired that well-known passage of Sir Walter Scott:

"Breathes there a man with soul so dead
Who never to himself hath said,
This is my own—my native land?
If such there be, go mark him well,
For him no minstrel numbers swell;
High though his title, proud his name,
Boundless his wealth as wish can claim,
The wretch concentred all in self,
Living shall forfeit fair renown,
And doubly dying shall go down
To the vile dust from which he sprung—
Unwept, unhonored, and unsung."

That is the temper which has made Scotland great, that is the temper which alone can make any country really great, and that is the temper which we must one and all try to cultivate and foster among our people if we ever expect to make Canada a great country. So, I say, be Canadians above all and before all, whatever else you are. It may well be that there are some among you whom I address to-night who may be destined to climb high, to whom it may be given to see clearly what we see only through a glass darkly, and who may come to enter into and possess the land we are only permitted to gaze upon from afar. To such I can only say that I hope they will cherish an honorable ambition. Such an ambition is perhaps the best safeguard of public morality, almost as good in its way as an honorable love is to defend you against vulgar profligacy, and how great a defence that is you may learn from Tennyson's splendid description of its effects in elevating the character, especially in youth and early manhood, where he bids you:

"To speak no slander—no, nor listen to it,
To lead sweet lives in purest chastity,
To love one maiden only—cleave to her,
And worship her by years of noble deeds
Until you win her. For, indeed I know
Of no more subtle master under Heaven
Than is the maiden passion for a maid.
Not only to subdue the base in man,
But teach high thoughts, and amiable words,
And courtliness—and the desire of fame
And love of truth—and all that makes a man."

SIR RICHARD CARTWRIGHT.

CANADIAN ARISTOCRACY.

Ours is a democratic country in an age of democracy. We here enjoy, at least in theory, what is called the reign of the common people. But the reign of the common people, that is to say, the right of the masses of mankind to govern themselves, requires on the part of those who govern, an earnest discharge of those duties, which are necessarily involved in the privileges which they enjoy. In politics as in other things, power and privilege bring with them an inevitable load of responsibility and duty, and we cannot hope to succeed in the noble task of self-government, unless each one of us, realizing this, shall do his duty in the situation which he occupies, and shall, within the sphere of his powers and influence, labor to promote the accomplishment of sound reforms in their due season. Now, in this democratic country we have but few, and I wish we had no examples of the class distinctions of the old world. I think they ought not to have been introduced. They are foreign to our soil; they are unsuited to our habits; they are relics of old times now past; they are not given under the advice of our own leaders of opinion; and I wish it might become part of our unwritten code, that these exotic distinctions should not be by us received. Yet, sir, I am a believer in a certain, and in a real sense, in the principle of aristocracy. I believe in the true aristocracy of energy, learning, ability, and integrity; an aristocracy whose marks and titles are found in the earnest efforts of a man to do his duty and to excel in its discharge; and whose distinctions are such as a free people themselves confer by the expression of their confidence, by mandates to the great council of the country, by selection for high offices of public trust, by the commission to regulate the affairs, to guide the high destinies of the people among whom they live. That is the aristocracy and the only aristocracy which is suited to our day and country.

EDWARD BLAKE.

Memories of the Old Land.

Attachment to the land from which we or our fathers came is not only compatible with intense devotion to the highest interests of the country where we dwell, but is a necessary condition of its birth, its growth, and its fervor. The dutiful son, the affectionate husband and father, will usually be the best and most patriotic subject or citizen; and he will love Canada best who draws his love of country in copious draughts from the old fountain-head across the sea. We have an example of strong devotion to the European stock, combined with unwavering attachment to Canada, in our French follow-countrymen of Quebec. No people can be more tenacious of their language, their institutions, and their religion than they are; they still love France and its past glories with all the passionate ardor of their warm and constant natures; and yet no people are more contented, more tenderly devoted to Canadian interests, more loyal to the Crown and the free institutions under which they live. Sir Etienne Taché gave expression to the settled feeling of his compatriots when he predicted that the last shot for British rule in America would be fired from the citadel of Quebec by a French-Canadian. The Norman and Breton root from which the Lower Canadians sprang was peculiarly patriotic, almost exclusively so, in a provincial or sectional sense, in old France; and they, like the Scot, brought their proud, hardy, and chivalrous nature with them, to dignify and enrich the future of colonial life.

The French-Canadian, moreover, can boast a thrilling history of the Dominion itself, to which the English portion of the population can lay no claim. Quebec has a Valhalla of departed heroes distinctly its own; yet still it does not turn its back upon the older France, but lives in the past, inspired by its spirit to work out the problem of a new nationality in its own way. There is no more patriotic Canadian that the Frenchman, and he is also the proudest of his origin and race. There is nothing, then, to forbid the English-speaking Canadian from revering the country of his fathers, be it England, Scotland, or Ireland; on the contrary, it may be laid down as a national maxim, that the unpatriotic Englishman, Scot, or Irishman, will be sure to prove a very inferior specimen of the Canadian.

W. J. Rattray.

CANADA: ITS SCENERY AND MAJESTIC PROPORTIONS.

He is not a wise Canadian who shuts himself up within the boundaries of his own little province, and, wasting life amidst the narrow prejudices and evil passions of his own contracted sphere, vegetates and dies, regardless of the growing communities and widely extending influences by which the interests of his country are affected every day, and which may at no distant period, if not watched and counteracted, control its destinies with an overmastering and resistless power.

The question has been put to me twenty times in a day, "what do you think of Canada?" and as it is likely to be many times repeated, I take this early opportunity of recording my conviction that it is one of the noblest countries that it has ever been my good fortune to behold. Canada wants two elements of prosperity which the lower colonies possess—open harbors for general commerce, and a homogeneous population; but it has got everything else that the most fastidious political economist would require. I knew that Canada was a very extensive province, that there was some fine scenery in it, and that much of the soil was good, for I had read all this a great many times; but yet it is only by spending some weeks in traversing the face of the country that one becomes really alive to its vast proportions, its great national features, boundless resources, and surpassing beauty. It is said, so exquisite is the architecture of St. Peter's at Rome, that it is not until a visitor has examined the fingers of a cherub, and found them as thick as his arm, or until he has attempted to fondle a dove, and found it far beyond his reach, and much larger than an eagle, that he becomes aware of the dimensions of the noble pile. So it is with Canada. A glance at the map or a perusal of a volume or two of description will give but a faint idea of the country. It must be seen to be understood.

But the mere extent of the country would not perhaps impress the mind so strongly if there were not so much of the vast, the magnificent, the national, in all its leading features. It is impossible to fancy that you are in a province—a colony; you feel at every step that Canada must become a great nation; and at every step you pray most devoutly for the descent upon the country of that wisdom, and foresight, and energy which shall make it the great treasury of British institutions upon this continent, and an honor to the British name. All the lakes of Scotland thrown together would not make one of those great inland seas, which form, as it were, a chain of Mediterraneans; all the rivers of England, old father Thames included, would scarcely fill the channel of the St. Lawrence. There is a grandeur in the mountain ranges, and a voice in the noble cataracts, which elevate the spirit above the ignorance and the passions of the past and the perplexities of the present, and make us feel that the great Creator of the universe never meant such a country to be the scene of perpetual discord and degradation; but will yet inspire the people with the union, the virtue, and the true patriotism by which alone its political and social condition shall be made to take more nearly than it does now the impress of its natural features. Canada is a country to be proud of; to inspire high thoughts; to cherish a love for the sublime and beautiful; and to take its stand among the nations of the earth in spite of all the circumstances which have hitherto retarded, and may still retard its progress.

JOSEPH HOWE.

THE BENEFITS OF BRITISH INSTITUTIONS.

We are a free and happy people; and we are so owing to the liberal institutions by which we are governed, institutions which we owe to the exertions of our forefathers and the wisdom of the mother country. Now, to properly estimate the value of the institutions by which we are ruled to-day, let us compare the present state of the country with what it was before they were granted to us.

Forty years ago the country was in a state of feverish commotion, a prey to an agitation which, a few months later, broke out in rebellion. The British crown was only maintained in the country by the force of powder and ball. And yet what were our predecessors seeking? They were asking for nothing more than the institutions which we have at present; those institutions were granted to us and loyally applied; and see the result; the British flag floats over the old citadel of Quebec; it floats to-night over our heads, without a single British soldier in the country to defend it, its sole defence resting in the gratitude which we owe it for our freedom and the security which we have found under its folds.

Where is the Canadian who, comparing his country with even the freest countries, would not feel proud of the institutions which protect him? Where is the Canadian who, passing through the streets of this old city and reaching the monument raised a few steps from here to the memory of the two brave men who died on the same field of battle while contending for empire in Canada, would not feel proud of his country? In what other country under the sun can you find a similar monument, reared to the memory of the conquered as well as of the conqueror? In what other country under the sun will you find the names of the conquered and conqueror equally honored and occupying the same place in the respect of the population? When, in that last battle which is recalled by the Wolfe and Montcalm monument, the iron hail was spreading death in the ranks of the French army; when the old heroes, whom victory had so often accompanied, saw at last victory snatched from them; when, stretching on the ground with their life-blood fast ebbing away, they saw, as the result of their defeat, Quebec in the hands of the enemy and the country forever lost; no doubt their last thought was of their children, whom they were leaving without protection and without defence; no doubt they pictured them as persecuted, enslaved and humiliated, and then, it is reasonable to believe, they drew their last breath with a cry of despair. But if Heaven had lifted the veil of the future from their dying eyes and enabled them for an instant, before they closed forever, to pierce what was hidden from their sight; if they could see their children free and happy, marching proudly in all spheres of society; if they could have seen, in the old cathedral, the seat of honor of the French Governors occupied by a French Governor; if they could have seen the church steeples rising in every valley from the shores of Gaspé to the prairies of the Red River; if they could have seen this old flag, which recalls the finest of their victories, carried triumphantly in all our public ceremonies; in fine, if they could have seen our free institutions, is it not permissible to think that their last breath would have been exhaled in a murmur of gratitude to Heaven and that they would have died consoled.

WILFRID LAURIER.

THE GRAVES OF THE PIONEERS.

He must have a dull and sluggish soul, who can look without emotion on the quiet graves of the early settlers of this country, who can tread upon their mouldering bones without a thought of their privations and their toils, who can, from their tombs, look out upon the rural loveliness—the fruitfulness and peace by which he is surrounded, nor drop a tear to the memories of the dead, who won, by the stoutness of their hearts, and the sweat of their brows, the blessings their children have only to cherish and enjoy. They plunged into the forest, not as we do now, for a summer day's ramble, or an hour of tranquil musing, but to win a home from the ruggedness of uncultivated nature, and in despite of the dusky savage thirsting for their blood. Oh! for the muse of Gray to pour out a befitting tribute to the dead. He caught from the sanctity and softened associations of an English graveyard an inspiration that rendered him immortal; but the graves among which he stood are the resting places of men whose lives had been tranquil and undisturbed; who had grown up amidst the fruitfulness of a civilized and cultivated country, and who had enjoyed the protection of institutions long firmly established, and the security and cheering influence of ancient usage.

How much deeper would have been the tones of his harp, had he stood where we now stand, had he been surrounded by the graves of those who found his country a wilderness and left it a garden; who pitched their tents among the solitudes of nature and left to their children her fairest charms, heightened by the soft touch of art; who had to build up institutions as they built up their lowly dwellings, but nevertheless bequeathed to their descendants the security of settled Government, the advantages of political freedom, the means of moral and religious improvement, which they labored to secure but never lived to enjoy. We have no Abbeys or Cathedrals where our warriors and statesmen are preserved. We have no monumental piles, fraught with the deeds of other days, to claim a tribute from the passer-by. The lapse of ages, political vicissitudes, violent struggles, and accumulated wealth are necessary to the possession of these; but in every village in our infant country we have the quiet graves of those who subdued the wilderness, who beautified the land by their toil, and left not only the fruits of their labors, but the thoughts and feelings that cheered them in their solitude, to cheer and stimulate us amidst the inferior trials and multiplied enjoyments of a more advanced state of society. May we while contrasting the present with the past never forget the debt of gratitude we owe and while standing beside the humble graves of our early settlers, may we ever feel our spirits awakened by the recollection of their lives, our thoughts ennobled by the remembrance of their trials, and our holiest and best resolves strengthened with a portion of their strength.

JOSEPH HOWE.

GREAT BRITAIN AND HER COLONIES.

From an address delivered by Silas Alward to the Alumni of Mount Allison University, New Brunswick, on Her Majesty's Jubilee.

In the record of the world's history never did nation occupy the proud position of Great Britain and her world-embracing colonies and dependencies. Gibbon, in his Decline and Fall, sketches with a master's hand the extent of the Roman Empire, when at the zenith of its greatness, stretching as it did from beyond the Euphrates in the east to the Pillars of Hercules in the west, a distance of three thousand miles; and from the arid sands of the Libyan desert in the south to the eternal snows of Sarmatia in the north, a distance of two thousand miles, embracing the fairest portions of the then habitable world. Yet the mighty expanse of the Roman Empire constituted in area only one-fourth part of the British Empire of to-day. Its population of 120,000,000 being only one-half that of India, one of its dependencies.

As by contrast we are the better able to form a just estimate of the qualities of an object, the characteristics of an individual and the progress of a nation, so in order adequately to appreciate the status of the British Empire it would be well to draw a parallel between the present and some other period in its history. To this end let us contrast the Victorian and Elizabethan periods.

What a striking contrast does the England of three hundred years ago present to the Great Britain of 1887. Then Scotland was a separate kingdom. Then Ireland, although a subject, was virtually an alien, nationally.

Then the population of England was less than five millions—not more than the Dominion of Canada to-day. The population of the empire is now three hundred millions, having increased sixty-fold. Then England was without colonies. Now her dependencies and colonies, constituting Greater Britain, embrace an area seventy-fold greater than the area of the United Kingdom. Then she was virtually without commerce. But as Spain and Holland had wrested from the free states of Italy the commercial primacy of the Mediterranean and the trade of the east, so England in turn wrested from Spain and Holland the commercial supremacy of the world. In 1582 the vessels of all sizes owned by England amounted to only 1,232, of which only 217 were above eight tons. Their united tonnage was 50,000, not one-fifth that of New Brunswick, only one-twenty-eighth that of the Dominion of Canada. Her seamen numbered only 14,295, less than those who go down from Canadian shores and smite the sounding furrows of our own waters. Now her great war-ships patrol the watery highways of the world unchallenged, and her merchant navy of 30,000 ships, manned by 270,000 sailors, are found on all seas. Her flag floats over forty-nine per cent. of the carrying power of the world. Nearly one-half of the world's commerce is moved in British bottoms.

The progress of the United Kingdom, during the present reign, evokes unqualified admiration. It is not measured solely by the growth of population, the expansion of trade and the accumulation of vast wealth. It is seen as well in the broadened liberty, which enlightened civilization brings and the thousand and one conveniences which add so much to the comfort of life and make it worth the living. The growth of population has been less in the United Kingdom than in the large colonies. Between 1837 and 1887 it increased in the former by only forty-one per cent., while in British North America, by two hundred and twenty-five per cent., and in the Australasian colonies, by two thousand three hundred and forty-five per cent. Wealth for the like period has made a gain of one hundred and twenty-four per cent., or at a rate three times greater than population. The repeal of the Corn Laws in 1846 and of the Navigation Laws in 1849 gave a wonderful impetus to trade and opened up a new era of prosperity to the country. The trade of the Empire expanded from two hundred and nine millions in 1837, to one thousand and seventy-nine millions in 1886, or over five hundred per cent. Steam power has proved a great factor in promoting the prosperity of the nation. The year Her Majesty ascended the throne the first two steamers, the "Great Western" and "Sirius," crossed the Atlantic. In shipping, including steamers, the effective carrying power has increased from three and a quarter million tons in 1837, to twenty-two million tons in 1887.

What Providence may have in store for the grand old nation we know not. There are those who believe, that the law of birth, growth, maturity, decline and death, which governs the animal and vegetable kingdoms, alike determines the destiny of nations.

They tell us, the fate which overtook Assyria, Greece and Rome, will eventually mark the career of England.

That as the course of Empire down the centuries may be traced by the broken arch and shattered column, so, in the lapse of time, within her island home will yet be seen the relics of a greatness and civilization forever departed. We indulge no such gloomy apprehension. Moved by the lever that is yet "to uplift the earth and roll it in another course," her career, we trust, lies along different lines. Those nations builded—as the foolish man in scripture—upon the sand. Our fathers builded, let us hope, more wisely. They digged deep and laid broad the foundations upon the eternal principles of truth and justice, and though the rains may descend, and the floods come, and the winds blow and beat upon it, they will spend their fury in vain upon the firm base of the superstructure. We believe it will never be said of her as of Rome—

> "The Niobe of nations, there she stands,
> Childless and crownless, in her voiceless woe,
> An empty urn within her wither'd hands,
> Whose holy dust was scatter'd long ago."

CULTURE AND PRACTICAL POWER.

From a Speech delivered by Nicholas Flood Davin, M.P., at the opening of Lansdowne College, Portage La Prairie, November 11th, 1889

The progress of civilization has equalized the physical qualities of man. In years gone by the strong arm ruled. It is the strong head rules to-day. Force is dethroned, and where brute violence wore a coronet which sometimes gleamed with chivalric ornament, intelligence, wearing a diadem in which there is no false glitter, in which every gem is of the purest water, now sits an omnipotent queen. A revolution, the most beneficent for man, has taken place, and it is the duty, as it should be the delight of every citizen to cultivate his faculties. Bacon has said "knowledge is power." Knowledge is also pleasure. I think it is Sir Arthur Helps that says a man who goes through life knowing only the trade or profession by which he gets his bread is a poor stunted creature. There is a close relation between all the arts—between poetry, painting, music, sculpture—and genuine proficiency in any one of these prepares the mind to enjoy the productions of the others. You cannot really wake any faculty of the mind and leave the rest asleep. Happy for the uncultured they know not what they have lost. When a man is destitute of some great physical attribute the most superficial observer recognizes his incompleteness. The blind can never see the purple coursers of morning chase night from marge to marge, or evening steep the landscape in every glorious and tender hue. In vain for the deaf do the birds sing, in vain is the voice of woman low and musical, and "the wind, that grand old harper, smites his thunder-harp of pines," for them in vain. So far as those who have no sense of smell are concerned, the care of nature in making every flower and shrub and grass odorous is bootless, while to the cripple the rapture of energetic movement is denied. In all these cases men recognize the absence of a faculty which would be cheaply purchased by colossal wealth. But how if we should want the seeing eye and hearing ear in a more important sense than is covered by any physical deprivation? How if there is a subtle aroma about what has been said by highly gifted men we cannot catch, a flavor we cannot appreciate; if nature and art teem with beauty which is for us as though it never was, if there is a music which our untrained ears cannot catch? The men of genius come to us each with his mission. One takes us up to the highest heaven of harmony; another purges our eyes that we may see God's glorious works as they are. George Macdonald says Burns' mission was to show men there was poetry immediately around them, at their very door. Now, beauty and utility go hand in hand in nature, and the same is true of all things which enable us to know her better. Drawing and designing for instance increase the power of observation along the whole line and develop accuracy in all matters on which the mind employs itself. We are unthankful when we are not dull. If we felt as we ought we should thank God at the sight of every flower, and send our hearts to heaven up the silver staircase of every starry beam. Think of all the beauty of the world; think of all that is glorious in literature from Homer to Tennyson—of all that is entrancing in song and music from David's harp, that could chase the evil spirit from an unworthy king, down to Handel, Beethoven, and the other great composers of modern times; think how a great historian like Thucydides, or Gibbon or Macaulay, makes us live in past ages and under strange climes; think of the joy that the lyric poet can evoke in the heart; think also that the mind thus awakened and nourished is capable of doing better whatever it applies itself to, and thank God we live in an age when all this may be brought within reach not merely of the rich and powerful, but almost of every child who has any aptitude, and who is blessed with parents and guardians not insensible to the possibilities of the time, and to their duty to their wards and offspring. Thank God that pioneers as you are—in a new country—in a small town—you can be not merely the architects of happier fortunes than could be within your reach in more crowded fields, but can have at your very door the means of the higher education of your children, where science, languages, history, the classics, political economy, the arts of commerce themselves, may be mastered, and on terms so moderate as to vindicate the essentially democratic character of the institution.

It is most auspicious in the capital of one of the richest and most salubrious belts of territory in the world to see you thus laying side by side with emporiums of material prosperity, the foundations of the higher learning, which, while in no way lessening, but rather increasing the capacity for dealing with agriculture and merchandise, will give us effective men in every field of human thought and endeavor; men who by a fruitful knowledge of the past, by clear conceptions of the duties of rulers and the ruled, by tempering and sweetening the disturbing envies and aspirations of democracy, will teach our youth to look forward to the same glorious future for Canada as has blessed the heroic efforts of young peoples in other days; men who will give us the art that beautifies and the song that thrills; men with brows full of practical wisdom which yet some muse shall have kissed, and with heroic hearts that bound at the promise of the great future which hovers over the twilight of the present, like the eagle the British Columbian sees in the early dawn above the highest of one of our own Rockies, burning in the light of a splendid but unrisen morrow.

THE FOUNDERS OF UPPER CANADA.

From an address delivered by Sir Oliver Mowat on the Centenary of Constitutional Government in Upper Canada.

The proclamation issued by Governor Simcoe at Kingston a hundred years ago this day, was the first step in the political history of the Province, and was doubtless an event of intense interest, as it was of great importance, to the white population of the Province at that time.

That population was small—10,000 souls only, as some estimated. These early settlers of Upper Canada were distinguished for industry, courage and a sense of religion and its duties. Take them all in all they were a noble ancestry, of whom a country may well feel proud. Whether their loyalty was a mistake and a misfortune as some aver, or whether, on the other hand, it is to be rejoiced over, as the people of Canada generally have always felt, there can be no denial that it was, at all events, a profound sentiment on their part. According to their view, in allowing this sentiment to guide their conduct, they were acting on principle and performing duty. They were as fond of the good things of this life as their neighbors were. They were as much attached to their houses and lands, their goods and their chattels, as others were, and as desirous of success in life for themselves and their children. But when the provinces in which they lived ceased to be British provinces and became parts of a new nation hostile to the old, they forsook all the material advantages and prospects which they had in their old homes, and followed the flag of Britain into the wilds of

Canada, preferring the privations and hardships and poverty which might be their lot there, rather than to live under the flag of the Revolution. The material sacrifices which they made at the call of what they believed to be duty and right, as well as just sentiment, constitute a glorious record, and that record has influenced the sentiment and conduct of the Canadian people ever since. Those early settlers had been born British subjects, they loved the British name; British subjects it was their determination under all temptations to remain, and on British soil to live out their lives, whatever the determination should cost them.

In view of the relations to it of us all, and in in view of the history of the country and of what is now known of its immense possibilities, there have grown up among its people, alongside of the old attachment to the British name and British nation and of the pride felt in British achievements in peace and war, a profound love for Canada also, a pride in Canada and hopes of Canada as one day to become a great British nation; British, whether in a political sense in connection or not with the United Kingdom of Great Britain and Ireland; British because Britain is the nation of the birth or origin of most of us, and has the profoundest respect and admiration of all; British because Canadians retain more of British institutions and British peculiarities than are possessed in other lands; British because of most of its people being more attached to Britain and more anxious for its well-being than they are with respect to any other nation of the world.

THE SPIRIT OF CANADIAN PATRIOTISM.

From a Speech by W. H. Withrow, D.D., on the Centenary of Upper Canada, 1892.

The patriotic feeling of the Jew to the land of his fathers and the city of the great king is to all lands and all ages a lesson of patriotic devotion. As the Jew walked round the goodly walls of Zion he said: "Mark ye well her bulwarks and consider her palaces, and tell it to the generations following." As he thought of the noble lives that had been spent therein, and of the sacred blood by which its walls had been cemented, of the historic achievements by which its annals had been made illustrious, his soul thrilled with patriotic emotion. So may we to-day, in looking back upon our national privileges, think with love and pride and exultation not only of this great and goodly land which is our heritage, but also of that old land from which we are sprung, which is either our birthland or the land of our fathers—that land whose noblest traditions, whose just and equal laws, whose heroic history, whose brilliant literature are ours to-day—that land from which we have derived the civil and religious privileges which we enjoy and to which we are under so great and lasting a debt and obligation.

But it is especially the mercies of the past century which we to-day commemorate. Beginning the century with extreme feebleness, few in numbers and with scant resources, under Divine Providence we have grown and increased and well nigh filled the land. Like Jacob, we may say, " With my staff I passed over this Jordan and now I am become two bands."

It is also befitting that on this historic ground we should recognize the blessings of Divine Providence in securing us the boon of self-government in this Province. This town of Niagara, indeed the whole of this frontier, have been consecrated to British liberty by sacrifices of our forefathers, by the blood which they shed and the hardships which they endured for the maintenance of British supremacy.

It has been said that the finest wheat of England was sifted for the planting of the New England colonies. If so, it is also true that the best wheat of American colonies was once more sifted to furnish the U. E. Loyalists and founders of Upper Canada. The true history of Canada, Goldwin Smith has said, is written upon the gravestones of these early pioneers in the old graveyards of our country.

Reverently let us mention their names, lightly let us tread upon their ashes. Let us seek to be worthy sons of such heroic sires. May their mantles fall on us, and may we live up to the privilege and obligation which they have entailed upon us by their strenuous toil and brave endurance. They have labored, and we have entered into their labors.

It is with no mere feeling of military jingoism that I speak. I am a man of peace. I am almost a Quaker in my sentiments of non-resistance. But there has been committed to us a precious heritage, which we may not lightly forego, which we may not squander, which, above all, we may not betray or barter for filthy lucre, " nor sell the mighty space of our large honors for as much gold as may be grasped thus." It is with no feeling of hostility or enmity to our republican neighbors who live across the river that I speak thus. If they prefer their institutions, let them enjoy them, as we wish to enjoy the institutions under which our country has flourished for one hundred years. I rejoice at the growing amenities between these two countries, and rejoice that on this platform we have been able to give cordial greeting to distinguished and friendly visitors from the neighboring republic.

A few days ago I stood on the steep escarpment at Queenston Heights which has been the scene of such fierce and bloody conflict; beneath my feet raved and chafed between its rugged banks the angry Niagara river. But a few miles above a wondrous wire-woven structure, spanned the deep abyss and furnished the means whereby the ceaseless currents of commerce might throb and pulsate across the raging torrent far beneath. So eighty years ago there flowed between these kindred peoples a raging, chafing, angry torrent of war. But by the kindly ministries of international commerce and international visits there has grown up a feeling of international friendship and good will. By the treaty of Washington, whereby, for the settlement of grave international questions, the kindly spirit of international arbitration was substituted for the dread arbitrament of war, the two nations have been linked together in bonds, we trust, of perpetual amity and peace. We, Canadians, wish to work out our destiny on the northern half of this continent. We believe that Providence has a mission for us to fulfil in this land. Of all lands which I have seen, and I have seen many, I do not know one where the conditions of the average mortal are so beneficent and happy as in our own. We have the largest fertile area for the food staples of the world that there is on this planet. Providence has dowered us with exhaustless resources of the field, the forest and the mine, of deep sea and lake and river fisheries. We have, I believe, the best system of constitutional government on the face of the earth. If our Legislatures do not carry out into practice the possibilities of our government system, the fault is our own, and if we have evils to complain of we can cure them any time we will by sending men of a different stamp to our legislative halls.

We are also destined, I believe, to live side by side with the neighboring republic, I trust, in a spirit of neighborliness and goodfellowship throughout all time. I would deprecate as a crime against humanity, against the common traditions which we hold, against the common language which we use, against the common literature which is our heritage, a strife with our American neighbors and friends. And only less distressing would be a war of retaliation in tariffs along our 4,000 miles of frontier. I trust that international treaties shall be interpreted by both countries, not in a narrow, peddling and huckstering spirit, but in a large, liberal and generous method. I would deprecate exceedingly anything looking like political union with the great country to the south of us. But I do hope that Great Britain and her eldest daughter, America, and her great colonial empire throughout the world will be united for the uplifting and the betterment of the whole world, for the disarmament of the war-burdened nations of the earth, and for the preservation of international peace throughout the world. Such an alliance would do much to hasten the coming of the millennial day, when the kingdoms of this world shall become the kingdom of our God and of His Christ, when the nations shall beat their swords into ploughshares and their spears into pruning hooks and

> "When the war drum throbs no longer, and the battle flag is furled,
> In the Parliament of man, the federation of the world."

Before I close I wish to drop a thought into the future, as men drop pebbles into deep wells to see what echo they return. I wish to try to conceive the destiny of this country towards the close of the twentieth century, whose threshold we have almost reached. As I have stood on the boundless prairies of the west, I seemed, with Whittier,

> "To hear the tread of pioneers
> Of nations yet to be,
> The first low wash of waves, where yet
> Shall roll a human sea."

I behold in my mind's eye a score of provinces each large enough for an old world empire, stretching from sea to sea. I doubt not that the child is yet living who shall lay his hand on the child's head who shall see 100,000,000 of people living on the broad and fertile area of our great Northwest—a great, free and happy people, dwelling in peace and prosperity under the folds of that Red Cross banner which is the symbol of liberty for the oppressed of every clime. Not merely one Pacific railway, but half a dozen shall stretch across the continent, uniting the Occident and the Orient, along which shall throb the pulses of commerce. Great cities, renowned as marts of trade throughout the world, shall stand thick along these highways of the nations. The church and school-house, those pioneers of civilization, shall crown every hill.

If that future is to be ours, out of the past and present, it must grow. If that goodly structure is to be realized we must lay broad and deep and sure and stable its foundation in those principles of integrity and righteousness, which are the sure defence of nations. These shall be the pledge of the permanence of our institutions; these shall be the corner stone of our national greatness. We owe much to the God-fearing men who a century ago laid the foundations of this commonwealth. We must build thereon in the same spirit of reverence for God's laws by which they were characterized. It is our proud boast that nowhere on earth is the Sabbath day so honored as in this land; nowhere is the sanctity of the family so maintained. There have not been, I believe, one hundred divorces in one hundred years in this broad Dominion. Nowhere is there a public press of purer character or of a higher moral tone. Without undue self-laudation we may say of our country, "Happy is the people whose God is the Lord; yea, happy is the people that is in such a case."

CANADA—A LINK IN THE EMPIRE.

From a Speech by Principal Grant, of Queen's University, at the Parliament of Religions, Chicago, 1893.

The supposed existence of a northwest passage to the Indies was the dream that allured hardy navigators who believed in the earth's rotundity but had not the data for determining its size. In our day it has been found that that great northwest passage is not by sea or river but by land. We have discovered that the shortest way from the old world to the world of Japan and China, is across Canada, and therefore Canada feels herself now to be the link between old Europe and the older East and also the link between the three great self-governing parts of the British Empire.

How is it possible for a people so situated to be parochial? How can they refuse to meet in a genial way the representatives of other races and religions? Across our broad lands thousands are coming and going from east to west, and we are obliged to meet them as man should always meet man. Not only so, but on that great ocean, which is the true Mediterranean—and which is to be the arena of the future commerce of the world—our sons are showing that they intend to play an important part. Our position, as the fourth maritime nation of the world as regards ocean tonnage, shows the aptitude of our people for foreign trade, and sailors owning the ships they sail are more likely than any others to learn the lesson that the life of the world is one, that truth is one, that all men are brothers, and that the service of humanity is the highest form of religion.

Therefore we feel that we have a right not so much to receive, as to join with you in extending, a welcome to brothers from different nations, whose forms of faith are different, but whose spiritual natures and necessities are the same, in whom dwelleth that Eternal Power and Person that is the true light which lighteth every man that cometh into the world, and by whom therefore He must be recognized when He is rightly presented to them, even as all needles must point to one pole.

Our racial, political, historical and religious evolution educates us along the same line as does our place in the world. Our racial evolution Parkman has described in pages glowing with purple light. He has told of the two centuries of conflict between France and Britain for the possession of this fair young continent, and he has shown that while outward failure was the part of the former, all the heroisms and enduring successes were not with the conquerors. France gave without stint the great explorers, whose names are sown over this continent, thick as a field, martyrs and missionaries of deathless fame and saintly women whose works do still follow them. Their blood was not lost in vast inland seas and on rugged Laurentian and Huronian rocks. It fell on good soil and we see its permanent memorial now in a noble French-speaking people, enjoying their own language, laws and institutions under a flag identified with their liberties and under a constitution which they and their fathers have helped to hammer out. Their children sit side by side in our federal parliament with the children of their ancestral foes and the only real contest between them is, which shall serve Canada best. The union of the two races and languages was needed to enable England to do her imperial work. Will not the same union enable Canada to do a like work, and does it not force us to see good, even in those whom our ancestors may have thought enemies?

Our political evolution has had the same lesson for us. It has taught us to borrow ideas with equal impartiality from sources apparently opposite. We have borrowed the federal idea from the United States, and our parliamentary and judicial systems from Britain, and so we have formed a constitution better than that which either the mother country or the older daughter enjoys. At any rate, we made it ourselves and it fits us: and we have thus been taught that ideas belong to no one people, that they are the common property of mankind, and that we should borrow new thoughts from every country that has found by experiment that they will work well.

Our religious evolution has taught us the same thing. We have been enabled to accomplish a measure of religious unification greater than either the mother land or the United States has found possible. Eighteen years ago, for instance, all the Presbyterian denominations united into one church, wide as the Dominion of Canada. Immediately thereafter the Methodist churches took the same step, and this very month the Anglicans are doing likewise. Still farther, these great Protestant churches have appointed committees to see whether it is not possible to have a wider union, and the young life of Canada says "Amen" to the proposal.

Our place in history is equally significant. Instead of violently disrupting ourselves from the past, we have gradually evolved from one stage of self-government to another. We have therefore not been obliged to sacrifice any of the inestimable treasures accumulated by our fathers, while at the same time we keep eyes and minds open to receive new teaching from this new world where everything is possible to man.

It is easy for a people with such an environment to understand that where men differ they must be in error that truth is the only thing which permanently unites, that every age has its problems to solve, that it is the glory of the human mind to solve, or try to solve them, and that no church or nation has a monopoly of the truth or of the spirit of the living God.

THE GRANDEUR OF CANADA.

From "Ocean to Ocean," by Principal Grant.

Other countries have had to spend, through long years of youth, their strength and substance to purchase freedom or the right to exist. Our lot is a happier one. Protected "against infection and the hand of war" by the might of Britain, we have but to go forward to open up for our children and the world what God has given into our possession, bind it together, consolidate it, and lay the foundations of an enduring future.

Looking back over the vast breadth of the Dominion when our journeyings were ended, it rolled out before us like a panorama varied and magnificent enough to stir the dullest spirit into patriotic emotion. For nearly 1,000 miles by railway between different points east of Lake Huron; 2,185 miles by coach, wagon, pack and saddle horses; 1,687 miles in steamers in the basin of the St. Lawrence and on Pacific waters, and 485 miles in canoes or row-boats; we had travelled in all 5,300 miles from ocean to ocean over a country with features and resources more varied than our modes of locomotion.

From the sea-pastures and coal-fields of Nova-Scotia and the forests of New Brunswick, from historic Louisburg up the St. Lawrence to historic Quebec, through the great Province of Ontario and on lakes that are really seas, by copper and silver mines so rich as to recall stories of the Arabian Nights, though only the rim of the land has been explored; on the chain of lakes where the Ojibway is at home in his canoe to the great plains where the Cree is at home on his horse; through the Prairie Province of Manitoba and rolling meadows and park-like country, equally fertile, out of which a dozen Manitobas shall be carved in the next quarter of a century; along the banks of

> "A full-fed river, winding slow
> By herds, upon an endless plain,"

full-fed from the exhaustless glaciers of the Rocky Mountains and watering the great lone land; over illimitable coal measures and deep woods to mountains which open their gates more widely than to our wealthier neighbors to lead us to the Pacific; down deep gorges filled with mighty timber and rivers whose ancient deposits are gold beds, sands like those of Pactolus and channels choked with fish; on to the harbors of mainland and island that look right across to the old Eastern Thulé, "with its rosy pearls and golden-roofed palaces," and offer trade and commerce to the swarming millions of Cathay; over all this we had travelled, and it was all our own.

> "Where's the coward that would not dare
> To fight for such a land."

Thank God, we have a country. It is not our poverty of land, or sea, or wood, or mine that shall ever urge us to be traitors. But the destiny of a country depends not on its material resources. It depends on the character of its people. Here, too, is full ground for confidence. We in everything "are sprung of earth's first blood, have titles manifold." We come of a race that never counted the number of its foes, nor the number of its friends when freedom, loyalty, or God was concerned.

Two courses are possible, though it is almost an insult to say there are two, for one requires us to be false to our traditions and history, to our future and to ourselves. Any number of courses may be proposed. The Abbé Sieges had a cabinet filled with pigeon-holes, in each of which was a cut-and-dried Constitution for France. *Doctrinaires* fancy that at any time they can say "Go to, let us make a Constitution," and that they can fit it on a nation as readily as new coats could be fitted to their backs. There never was a profounder mistake. A nation grows and its Constitution must grow with it. The nation cannot be pulled up by the roots, cannot be dissociated from its past, without danger to its highest interests. Loyalty is essential to its fulfilment of a distinctive mission, essential to its true glory. Only one course therefore is possible for us, consistent with the self-respect that alone gains the respect of others; to seek, in the consolidation of the Empire, a common Imperial citizenship with common responsibilities and a common inheritance.

We are sometimes told that a Republican form of government and Republican institutions are the same as our own. But they are not ours. Besides, they are not the same either in themselves or in their effects on character. And, as we are the children even more than we are the fathers and framers of our national institutions, our first duty is to hold fast those political forms the influences of which on national character have been proved by the tests of time and comparison to be the most ennobling. Republicanism is one-sided. Despotism is other-sided. The tiue form should combine and harmonize both sides.

The favorite principle of Robertson, of Brighton, that the whole truth in the realm of the spiritual consists in the union of two truths that are contrary but not contradictory, applies to the social and political realms. What two contrary truths then lie at the basis of a complete national Constitution? First, that the will of the people is the will of God. Secondly, that the will of God must be the will of the people. That the people are the ultimate fountain of all power is one truth. That government is of God and should be strong, stable, and above the people, is another. In other words, the elements of liberty and of authority should both be represented. A republic recognizes only the first. In consequence, popular appeals are made to that which is lowest in our nature, for such appeals are made to the greatest number and are most likely to be immediately successful. The character of public men and the national character deteriorate. Neither dignity, elevation of sentiment, nor refinement of manners is cultivated. Still more fatal consequences, the ark of the nation is carried periodically into party fights. For the time being, the citizen has no country; he has only his party, and the unity of the country is constantly imperilled. On the other hand, a despotism is based entirely on the element of authority.

To unite those elements in due proportions has been and is the aim of every true statesman. Let the history of liberty and progress, of the development of human character to all its rightful issues, testify where they have been more wisely blended than in the British Constitution.

We have a fixed centre of authority and government, a fountain of honor above us that all reverence, from which a thousand gracious influences come down to every rank; and along with that fixity we have, instead of a cast-iron yoke for four years, representative institutions so elastic that they respond within their own sphere to every breath of popular sentiment. In harmony with this central part of our Constitution, we have an independent judiciary instead of judges—too often the creatures of wealthy adventurers or the echoes of passing popular sentiment. And more valuable than the direct advantages are the subtle, indirect influences that flow from our unbroken connection with the past, the dynamical though imponderable forces that determine the tone and mould the character of a people.

"In our halls is hung armory of the invincible knights of old."

Ours are the graves of our forefathers and a historical continuity that is the best safeguard against revolutionary fever; ours the names "to which a thousand memories call"; ours is the flag that symbolizes the highest thoughts that have ever descended from Heaven to earth; ours the Queen whose virtues transmute the sacred principle of loyalty into a personal affection.

PART III.

UNIVERSAL PATRIOTISM.

PART III.

UNIVERSAL PATRIOTISM.

MY COUNTRY.

There is a land, of every land the pride,
Beloved of Heaven o'er all the world beside,
Where brighter suns dispense serener light,
And milder moons imparadise the night;
A land of beauty, virtue, valor, truth,
Time-tutored age, and love exalted youth.
The wandering mariner, whose eye explores
The wealthiest isles, the most enchanting shores,
Views not a realm so beautiful and fair,
Nor breathes the spirit of a purer air.

In every clime, the magnet of his soul,
Touched by remembrance, trembles to that pole;
For in this land of Heaven's peculiar race,
The heritage of Nature's noblest grace,
There is a spot of earth supremely blest,
A dearer, sweeter spot than all the rest,
Where man, creation's tyrant, casts aside
His sword and sceptre, pageantry and pride,
While in his softened looks benignly blend
The sire, the son, the husband, brother friend.

Here woman reigns; the mother, daughter, wife,
Strew with fresh flowers the narrow way of life;
In the clear heaven of her delightful eye
An angel-guard of love and graces lie;
Around her knees domestic duties meet,
And fireside pleasures gambol at her feet.
Where shall that land, that spot of earth be found?
Art thou a man?—a patriot?—look around;
Oh, thou shalt find, howe'er thy footsteps roam,
That land thy country, and that spot thy home.

JAMES MONTGOMERY.

BRITANNIA.

All hail, my country! hail to thee,
Thou birthplace of the brave and free,
Thou ruler upon land and sea,
Britannia!

No thing of change, no mushroom state,
In wisdom thou canst work and wait,
Or wield the thunderbolts of Fate,
Britannia!

Oh, nobly hast thou played thy part!
What struggles of the head and heart
Have gone to make thee what thou art,
Britannia!

Great mother of the mighty dead!
Sir Walter sang and Nelson bled
To weave a garland for thy head,
Britannia!

And Watt, the great magician, wrought.
And Shakespeare ranged the realms of thought,
And Newton soared, and Cromwell fought,
Britannia!

And Milton's high seraphic art,
And Bacon's head and Burns' heart
Are glories that shall ne'er depart,
Britannia!

These are the soul of thy renown,
The gems immortal in thy crown,
The suns that never shall go down,
Britannia!

O, still have faith in truth divine!
Aye sacred be thy seal and sign,
And power and glory shall be thine,
Britannia!

A. McLachlan.

ST. GEORGE'S FLAG.

St. George for merry England, ho, up with the pennon brave,
It hath streamed o'er many a conquered land, o'er many a distant wave;
Up with the red-cross banner, 'tis a glorious sight to see,
The noblest flag that ever flew, stream out so fair and free.

It floated o'er proud Acre's towers in days long passed away,
When Lion Richard led his host at the holy tomb to pray;
And still the crescent paler waned before the hallowed sign,
That flew in triumph o'er thy fields, oh, sacred Palestine.

It cheered old England's stalwart sons thro' Cressy's hard won fray.
It waved o'er Royal Henry's head on Agincourt's proud day;
The sultry breath of sunny Spain its crimson cross has fanned,
And gallant hosts have borne it on through India's burning land.

Oh, many a flag of gaudier hue the fanning breeze may wave,
But none that bears a nobler name, more stainless or more brave;
None that hath led more dauntless hearts to battle for the right,
None that have flown more proudly o'er the crimson field of fight

Up with the brave old banner then, the peerless and the bold,
True hearts will rally round it yet as in the days of old;
And still on every English lip the thrilling cry shall be
St. George for merry England, ho, God and our own country.

Mrs. Faulkner.

THE HOMES OF ENGLAND.

The stately homes of England,
How beautiful they stand!
Amidst their tall ancestral trees!
O'er all the pleasant land!
The deer across the greensward bound
Through shade and sunny gleam,
And the swan glides past them with the sound
Of some rejoicing stream.

The merry homes of England!
Around their hearths by night,
What gladsome looks of household love
Meet in the ruddy light!
There woman's voice flows forth in song,
Or childhood's tale is told;
Or lips move tunefully along
Some glorious page of old.

The cottage homes of England!
By thousands on her plains,
They are smiling o'er the silvery brook,
And round the hamlet fanes.
Through glowing orchards forth they peep,
Each from its nook of leaves;
And fearless there the lowly sleep,
As the bird beneath their eaves.

The free, fair homes of England,
Long, long in hut and hall,
May hearts of native proof be reared
To guard each hallow'd wall.
And green forever be the groves,
And bright the flowery sod,
Where first the child's glad spirit loves
Its country and its God.

Mrs. Hemans.

SCOTLAND.

O, Caledonia ! can it be
  A wonder that we love thee ?
And tho' we be afar from thee,
  We place no land above thee.
For tho' in foreign lands we dwell,
  A sacred tie has bound us ;
Our hearts can never lose the spell
  Thy mountains threw around us.

And tho' thy breath is cold and keen,
  And rugged are thy features ;
Yet, O, my country ! Thou hast been
  The nurse of noble natures.
Does not thine humblest peasant know
  The truth of truths supernal—
That rank is but a passing show,
  But moral worth's eternal.

Scotland ! the humblest son of thine
  Is heir to living pages
Heir to a literature divine,
  Bequeathed to all the ages ;
Heir to those songs and ballads old,
  Brimful of love and pity,
Which fall like showers of living gold,
  In many a homely ditty.

O, we may leave our mountains high,
  Our grand old hills of heather ;
Yet song's the tie—the sacred tie—
  Which binds our hearts together.
Then here's to all who fight the wrong,
  And may their hopes ne'er wither—
To Scotland, freedom, love and song,
  For aye they go together.

A. McLachlan.

THE IRISH HARP.

The harp that in darkness and silence forsaken,
Had slumbered while ages rolled slowly along,
Once more in its own native land shall awaken,
And pour from its chords all the raptures of song.

Unhurt by the mildews that o'er it were stealing,
Its strings in full chorus shall warble sublime,
Shall rouse all the ardor of patriot feeling,
And snatch a bright wreath from the relics of time.

Sweet harp! on some tale of past sorrow while dwelling,
Still plaintive and sad breathes the murmuring sound;
The bright, sparkling tear of fond sympathy swelling,
Shall freshen the shamrock that twines thee around.

Sweet harp! o'er thy tones, though with fervent devotion,
We mingle a patriot smile with a tear,
Not fainter the smiles, not less pure the emotion,
That waits on the cause which assembles us here.

Behold where the child of affliction and sorrow,
Whose eyes never gazed on the splendor of light,
Is taught from thy trembling vibration to borrow
One mild ray of joy, midst the horrors of night.

No more shall he wander unknown and neglected,
From Winter's loud tempests a shelter to find;
No more a sad outcast, forlorn and dejected,
Shall poverty add to the woes of the blind.

Miss Balfour.

THE DEFENCE OF LUCKNOW.

Banner of England, not for a season, O banner of Britain, hast thou
Floated in conquering battle or flapt to the battle-cry!
Never with mightier glory than when we had rear'd thee on high
Flying at top of the roofs in the ghastly siege of Lucknow
Shot thro' the staff or the halyard, but ever we raised thee anew,
And ever upon the topmost roof our banner of England blew.

Frail were the works that defended the hold that we held with our lives—
Women and children among us, God help them, our children and wives!
Hold it we might—and for fifteen days or for twenty at most.
"Never surrender, I charge you, but every man die at his post!"
Voice of the dead whom we loved, our Lawrence the best of the brave.
Cold were his brows when we kiss'd him—we laid him that night in his grave.
"Every man dies at his post!" and there hail'd on our houses and halls
Death from their rifle-bullets, and death from their cannon-balls,
Death in our innermost chamber, and death at our slight barricade,
Death while we stood with the musket, and death while we stoopt to the spade.
Handful of men as we were, we were British in heart and in limb,
Strong with the strength of the race to command, to obey, to endure,
Each of us fought as if hope for the garrison hung but on him;
Still, could we watch at all points? we were every day fewer and fewer.
There was a whisper among us, but only a whisper that passed,
"Children and wives—if the tigers leap into the fold unawares—
Every man die at his post—and the foe may outlive us at last—
Better to fall by the hands that they love, than to fall into theirs."

Men will forget what we suffer and not what we do. We can fight!
But to be soldier all day and be sentinel thro' the night—

Ever the mine and assault, our sallies, their lying alarms,
Bugles and drums in the darkness, and shoutings and soundings of arms,
Ever the labor of fifty that had to be done by five,
Ever the marvel among us that one should be left alive,
Ever the day with its traitorous death from the loopholes around,
Ever the night with its coffinless corpse to be laid in the ground,
Grief for our perishing children, and never a moment for grief,
Toil and ineffable weariness, faltering hopes of relief,
Havelock baffled, or beaten, or butcher'd for all that we knew—
Then day and night, day and night, coming down on the still-shatter'd walls
Millions of musket-bullets, and thousands of cannon-balls—
But ever upon the topmast roof our banner of England blew.

Hark cannonade, fusilade ! is it true what was told by the scout,
Outram and Havelock breaking their way through the fell mutineers?
Surely the pibroch of Europe is ringing again in our ears !
All on a sudden the garrison uttered a jubilant shout,
Havelock's glorious Highlanders answer with conquering cheers,
Sick from the hospital echo them, women and children come out,
Blessing the wholesome white faces of Havelock's good fusileers,
Kissing the war-harden'd hand of the Highlander wet with their tears.
Dance to the pibroch ! saved ! we are saved ! is it you ? is it you ?
Saved by the valor of Havelock, saved by the blessing of Heaven !
"Hold it for fifteen days !" we have held it for eighty-seven.
And ever aloft on the palace roof the old banner of England blew.

TENNYSON.

THE SONG OF THE CAMP.

An Incident of the Crimean War.

"Give us a song!" the soldier cried,
The outer trenches guarding,
When the heated guns of the camp allied
Grew weary of bombarding.

The dark Redan, in silent scoff,
Lay, grim and threatening, under;
And the tawny mound of the Malakoff
No longer belched its thunder.

There was a pause. A guardsman said:
"We storm the forts to-morrow;
Sing while we may, another day,
Will bring enough of sorrow."

They lay along the battery's side,
Below the smoking cannon;
Brave hearts, from Severn and from Clyde,
And from the banks of Shannon.

They sang of love and not of fame;
Forgot was Britain's glory;
Each heart recallèd a different name,
But all sang "Annie Laurie."

Voice after voice caught up the song,
Until its tender passion
Rose, like an anthem, rich and strong,—
Their battle-eve confession.

Dear girl, her name he dared not speak,
But, as the song grew louder,
Something upon the soldier's cheek
Washed off the stains of powder.

Beyond the darkening ocean burned
The bloody sunset's embers,
While the Crimean valleys learned
How English love remembers.

And once again a fire of hell
Rained on the Russian quarters,
With scream of shot, and burst of shell,
And bellowing of the mortars!

And Irish Nora's eyes are dim
For a singer, dumb and gory;
And English Mary mourns for him
Who sang of "Annie Laurie."

Sleep, soldiers! still in honored rest
Your truth and valor wearing.
The bravest are the tenderest,—
The loving are the daring.

BAYARD TAYLOR.

THE BETTER WAY.

Who serves his country best?
Not he who, for a brief and stormy space,
Leads forth her armies to the fierce affray.
Short is the time of turmoil and unrest,
Long years of peace succeed it and replace;
  There is a better way.

He serves his country best
Who joins the tide that lifts her nobly on;
For speech has myriad tongues for every day,
And song but one; and law within the breast
Is stronger than the graven law on stone;
  There is a better way.

He serves his country best
Who lives pure life, and doeth righteous deed,
And walks straight paths, however others stray
And leaves his sons as uttermost bequest
A stainless record which all men may read;
  This is a better way.

No drop but serves the slowly lifting tide,
No dew but has an errand to some flower,
No smallest star but sheds some helpful ray,
And man by man, each giving to the rest,
Makes the firm bulwark of the country's power;
  There is no better way.

SUSAN COOLIDGE.

WHAT MAKES A HERO?

What makes a hero? Not success, not fame,
Inebriate merchants, and the loud acclaim
  Of glutted Avarice, caps tossed up in air,
  Or pen of journalist, with flourish fair,
Bells pealed, stars, ribbons and a titular name,—
  These, though his rightful tribute, he can spare;
His rightful tribute,—not his end or aim,
  Or true reward; for never yet did these
  Refresh the soul, or set the heart at ease.

What makes a hero? An heroic mind,
Expressed in action, in endurance proved.
  And if there be pre-eminence of right,
  Derived through pain well suffered, to the height
Of rank heroic, 'tis to bear unmoved,
Not toil, not risk, not rage of sea or wind,
Not the brute fury of barbarians blind,
  But worse,—ingratitude and poisonous darts
Launched by the country he had served and loved;
This, with a free, unclouded spirit pure,
This, in the strength of silence to endure,
  A dignity to noble deeds imparts.
  Beyond the gauds and trappings of renown;
  This is the hero's complement and crown;
This missed, one struggle had been wanting still,
One glorious triumph of the heroic will,
  One self-approved in his heart of hearts.

HENRY TAYLOR.

AMERICA'S GREETING TO ENGLAND.

All hail! thou noble land,
Our fathers' native soil!
Oh! stretch thy mighty hand,
Gigantic grown by toil,
O'er the vast Atlantic wave to our shore!
For thou, with magic might,
Canst reach to where the light
Of Phœbus travels bright
The world o'er!

The genius of our clime,
From pine-embattled steep,
Shall hail the guest sublime;
While the Tritons of the deep
With their conchs the kindred league shall proclaim.
Then let the world combine,—
O'er the main, our naval line,
Like the Milky Way, shall shine
Bright in fame!

Though ages long have passed
Since our fathers left their home,
Their pilot in the blast,
O'er untravelled seas to roam,—
Yet lives the blood of England in our veins!
And shall we not proclaim
That blood of honest fame,
Which no tyranny can tame
By its chains?

While the language free and bold,
Which the bard of Avon sung,
In which our Milton told
How the vault of heaven rung,

When Satan, blasted, fell with all his host,—
While this, with reverence meet,
Ten thousand echoes greet,
From rock to rock repeat
Round our coast!

While the manners, while the arts,
That mould a nation's soul,
Still cling around our hearts,—
Between let ocean roll,
Our joint communion breaking with the Sun;
Yet, still, from either beach
The voice of blood shall reach,
More audible than speech,
"We are one!"

WASHINGTON ALLSTON.

LUCKNOW AND JESSIE BROWN.

Oh, that last day in Lucknow fort!
We knew that it was the last;
That the enemy's lines crept surely on,
And the end was coming fast.

To yield to that foe was worse than death,
And the men and we all worked on;
It was one day more of smoke and roar,
And then it would all be done.

There was one of us, a corporal's wife,
A fair, young, gentle thing,
Wasted with fever in the siege,
And her mind was wandering.

She lay on the ground in her Scottish plaid,
And I took her head on my knee;
"When my father comes hame frae the pleugh," she said
"Oh! then please waken me."

She slept like a child on her father's floor,
In the flecking of woodbine-shade,
When the house-dog sprawls by the open door,
And the mother's wheel is staid.

It was smoke and roar and powder-stench,
And hopeless waiting for death;
And the soldier's wife, like a full-tired child,
Seemed scarce to draw her breath.

I sank to sleep; and I had my dream
Of an English village-lane
And wall and garden—but one wild scream
Brought me back to the roar again.

There Jessie Brown stood listening,
  Till a sudden gladness broke
All over her face, and she caught my hand
  And drew me near, as she spoke:

"The Hielanders! Oh! dinna ye hear
  The slogan far awa?
The McGregor's! Oh! I ken it weel;
  It's the grandest o' them a'!

"God bless the bonny Hielanders!
  We're saved! we're saved!" she cried;
And fell on her knees, and thanks to God
  Flowed forth like a full flood-tide.

Along the battery-line her cry
  Had fallen among the men
And they started back—they were there to die;
  But was life so near them then?

They listened for life; the rattling fire
  Far off, and the far-off roar
Were all; and the colonel shook his head,
  And they turned to their guns once more.

But Jessie said: "The slogan's done;
  But winna ye hear it noo?
The Campbells are comin'! It's nae a dream;
  Our succors hae broken through!"

We heard the roar and the rattle afar,
  But the pipes we could not hear;
So the men plied their work of hopeless war,
And knew that the end was near.

It was not long ere it made its way—
  A shrilling, ceaseless sound;
It was no noise from the strife afar,
  Or the sappers underground.

It *was* the pipes of the Highlanders!
  And now they played *Auld Lang Syne*;
It came to our men like the voice of God,
  And they shouted along the line.

And they wept, and shook one another's hands,
  And the women sobbed in a crowd;
And everyone knelt down where he stood
  And we all thanked God aloud.

That happy time, when we welcomed them,
  Our men put Jessie first;
And the general gave her his hand, and cheers
  Like a storm from the soldiers burst.

And the pipers' ribbons and tartans streamed,
  Marching round and round our line;
And our joyful cheers were broken with tears
  As the pipes played *Auld Lang Syne*.

ROBERT LOWELL.

———

FREEDOM.

Of old sat Freedom on the heights,
The thunders breaking at her feet:
Above her shook the starry lights:
She heard the torrents meet.

There in her place she did rejoice,
Self-gather'd in her prophet-mind;
But fragments of her mighty voice
Came rolling on the wind.

Then stept she down through town and field
To mingle with the human race,
And part by part to men reveal'd
The fullness of her face.

Grave mother of majestic works,
From her isle-altar gazing down,
Who, God-like, grasps the triple forks,
And, King-like, wears the crown.

Her open eyes desire the truth,
The wisdom of a thousand years
Is in them. May perpetual youth
Keep dry their light from tears.

That her fair form may stand and shine,
Make bright our days and light our dreams,
Turning to scorn with lips divine
The falsehood of extremes!

TENNYSON.

THE STAMP OF MANHOOD.

Come, let us sing to human worth,
'Tis big hearts that we cherish,
For they're the glory of the earth
And never wholly perish.
All nature loves the good and brave,
And showers her gifts upon them ;
She hates the tyrant and the slave
For manhood's stamp's not on them.

Thine eye shall be the index true
Of what thy soul conceiveth ;
Thy words shall utter firm and few
The things thy heart believeth ;
Thy voice shall have the ring of steel,
The good and brave will own thee ;
Where'er thou art each heart shall feel
That manhood is upon thee.

And if stern duties are assign'd
And no one near to love thee,
Be resolute, nor look behind,
The Heavens are still above thee ;
And follow truth where'er she leads,
Though bigots frown npon thee,
Your witnesses will be your deeds
If manhood's stamp is on thee.

Let hope around thy heart entwine
Thy loadstar's love and duty,
And every word and deed of thine
Will be embalmed in beauty,
And goodness from her highest throne
Will blessings pour upon thee,
Thee Nature's soul will love to own
If manhood's stamp is on thee.

 A. McLachlan.

A PLEA FOR LIBERTY.

It stirs the pulses of the blood
  With thrills of joy, to hear again
How lion-hearted heroes stood
  And fought, on many a gory plain,
For freedom in the olden days
  When stern oppression ruled the world ;—
Or read, in warm impassioned lays,
  How tyrants from their thrones were hurled.

And shall we tamely wear a yoke,
  And slavish fetters on the mind,
Esteeming all, some teacher spoke
  Or wrote, as gold refined ?
Opinion, sentiment or creed
  Which others firmly held and taught,
Cannot to us be truth indeed,
  Till it becomes our living thought.

When round the walls the foemen fight,
  New points to higher interest rise ;
The truths, which once were lost to sight,
  May be the pearls which most we prize.
Each tone from ages past possessed
  Whatever guiding light it brings,
Is not a goal in which to rest,
  But steps to climb to higher things.

As one who climbs some mountain height,
  That grandly lifts its peaks of snow,
Beholds, with wonder and delight,
  Wild scenes, invisible below,
So through the gliding years of time,
  As suns revolve and earth grows old,
The snowy hills of thought we climb,
  And broader fields of truth behold.

Shall I condemn, with stern disdain,
  The man who will not sign my creed;
Though he is with me in the main,
  And side by side in kindly deed?
If history's darkest page is traced
  In blood, by Christian bigots stern,
The war of creeds will never cease,
  Till charity from Christ we learn.

In thought, there must be false and true,—
  There must be wrong and right in deed;
Yet truth should value what we do,
  As highly as a lifeless creed.
The thoughts despised, as new or strange,
  May yet in real triumph reign;—
The form and garb of truth may change,
  And yet the inner life remain.

E. H. DEWART, D.D.

BATTLE-HYMN OF THE REPUBLIC.

Mine eyes have seen the glory of the coming of the Lord ;
He is tramping out the vintage where the grapes of wrath are stored ;
He hath loosed the fateful lightning of his terrible swift sword ;
His truth is marching on.

I have seen him in the watch-fires of a hundred circling camps ;
They have builded him an altar in the evening dews and damps ;
I have read his righteous sentence by the dim and flaring lamps :
His day is marching on.

I have read a fiery gospel writ in burnished rows of steel :
" As ye deal with my contemners, so with you my grace shall deal ;
Let the Hero, born of woman, crush the serpent with his heel,
Since God is marching on."

He has sounded forth the trumpet that shall never call retreat ;
He is sifting out the hearts of men before his judgment seat ;
Oh, be swift, my soul, to answer him ! be jubilant, my feet !
Our God is marching on.

In the beauty of the lilies, Christ was born across the sea,
With a glory in his bosom that transfigures you and me ;
As he died to make men holy, let us die to make men free,
While God is marching on.

JULIA WARD HOWE.

THE LAUNCH OF THE SHIP.

" Build me straight, O worthy Master !
Staunch and strong, a goodly vessel,
That shall laugh at all disaster,
And with wave and whirlwind wrestle ! "

The merchant's word
Delighted the Master heard ;
For his heart was in his work, and the heart
Giveth grace unto every art.
And with a voice that was full of glee,
He answered, " Ere long we will launch
A vessel as goodly, and strong, and staunch
As ever weathered a wintry sea ! "

All is finished ! and at length
Has come the bridal day
Of beauty and of strength.
To-day the vessel shall be launched !
With fleecy clouds the sky is blanched ;
And o'er the bay,
Slowly, in all his splendors dight,
The great sun rises to behold the sight.
The ocean old
Centuries old,
Strong as youth, and as uncontrolled,
Paces restless to and fro,
Up and down the sands of gold.
His beating heart is not at rest ;
And far and wide,
With ceaseless flow,
His beard of snow
Heaves with the heaving of his breast.
He waits impaitent for his bride.
There she stands,
With her foot upon the sands,

Decked with flags and streamers gay,
In honor of her marriage-day,
Her snow-white signals fluttering, blending,
Round her like a veil descending,
Ready to be
The bride of the gray old sea.

Then the Master,
With a gesture of command,
Waved his hand;
And at the word,
Loud and sudden there was heard,
All around them and below,
The sound of hammers, blow on blow,
Knocking away the shores and spurs,
And see! she stirs!
She starts,—she moves,—she seems to feel
The thrill of life along her keel,
And spurning with her foot the ground,
With one exulting, joyous bound,
She leaps into the ocean's arms!
And lo! from the assembled crowd
There rose a shout, prolonged and loud,
That to the ocean seemed to say,—
"Take her, O bridegroom, old and gray;
Take her to thy protecting arms,
With all her youth, and all her charms!"
How beautiful she is! how fair
She lies within those arms that press
Her form with many a soft caress
Of tenderness and watchful care!
Sail forth into the sea, O ship!
Through wind and wave, right onward steer!
The moistened eye, the trembling lip,
Are not the signs of doubt or fear.

Thou, too, sail on, O Ship of State!
Sail on, O Union, strong and great!
Humanity, with all its fears,
With all the hopes of future years,
Is hanging breathless on thy fate!

We know what Master laid thy keel,
What Workman wrought thy ribs of steel,
Who made each mast, and sail and rope,
What anvils rang, what hammers beat,
In what a forge and what a heat,
Were shaped the anchors of thy hope!

Fear not each sudden sound and shock.
'Tis of the wave and not the rock;
'Tis but the flapping of the sail,
And not a rent made by the gale!
In spite of rock and tempest's roar,
In spite of false lights on the shore,
Sail on, nor fear to breast the sea!
Our hearts, our hopes, are all with thee;
Our hearts, our hopes, our prayers, our tears,
Our faith triumphant o'er our fears,
Are all with thee,—are all with thee!

LONGFELLOW.

THE GOOD TIME COMING.

There's a good time coming, boys,
A good time coming:
We may not live to see the day,
But earth shall glisten in the ray
Of the good time coming.
Cannon balls may aid the truth,
But thought's a weapon stronger;
We'll win the battle by its aid—
Wait a little longer.

There's a good time coming, boys,
A good time coming:
The pen shall supersede the sword,
And Right, not Might, shall be the lord,
In the good time coming.
Worth, not Birth, shall rule mankind,
And be acknowledged stronger;
The proper impulse has been given;
Wait a little longer.

There's a good time coming, boys,
A good time coming;
War in all men's eyes should be
A monster of iniquity
In the good time coming.
Nations shall not quarrel then,
To prove which is the stronger;
The proper impulse has been given;
Wait a little longer.

There's a good time coming, boys,
A good time coming:
Hateful rivalries of creed
Shall not make their martyrs bleed

In the good time coming.
Religion shall be shorn of pride,
And flourish all the stronger ;
And Charity shall trim her lamp ;
Wait a little longer.

There's a good time coming, boys,
A good time coming ;
Let us aid it all we can—
Every woman, every man,—
The good time coming.
Smallest helps, if rightly given,
Make the impulse stronger ;
'Twill be strong enough one day ;
Wait a little longer.

CHARLES MACKAY.

CARDINAL WOLSEY.

Nay, then, farewell!
I have touched the highest point of all my greatness,
And, from that full meridian of my glory,
I haste now to my setting: I shall fall
Like a bright exhalation in the evening,
And no man see me more.

Farewell, a long farewell, to all my greatness!
This is the state of man: to day he puts forth
The tender leaves of hope; to-morrow blossoms,
And bears his blushing honors thick upon him:
The third day comes a frost, a killing frost;
And when he thinks,—good, easy man,—full surely
His greatness is a-ripening, nips his root,
And then he falls, as I do. I have ventured,
Like little wanton boys that swim on bladders,
These many summers in a sea of glory;
But far beyond my depth: my high-blown pride
At length broke under me; and now has left me,
Weary and old with service, to the mercy
Of a rude stream that must forever hide me.
Vain pomp and glory of this world, I hate ye!
I feel my heart new opened. Oh, how wretched
Is that poor man that hangs on princes' favors!
There is, betwixt that smile he would aspire to,
That sweet aspect of princes, and their ruin,
More pangs and fears than wars or women have,
And when he falls, he falls like Lucifer,
Never to hope again!

Cromwell, I did not think to shed a tear
In all my miseries: but thou hast forced me,
Out of thy honest truth to play the woman.

Let's dry our eyes : and thus far hear me, Cromwell ;
And when I am forgotten, as I shall be,
And sleep in dull cold marble, where no mention
Of me more must be heard of,—say I taught thee,—
Say Wolsey, that once trod the ways of glory,
And sounded all the depths and shoals of honor,
Found thee a way, out of his wreck, to rise in ;
A sure and safe one, though thy master missed it.
Mark but my fall, and that which ruined me !

Cromwell, I charge thee, fling away ambition ;
By that sin fell the angels : how can man, then,
The image of his Maker, hope to win by't ?
Love thyself last ; cherish those hearts that hate thee,—
Corruption wins not more than honesty ;
Still in thy right hand carry gentle peace,
To silence envious tongues. Be just, and fear not.
Let all the ends thou aim'st at be thy country's
Thy God's, and truth's ; then, if thou fall'st, O Cromwell,
Thou fall'st a blessed martyr !

SHAKESPEARE.

CLEAR THE WAY.

Men of thought, be up and stirring,
    Night and day !
Sow the seed—withdraw the curtain—
    Clear the way !
Men of action, aid and cheer them
    As ye may !
There's a fount about to stream,
There's a light about to beam,
There's a warmth about to glow,
There's a flower about to blow,
There's a midnight blackness changing
    Into gray.
Men of thought, and men of action,
    Clear the way !

Once the welcome light has broken,
    Who shall say
What the unmingled glories
    Of the day ?
What the evil that shall perish
    In its ray ?
Aid the dawning, tongue and pen ;
Aid it, hopes of honest men ;
Aid it, paper—aid it, type—
Aid it, for the hour is ripe,
And our earnest must not slacken
    Into play.
Men of thought, and men of action,
    Clear the way.

Lo ! a cloud's about to vanish
    From the day ;
Lo ! a right's about to conquer—
    Clear the way !
And a brazen wrong to crumble
    Into clay.
With that right shall many more
Enter smiling at the door ;
With the giant wrong shall fall
Many others, great and small,
That for ages long have held us
    For their prey ;
Men of thought, and men of action,
    Clear the way !

ANON.

HYMN OF THE VAUDOIS MOUNTAINEERS.

For the strength of the hills we bless Thee, our God, our fathers' God.
Thou hast made Thy children mighty by the touch of the mountain sod,
Thou hast fixed our ark of refuge where the spoiler's foot ne'er trod ;
For the strength of the hills we bless Thee, our God, our fathers' God.

We are watchers of a beacon whose light must never die ;
We are guardians of an altar 'midst the silence of the sky ;
The rocks yield founts of courage, struck forth as by thy rod ;
For the strength of the hills we bless Thee, our God, our fathers' God.

For the dark-resounding caverns, where Thy still, small voice is heard ;
For the strong pines of the forests, that by Thy breath are stirred ;
For the storms, on whose free pinions thy spirit walks abroad ;
For the strength of the hills we bless Thee, our God, our fathers God.

The royal eagle darteth on his quarry from the heights,
And the stag that knows no master seeks there his wild delights ;
But we for Thy communion have sought the mountain sod ;
For the strength of the hills we bless Thee, our God, our fathers' God.

The banner of the chieftain, far, far below us waves ;
The war-horse of the spearman cannot reach our lofty caves ;
The dark clouds wrap the threshold of Freedom's last abode ;
For the strength of the hills we bless Thee, our God, our fathers' God.

For the shadow of Thy presence, round our camp of rock outspread ;
For the stern defiles of battle, bearing record of our dead ;
For the snows, and for the torrents, for the free heart's burial sob ;
For the strength of the hills we bless Thee, our God, our fathers' God.

Mrs. Hemans.

BURIAL OF SIR JOHN MOORE.

Not a drum was heard, not a funeral note,
As his corse to the rampart we hurried:
Not a soldier discharged his farewell shot,
O'er the grave where our hero was buried.

We buried him darkly, at dead of night,
The sods with our bayonets turning;
By the struggling moon-beam's misty light,
And the lantern dimly burning.

No useless coffin enclosed his breast,
Not in sheet nor in shroud we wound him;
But he lay like a warrior taking his rest—
With his martial cloak around him.

Few and short were the prayers we said,
And we spoke not a word of sorrow;
But we steadfastly gazed on the face of the dead,
And we bitterly thought of the morrow.

We thought, as we hollow'd his narrow bed,
And smooth'd down his lonely pillow,
That the foe and the stranger would tread o'er his head,
And we far away on the billow.

Lightly they'll talk of the spirit that's gone,
And o'er his cold ashes upbraid him;
But little he'll reck if they let him sleep on,
In the grave where a Briton has laid him.

But half of our heavy task was done,
When the clock struck the hour for retiring;
And we heard the distant and random gun,
That the foe was sullenly firing.

Slowly and sadly we laid him down,
From the field of his fame fresh and gory;
We carved not a line, and we raised not a stone—
But we left him alone in his glory!

C. WOLFE.

DUTY TO ONE'S COUNTRY.

Our country is a whole, my Publius,
Of which we all are parts ; nor should a citizen
Regard his interests as distinct from hers ;
No hopes or fears should touch his patriot soul
But what affect her honor or her shame.
E'en when in hostile fields he bleeds to save her,
'Tis not his blood he loses, 'tis his country's ;
He only pays her back a debt he owes.
To her he's bound for birth and education,
Her laws secure him from domestic feuds,
And from the foreign foe her arms protect him.
She lends him honors, dignity, and rank,
His wrongs revenges, and his merits pays ;
And, like a tender and indulgent mother,
Loads him with comforts, and would make his state
As blessed as nature and the gods designed it.
Such gifts my son, have their alloy of pain,
And let the unworthy wretch, who will not bear
His portion of the public burden, lose
The advantages it yields ; let him retire
From the dear blessings of a social life,
And from the sacred laws which guard those blessings !
Renounce the civilized abodes of man ;
With kindred brutes, one common shelter seek
In horrid wilds, and dens, and dreary caves,
And with their shaggy tenants share the spoils ;
Or, if the shaggy hunters miss their prey,
From scattered acorns pick a scanty meal,
Far from the sweet civilities of life ;
There let him live, and vaunt his wretched freedom,
While we, obedient to the laws that guard us,
Guard them, and live or die, as they decree.

WILLIAM COWPER.

"THE GLORIOUS STRIFE."

The following lines by an unknown author, written at the time of the struggle of modern Greece for independence, in 1822, are in the spirit of patriotic aspiration.

On, on to the just and glorious strife !
With your swords your freedom shielding ;
Nay, resign, if it must be so, even life,
But die, at least, unyielding.

On to the strife, for 'twere far more meet
To sink with the foes who bay you,
Than crouch like dogs at your tyrants' feet,
And smile on the swords that slay you.

Shall the Pagan slaves, be masters, then,
Of the land which your fathers gave you ?
Shall the infidel lord it o'er Christian men,
When your own good swords may save you ?

No ! let him feel that their arms are strong,
That their courage will fail them never,
Who strike to repay long years of wrong,
And bury past shame forever.

Let him know there are hearts, however bowed,
By the chains which he threw around them,
That will rise, like a spirit, from pall and shroud,
And cry " ' woe ! " to the slaves who bound them.

Let him learn how weak is a tyrant's might
Against Liberty's sword contending ;
And find how the sons of Greece can fight,
Their freedom and land defending.

Then on, then on to the glorious strife !
With your swords your country shielding ;
And resign, if it must be so, even life,
But die, at least, unyielding.

ANON.

WILLIAM TELL TO HIS MEN.

My friends, our country must be free ! The land
Is never lost that has a son to right her,—
And here are troops of sons, and loyal ones !
Strong in her children should a mother be :
Shall ours be helpless, that has sons like us ?
God save our native land, whoever pays
The ransom that redeems her ! Now, what wait we ?
For word to move upon the dastard foe ?
Upon him, then ! Now think ye on the things
Ye most do love !—husbands and fathers, on
Their wives and children ; lovers, on their beloved ;
And all, upon their country ! When you use
Your weapons, think on the beseeching eyes,
To whet them could have lent you tears for water !
Still, wheresoe'er men strike for justice, there
Is God ; and now beneath His heaven we stand.
The nations round us bear a foreign yoke,
For they have yielded to the conqueror.
Nay, e'en within our frontiers may be found
Some that owe villain service to a lord,—
A race of bonded serfs, from sire to son.
But we, the genuine race of ancient Swiss,
Have kept our freedom, from the first, till now.
Never to princes have we bowed the knee.
What said our fathers when the Emperor
Pronounced a judgment in the Abbey's favor
Awarding lands beyond his jurisdiction ?
What was their answer ? This : "The grant is void.
No Emperor can bestow what is our own ;
And if the Empire shall deny us justice,
We can, within our mountains, right ourselves."
Thus spake our fathers ; and shall we endure
The shame and infamy of this new yoke,
And from the vassal brook what never king
Dared, in the fullness of his power, attempt ?

This soil we have created for ourselves,
By the hard labor of our hands; we've changed
The giant forest, that was erst the haunt
Of savage bears, into a home for man;
Blasted the solid rock; o'er the abyss
Thrown the firm bridge for the wayfaring man.
By the possession of a thousand years,
The soil is ours. And shall an alien lord,
Himself a vassal, dare to venture here,
On our own hearths insult us, and attempt
To forge the chains of bondage for our hands,
And do us shame on our own proper soil?
Is there no help against such wrong as this?
Yes! there's a limit to the despot's power.
When the oppressed looks round in vain for justice,
When his sore burden may no more be borne,
With fearless heart he makes appeal to Heaven,
And thence brings down his everlasting rights,
Oh, now be men, or never! From your hearts
Thrust the unbidden feet, that from their nooks
Drove forth your aged sires, your wives and babes!
The couches, your fair-handed daughters used
To spread, let not the vaunting stranger press,
Weary from spoiling you! Your roofs, that hear
The wanton riot of the intruding guest,
That mocks their masters,—clear them for the sake
Of the manhood to which all that's precious clings,
Else perishes. The land that bore you—oh,
Do honor to her! Let her glory in
Your breeding! Rescue her! Revenge her,—or
Ne'er call her mother more! Come on, my friends,
And where you take your stand upon the field,
However you advance, resolve on this,
That you will ne'er recede, while from the tongues
Of age, and womanhood, and infancy,
The helplessness, whose safety in you lies,
Invokes you to be strong! Come on! Come on!
I'll bring you to the foe! And when you meet him,
Strike hard! Strike home! Strike, while a dying blow
Is in an arm! Strike, till you're free, or fall!

Arranged from J. S. KNOWLES by EPES SARGENT.

ARNOLD VON WINKELRIED.

"Make way for liberty!" he cried,—
Made way for liberty, and died!

In arms the Austrian phalanx stood,
A living wall, a human wood;
Impregnable their front appears,
All horrent with projected spears.
Opposed to these, a hovering band
Contended for their native land,
Peasants whose new-found strength had broke
From manly necks the ignoble yoke,
And forged their fetters into swords,
On equal terms to fight their lords;
Marshalled once more at Freedom's call,
They came to conquer or to fall.

And now the work of life and death
Hung on the passing of a breath;
The fire of conflict burned within;
The battle trembled to begin;
Yet, while the Austrians held their ground,
Point for attack was nowhere found;
Where'er the impatient Switzers gazed,
The unbroken line of lances blazed;
That line 'twere suicide to meet,
And perish at their tyrants' feet.
How could they rest within their graves,
And leave their homes the haunts of slaves?
Would they not feel their children tread
With clanking chains above their head?

It must not be; this day, this hour,
Annihilates the oppressor's power!
All Switzerland is in the field,
She will not fly; she cannot yield.
She must not fall; her better fate

Here gives her an immortal date.
Few were the numbers she could boast,
But every freeman was a host,
And felt as 'twere a secret known
That one should turn the scale alone,
While each unto himself was he
On whose sole arm hung Victory.

It did depend on *one*, indeed;
Behold him—Arnold Winkelried!
There sounds not to the trump of Fame
The echo of a nobler name.
Unmarked he stood amid the throng,
In rumination deep and long,
Till you might see, with sudden grace,
The very thought come o'er his face,
And by the motion of his form
Anticipate the bursting storm;
And by the uplifting of his brow
Tell where the bolt would strike, and how.

But 'twas no sooner thought than done,—
The field was in a moment won!
"Make way for liberty!" he cried,
Then ran, with arms extended wide,
As if his dearest friend to clasp;
Ten spears he swept within his grasp.
"Make way for liberty!" he cried;
Their keen points met from side to side;
He bowed amongst them like a tree,
And thus made way for liberty.

Swift to the breach his comrádes fly,—
"Make way for liberty!" they cry,
And through the Austrian phalanx dart,
As rushed the spears through Arnold's heart,
While, instantaneous as his fall,
Rout, ruin, panic, scattered all.
An earthquake could not overthrow
A city with a surer blow.
Thus Switzerland again was free;
Thus death made way for liberty!

James Montgomery.

THE SONGS OF OUR FATHERS.

Sing them upon the sunny hills,
  When days are long and bright,
And the blue gleam of shining rills
  Is loveliest to thy sight;
Sing them along the misty moor,
  Where ancient hunters roved,
And swell them through the torrent's roar,—
  The songs our fathers loved.

The songs their souls rejoiced to hear
  When harps were in the hall,
And each proud note made lance and spear
  Thrill on the bannered wall;
The songs that through our valley green,
  Sent on from age to age,
Like his own river's voice, have been
  The peasant's heritage.

The reaper sings them when the vale
  Is filled with plumy sheaves;
The woodman, by the starlight pale
  Cheered homeward through the leaves;
And unto them the glancing oars
  A joyous measure keep,
Where the dark rocks that crest our shores
  Dash back the foaming deep.

So let it be,—a light they shed
  O'er each old fount and grove;
A memory of the gentle dead,
  A spell of lingering love;

Murmuring the names of mighty men,
  They bid our streams roll on,
And link high thoughts to every glen
  Where valiant deeds were done.

Teach them your children round the hearth,
  When evening fires burn clear,
And in the fields of harvest mirth,
  And on the hills of deer.
So shall each long-forgotten word,
  When far those loved ones roam,
Call back the hearts that once it stirred,
  To childhood's holy home.

The green woods of their native land
  Shall whisper in the strain,
The voices of their household band
  Shall sweetly speak again;
The heathery heights in vision rise
  Where like the stag they roved,—
Sing to your sons those melodies,
  The songs your fathers loved.

MRS. HEMANS.

THE SOLDIER'S DREAM.

Our bugles sang truce, for the night-cloud had lowered,
And the sentinel stars set their watch in the sky;
And thousands had sunk on the ground overpowered,
The weary to sleep, and the wounded to die.

When reposing that night on my pallet of straw,
By the wolf-scaring faggot that guarded the slain,
At the dead of the night, a sweet vision I saw,
And thrice ere the morning I dreamt it again.

Methought from the battle-field's dreadful array,
Far, far I had roamed on a desolate track;
'Twas autumn, and sunshine arose on the way
To the home of my fathers, that welcomed me back.

I flew to the pleasant fields, traversed so oft
In life's morning march, when my bosom was young,
I heard my own mountain goats bleating aloft,
And knew the sweet strain that the corn-reapers sung.

Then pledged we the wine-cup, and fondly I swore
From my home and my weeping friends never to part;
My little ones kissed me a thousand times o'er,
And my wife sobbed aloud in her fullness of heart.

"Stay, stay with us, rest, thou art weary and worn!"
And fain was the war-broken soldier to stay,—
But sorrow returned with the dawning of morn,
And the voice of my dreaming then melted away!

THOMAS CAMPBELL.

HOW HE SAVED ST. MICHAEL'S.

It was long ago it happened, ere ever the signal gun
That blazed above Fort Sumter had wakened the North as one ;
Long ere the wondrous pillar of battle-cloud and fire,
Had marked where the unchained millions marched on to their hearts' desire.

On the roofs and the glittering turrets, that night, as the sun went down,
The mellow glow of the twilight shone like a jewelled crown ;
And, bathed in the living glory, as the people lifted their eyes,
They saw the pride of the city, the spire of St. Michael's, rise.

High over the lesser steeples tipped with a golden ball,
That hung like a radiant planet caught in its earthward fall,
First glimpse of home to the sailor who made the harbor-round,
And last, slow-fading vision dear to the outward bound.

The gentle gathering shadows shut out the waning light ;
The children prayed at their bedsides, as you will pray to-night ;
The noise of buyer and seller from the busy mart was done ;
And in dreams of a peaceful morrow the city slumbered on.

But another light than sunrise aroused the sleeping street,
For a cry was heard at midnight, and the rush of trampling feet ;
Men stared in each other's faces through mingled fire and smoke,
While the frantic bells went clashing, clamorous stroke on stroke,

By the glare of her blazing roof-tree the houseless mother fled,
While the babe she pressed to her bosom shrieked in nameless dread,
While the fire-king's wild battalions scaled wall and capstone high,
And planted their flaring banners against an inky sky.

For the death that raged behind them, and the crash of ruin loud,
To the great square of the city were driven the surging crowd;
Where yet, firm in all the tumult, unscathed by the fiery flood,
With its heavenward-pointing finger the Church of St. Michael stood.

But e'en as they gazed upon it there rose a sudden wail,
A cry of horror, blended with the roaring of the gale,
On whose scorching wings up-driven, a single flaming brand
Aloft on the towering steeple clung like a bloody hand.

"Will it fade?" The whisper trembled from a thousand whitening lips;
Far out on the lurid harbor, they watched it from the ships,
A baleful gleam that brighter and ever brighter shone,
Like a flickering, trembling will-o'-wisp to a steady beacon grown.

"Uncounted gold shall be given to the man whose brave right hand,
For the love of the perilled city, plucks down yon burning brand,"
So cried the Mayor of Charleston, that all the people heard;
But they looked each one at his fellow, and no man spoke a word.

Who is it leans from the belfry, with face upturned to the sky,
Clings to a column, and measures the dizzy spire with his eye?
Will he dare it, the hero undaunted, that terrible sickening height?
Or will the hot blood of his courage freeze in his veins at the sight?

But see! he has stepped on the railing, he climbs with his feet and his hands,
And firm on a narrow projection, with the belfry beneath him, he stands,
Now once, and once only, they cheer him, a single tempestuous breath,
And there falls on the multitude gazing a hush like the stillness of death.

Slow, steadily mounting, unheeding aught save the goal of the fire,
Still higher and higher, an atom, he moves on the face of the spire,
He stops. Will he fall? Lo, for answer, a gleam like a meteor's track,
And, hurled on the stones of the pavement, the red brand lies shattered and black.

Once more the shouts of the people have rent the quivering air,
At the church door mayor and council wait with their feet on the stair,
And the eager throng behind them press for a touch of his hand,
The unknown savior, whose daring could compass a deed so grand.

But why does a sudden tremor seize on them while they gaze?
And what meaneth that stifled murmur of wonder and amaze?
He stood in the gate of the temple he had perilled his life to save;
And the face of the hero undaunted, was the sable face of a slave.

With folded arms he was speaking, in tones that were clear, not loud
And his eyes, ablaze in their sockets, burnt into the eyes of the crowd.
"You may keep your gold; I scorn it. But answer me, ye who can,
If the deed I have done before you be not the deed of a man?"

He stepped but a short space backward; and from all the women and men
There were only sobs for answer; and the mayor called for a pen,
And the great seal of the city, that he might read who ran.
And the slave who saved St. Michael's went out of its door—a man.

HORATIUS AT THE BRIDGE.

The Consul's brow was sad, and the Consul's speech was low,
And darkly looked he at the wall, and darkly at the foe.
"Their van will be upon us before the bridge goes down ;
And if they once may win the bridge, what hope to save the town ?"

Then out spoke brave Horatius, the Captain of the gate ;
"To every man upon this earth death cometh, soon or late.
Hew down the bridge, Sir Consul, with all the speed ye may,
I, with two more to help me, will hold the foe at bay.

"In yon straight path a thousand may well be stopped by three.
Now who will stand on either hand and keep the bridge with me ?"
Then out spoke Spurius Lartius—a Ramnian proud was he,
"Lo, I will stand at thy right hand, and keep the bridge with thee ?"

And out spake strong Herminius—of Titian blood was he,
"I will abide on thy left side, and keep the bridge with thee."
"Horatius," quoth the Consul, "as thou sayest, so let it be,"
And straight against that great array, forth went the dauntless Three.

Soon all Etruria's noblest felt their hearts sink to see
On the earth the bloody corpses, in the path the dauntless Three.
And from the ghastly entrance, where those bold Romans stood,
The bravest shrank like boys who rouse an old bear in the wood.

But meanwhile axe and lever have manfully been plied,
And now the bridge hangs tottering above the boiling tide.
"Come back, come back, Horatius !" loud cried the Fathers all,
"Back, Lartius ! Back, Herminius ! Back ere the ruin fall !"

Back darted Spurius Lartius ; Herminius darted back ;
And, as they passed, beneath their feet they felt the timbers crack ;
But when they turned their faces, and on the further shore
Saw brave Horatius stand alone, they would have crossed once more.

But, with a crash like thunder, fell every loosened beam,
And, like a dam the mighty wreck lay right athwart the stream :
And a long shout of triumph rose from the walls of Rome,
As to the highest turret-tops was splashed the yellow foam.

And, like a horse unbroken when first he feels the rein,
The furious river struggled hard, and tossed his tawny mane,
And burst the curb, and bounded, rejoicing to be free,
And battlement, and plank, and pier, whirled headlong to the sea

Alone stood brave Horatius, but constant still in mind,
Thrice thirty thousand foes before, and the broad flood behind:
"Down with him!" cried false Sextus, with a smile on his pale face,
"Now yield thee," cried Lars Porsena, "now yield thee to our grace."

Round turned he, as not deigning those craven ranks to see;
Naught spake he to Lars Porsena, to Sextus naught spake he;
But he saw on Palatinus the white porch of his home,
And he spake to the noble river that rolls by the towers of Rome.

"O Tiber! Father Tiber! to whom the Romans pray,
A Roman's life, a Roman's arms take thou in charge this day!"
So he spake, and, speaking, sheathed the good sword by his side,
And, with his harness on his back, plunged headlong in the tide.

No sound of joy or sorrow was heard on either bank;
But friends and foes, in dumb surprise, stood gazing where he sank;
And when above the surges they saw his crest appear,
Rome shouted, and e'en Tuscany could scarce forbear to cheer.

But fiercely ran the current, swollen high by months of rain,
And fast his blood was flowing; and he was sore in pain,
And heavy with his armor, and spent with changing blows;
And oft they thought him sinking, but still again he rose.

Never, I ween, did swimmer, in such an evil case,
Struggle through such a raging flood safe to the landing place;
But his limbs were borne up bravely by the brave heart within,
And our good father Tiber bare bravely up his chin.

"Curse on him!" quoth false Sextus, "will not the villain drown?
But for this stay, ere close of day we should have sacked the town!"
"Heaven help him!" quoth Lars Porsena, "and bring him safe to shore,
For such a gallant feat of arms was never seen before."

And now he feels the bottom; now on dry earth he stands,
Now round him throng the Fathers to press his gory hands.
And now, with shouts and clapping, and noise of weeping loud,
He enters through the River Gate, borne by the joyous crowd.

MACAULAY.

UP AND BE A HERO.

Up, my friend, be bold and true,.
There is noble work to do,
Hear the voice which calls on you,
"Up, and be a hero!"

What, tho' fate has fixed thy lot,
To the lowly russet cot;
Tho' thou art not worth a groat,
Thou mayest be a hero!

High heroic deeds are done,
Many a battle's lost or won,
Without either sword or gun,
Up, and be a hero!

Not to gain a worldly height,
Not for sensual delight,
But for very love of right,
Up, and be a hero!

Follow not the worldling's creed,
Be an honest man indeed,
God will help thee in thy need,
Only be a hero!

There is seed which must be sown,
Mighty truths to be made known,
Tyrannies to be o'erthrown,
Up, and be a hero!

There are hatreds and suspicions,
There are social inquisitions,
Worse than ancient superstitions,
Strike them like a hero!

In the mighty field of thought,
There are battles to be fought,
Revolutions to be wrought,
Up, and be a hero!

Bloodless battles to be gained,
Spirits to be disenchained,
Holy heights to be attained,
Up, and be a hero!

To the noble soul alone,
Nature's mystic art is shown,
God will make His secrets known,
Only to the hero!

If thou only art but true,
What may not thy spirit do,
All is possible to you,
Only be a hero!

A. McLachlan.

MY COUNTRY.

I love my country's pine-clad hills,
Her thousand bright and gushing rills,
  Her sunshine and her storms ;
Her rough and rugged rocks that rear
Their hoary heads high in the air
  In wild fantastic forms.

I love her rivers, deep and wide,
Those mighty streams that seaward glide
  To seek the ocean's breast ;
Her smiling fields, her pleasant vales,
Her shady dells, her flowery dales,
  The haunts of peaceful rest.

I love her forests, dark and lone,
For there the wild bird's merry tone
  Is heard from morn till night,
And there are lovelier flowers, I ween,
Than e'er in Eastern lands were seen,
  In varied colors bright.

Her forests and her valleys fair,
Her flowers that scent the morning air,
  Have all their charms for me ;
But more I love my country's name,
Those words that echo deathless fame,—
  "The land of liberty."

Oh, give me back my native hills,
My daisied meads, and trouted rills,
  And groves of pine !
Oh, give me, too, the mountain air,—
My youthful days without a care,
When rose for me a mother's prayer,
  In tones divine !

Long years have passed, and I behold
My father's elms and mansion old,—
  The brook's bright wave;
But, ah! the scenes which fancy drew
Deceived my heart,—the friends I knew,
Are sleeping now, beneath the yew,—
  Low in the grave!

The sunny sports I loved so well,
When but a child, seem like a spell
  Flung round the bier!
The ancient wood, the cliff, the glade,
Whose charms methought could never fade,
Again I view,—yet shed, unstayed,
  The silent tear!

Here let me kneel, and linger long,
And pour, unheard, my native song,
  And seek relief!
Like Ocean's wave that restless heaves,
My days roll on, yet memory weaves
Her twilight o'er the past, and leaves
  A balm for grief!

Oh that I could again recall
My early joys, companions, all,
  That cheered my youth!
But, ah! 'tis vain,—how changed am I!
My heart hath learned the bitter sigh!
The pure shall meet beyond the sky,—
  How sweet the truth!

HESPERIAN.

THE WAY TO SUCCESS.

Heaven is not gained at a single bound ;
  But we build the ladder by which we rise
  From the lowly earth to the vaulted skies,
And we mount to its summit round by round.

I count this thing to be grandly true,
  That a noble deed is a step toward God,—
  Lifting the soul from the common sod
To a purer air and a broader view.

We rise by things that are 'neath our feet ;
  By what we have mastered of good and gain ;
  By the pride deposed and the passion slain,
And the vanquished ills that we hourly meet.

We hope, we aspire, we resolve, we trust,
  When the morning calls us to life and light
  But our hearts grow weary, and, ere the night,
Our lives are trailing the sordid dust.

We hope, we resolve, we aspire, we pray,
  And we think that we mount the air on wings
  Beyond the recall of sensual things,
While our feet still cling to the heavy clay.

Wings for the angels, but feet for men !
  We may borrow the wings to find the way,—
  We may hope, and resolve, and aspire, and pray,
But our feet must rise or we fall again.

Only in dreams is a ladder thrown
  From the weary earth to the sapphire walls ;
  But the dream departs and the vision falls,
And the sleeper awakes on his pillow of stone.

Heaven is not reached at a single bound ;
  But we build the ladder by which we rise
  From the lowly earth to the vaulted skies,
And we mount to its summit round by round.

 JOSIAH GILBERT HOLLAND.

THE CHARGE OF THE LIGHT BRIGADE.

Half a league, half a league,
Half a league onward,
All in the valley of Death
Rode the six hundred.
"Forward, the Light Brigade!
Charge for the guns!" he said;
Into the valley of Death
Rode the six hundred.

"Forward, the Light Brigade!"
Was there a man dismayed?
Not though the soldier knew
Some one had blundered;
Theirs not to make reply,
Theirs not to reason why,
Theirs but to do and die:
Into the valley of Death
Rode the six hundred.

Cannon to right of them,
Cannon to left of them,
Cannon in front of them
Volleyed and thundered;
Stormed at with shot and shell,
Boldly they rode and well;
Into the jaws of Death,
Into the mouth of Hell,
Rode the six hundred.

Flashed all their sabres bare,
Flashed as they turned in air,
Sabring the gunners there,
Charging an army, while
All the world wondered;

Plunged in the battery smoke,
Right through the line they broke ;
Cossack and Russian
Reeled from the sabre stroke,
  Shattered and sundered.
Then they rode back, but not—
Not the six hundred.

Cannon to right of them,
Cannon to left of them,
Cannon behind them
  Volleyed and thundered ;
Stormed at with shot and shell,
While horse and hero fell,
They that had fought so well
Came through the jaws of Death,
Back from the mouth of Hell—
All that was left of them,
Left of six hundred.

When can their glory fade ?
Oh, the wild charge they made !
  All the world wondered.
Honor the charge they made !
Honor the Light Brigade.
Noble six hundred !

TENNYSON.

THE SLAVE'S DREAM.

Beside the ungathered rice he lay,
His sickle in his hand ;
His breast was bare, his matted hair
Was buried in the sand.
Again, in the mist and shadow of sleep,
He saw his native land.

Wide through the landscape of his dreams
The lordly Niger flowed ;
Beneath the palm-trees on the plain
Once more a king he strode ;
And heard the tinkling caravans
Descend the mountain road.

He saw once more his dark-eyed queen
Among her children stand ;
They clasped his neck, they kissed his cheeks,
They held him by the hand !—
A tear burst from the sleeper's lids,
And fell into the sand.

And then at furious speed he rode
Along the Niger's bank ;
His bridle reins were golden chains,
And, with a martial clank,
At each leap he could feel his scabbard of steel
Smiting his stallion's flank.

Before him, like a blood-red flag,
The bright flamingoes flew ;
From morn till night he followed their flight,
O'er plains where the tamarind grew,
Till he saw the roofs of Caffre huts,
And the ocean rose to view.

At night he heard the lion roar,
  And the hyæna scream,
And the river-horse, as he crushed the reeds
  Beside some hidden stream;
And it passed, like a glorious roll of drums,
  Through the triumph of his dream.

The forests, with their myriad tongues,
  Shouted of liberty;
And the Blast of the Desert cried aloud,
  With a voice so wild and free,
That he started in his sleep and smiled
  At their tempestuous glee.

He did not feel the driver's whip,
  Nor the burning heat of day;
For Death had illumined the Land of Sleep,
  And his lifeless body lay
A worn-out fetter, that the soul
  Had broken and thrown away!

LONGFELLOW.

THE DOWNFALL OF POLAND.

O sacred Truth ! thy triumph ceased awhile,
And Hope, thy sister, ceased with thee to smile,
When leagued Oppression poured to Northern wars
Her whiskered pandoors and her fierce hussars,
Waved her dread standard to the breeze of morn,
Pealed her loud drum, and twanged her trumpet horn :
Tumultuous horror brooded o'er her van,
Presaging wrath to Poland—and to man !

Warsaw's last champion from her height surveyed,
Wide o'er the fields, a waste of ruin laid ;
"O Heaven !" he cried, "my bleeding country save !
Is there no hand on high to shield the brave ?
Yet though destruction sweep these lovely plains,
Rise, fellow-men ! our country yet remains !
By that dread name, we wave the sword on high,
And swear for her to live, with her to die !"

He said, and on the rampart-heights arrayed
His trusty warriors, few, but undismayed ;
Firm-paced and slow, a horrid front they form,
Still as the breeze, but dreadful as the storm ;
Low murmuring sounds along their banners fly,
"Revenge, or death,"—the watchword and reply ;
Then pealed the notes, omnipotent to charm,
And the loud tocsin tolled their last alarm !

In vain, alas ! in vain, ye gallant few,
From rank to rank your volleyed thunder flew :
Oh ! bloodiest picture in the book of Time,
Sarmatia fell, unwept, without a crime ;
Found not a generous friend, a pitying foe,
Strength in her arms, nor mercy in her woe !
Dropped from her nerveless grasp the shattered spear,
Closed her bright eye, and curbed her high career ;
Hope for a season, bade the world farewell,
And Freedom shrieked—as Kosciusko fell.

The sun went down, nor ceased the carnage there;
Tumultuous murder shook the midnight air.
On Prague's proud arch the fires of ruin glow,
His blood-dyed waters murmuring far below;
The storm prevails, the rampart yields away,
Bursts the wild cry of horror and dismay!
Hark! as the mouldering piles with thunder fall,
A thousand shrieks for hopeless mercy call!
Earth shook, red meteors flashed along the sky,
And conscious Nature shuddered at the cry!

O righteous Heaven! ere Freedom found a grave,
Why slept the sword, omnipotent to save?
Where was thine arm, O Vengeance! where thy rod,
That smote the foes of Sion and of God;
That crushed proud Ammon, when his iron car
Was yoked in wrath, and thundered from afar?
Where was the storm that slumbered till the host
Of blood-stained Pharaoh left their trembling coast,
Then bade the deep in wild commotion flow,
And heaved an ocean on their march below?

Departed spirits of the mighty dead!
Ye that at Marathon and Leuctra bled!
Friends of the world! restore your swords to man,
Fight in his sacred cause, and lead the van!
Yet for Sarmatia's tears of blood atone,
And make her arm puissant as your own!
Oh! once again to freedom's cause return
The patriot Tell,—the Bruce of Bannockburn!

THOMAS CAMPBELL.

THE GRAVES OF THE PATRIOTS.

Here rest the great and good,—here they repose
After their generous toil. A sacred band,
They take their sleep together, while the year
Comes with its early flowers to deck their graves,
And gathers them again, as winter frowns.
Theirs is no vulgar sepulchre,—green sods
Are all their monument ; and yet it tells
A nobler history than pillared piles,
Or the eternal pyramids. They need
No statue nor inscription to reveal
Their greatness. It is round them ; and the joy
With which their children tread the hallowed ground
That holds their venerated bones, the peace
That smiles on all they fought for, and the wealth
That clothes the land they rescued,—these though mute,
As feeling ever is when deepest,—these
Are monuments more lasting than the fanes
Reared to the kings and demi-gods of old.
Touch not the ancient elms, that bend their shade
Over the lowly graves ; beneath their boughs
There is a solemn darkness, even at noon,
Suited to such as visit at the shrine
Of serious liberty. No factious voice
Called them unto the field of generous fame,
But the pure consecrated love of home.
No deeper feeling sways us, when it wakes
In all its greatness. It has told itself
To the astonished gaze of awe-struck kings,
At Marathon, at Bannockburn, and here,
When first our patriots sent the invader back,
Broken and cowed. Let these green elms be all
To tell us where they fought, and where they lie.

Their feelings were all nature ; and they need
No art to make them known. They live in us,
While we are like them, simple, hardy, bold,
Worshipping nothing but our own pure hearts
And the one universal Lord. They need
No column pointing to the heaven they sought,
To tell us of their home. The heart itself,
Left to its own free purposes, hastens there,
And there alone reposes. Let these elms
Bend their protecting shadow o'er their graves,
And build with their green roof the only fane,
Where we may gather on the hallowed day,
That rose to them in blood, and set in glory.
Here let us meet ; and while our motionless lips
Give not a sound, and all around is mute
In the deep Sabbath of a heart too full
For words or tears,—here let us strew the sod
With the first flowers of spring, and make to them
An offering of the plenty, Nature gives,
And they have rendered ours,—perpetually.

James Gates Percival.

THE ENGLISHMAN.

There's a land that bears a world-known name,
Though it is but a little spot ;
I say 'tis first on the scroll of Fame,
And who shall say it is not ?
Of the deathless ones who shine and live
In Arms, in Art, or Song ;
The brightest the whole wide world can give
To that little land belong.
'Tis the star of earth, deny it who can ;
The island home of an Englishman.

There's a flag that waves over every sea,
No matter when or where ;
And to treat that flag as aught but the free
Is more than the strongest dare.
For the lion spirits that tread the deck
Have carried the palm of the brave ;
And that flag may sink with a shot-torn wreck,
But never float over a slave.
Its honor is stainless, deny it who can ;
And this is the flag of an Englishman.

There's a heart that leaps with burning glow,
The wrong'd and the weak to defend ;
And strikes as soon for a trampled foe ;
As it does for a soul-bound friend.
It nurtures a deep and honest love :
It glows with faith and pride ;
And yearns with the fondness of a dove,
To the light of its own fireside.
'Tis a rich, rough gem, deny it who can ;
And this is the heart of an Englishman.

The Briton may traverse the pole or the zone
  And boldly claim his right ;
For he calls such a vast domain his own,
  That the sun never sets on his might.
Let the haughty stranger seek to know
  The place of his home and birth ;
And a flush will pour from cheek to brow ;
  While he tells his native earth.
For a glorious charter, deny it who can ;
  Is breathed in the words "I'm an Englishman."

ELIZA COOK.

BARBARA FRIETCHIE.

Up from the meadows rich with corn,
Clear in the cool September morn,
The clustered spires of Frederick stand
Green-walled by the hills of Maryland.

Round about them orchards sweep,
Apple and peach tree fruited deep,
Fair as the garden of the Lord
To the eyes of the famished rebel horde.

On that pleasant morn of the early fall
When Lee marched over the mountain-wall—
Over the mountains winding down,
Horse and foot, into Frederick town.

Forty flags with their silver stars,
Forty flags with their crimson bars,
Flapped in the morning wind ; the sun
Of noon looked down, and saw not one.

Up rose old Barbara Frietchie then,
Bowed with her four score years and ten ;
Bravest of all in Frederick town,
She took up the flag the men hauled down ;

In her attic window the staff she set,
To show that one heart was loyal yet.
Up the street came the rebel tread,
Stonewall Jackson riding ahead.

Under his slouched hat left and right
He glanced : the old flag met his sight.
"Halt !"—the dust-brown ranks stood fast.
"Fire !"—out blazed the rifle-blast.

It shivered the window, pane and sash ;
It rent the banner with seam and gash.
Quick, as it fell, from the broken staff
Dame Barbara snatched the silken scarf.

She leaned far out on the window-sill,
And shook it forth with a royal will.
" Shoot, if you must, this old gray head,
But spare your country's flag," she said.

A shade of sadness, a blush of shame,
Over the face of the leader came ;
The nobler nature within him stirred
To life at that woman's deed and word ;

" Who touches a hair of yon gray head
Dies like a dog ! March on ! " he said.
All day long through Frederick street
Sounded the tread of marching feet ;

All day long that free flag tossed
Over the heads of the rebel host.
Ever its torn folds rose and fell
On the loyal winds that loved it well ;

And through the hill-gaps sunset light
Shone over it with a warm good-night.
Barbara Frietchie's work is o'er,
And the rebel rides on his raids no more.

Honor to her ! and let a tear
Fall, for her sake, on Stonewall's bier.
Over Barbara Frietchie's grave,
Flag of Freedom and Union, wave !

Peace and order and beauty draw
Round thy symbol of light and law ;
And ever the stars above look down
On thy stars below in Frederick town !

WHITTIER.

HERVE RIEL.

I.

On the sea and at the Hogue, sixteen hundred and ninety-two,
Did the English fight the French—woe to France!
And, the thirty-first of May, helter-skelter thro' the blue,
Like a crowd of frightened porpoises a shoal of sharks pursue,
Came crowding ship on ship to St. Malo on the Rance,
With the English fleet in view.

II.

'Twas the squadron that escaped, with the victor in full chase;
First and foremost of the drove, in his great ship, Damfreville:
Close on him fled, great and small,
Twenty-two good ships in all;
And they signalled to the place,
"Help the winners of a race!
Get us guidance, give us harbor, take us quick—or, quicker still,
Here's the English can and will!"

III.

Then the pilots of the place put out brisk and leapt on board;
"Why, what hope or chance have ships like these to pass?" laughed they:
"Rocks to starboard, rocks to port, all the passage scarred and scored,
Shall the *Formidable* here with her twelve and eighty guns,
Think to make the river-mouth by the single narrow way,
Trust to enter where 'tis ticklish for a craft of twenty tons,
And with flow at full ebb beside?
Now, 'tis slackest ebb of tide.
Reach the mooring? Rather say,
While rock stands or water runs,
Not a ship will leave the bay?"

IV.

Then was called a council straight.
Brief and bitter the debate :
"Here's the English at our heels ; would you have them take in
tow
All that's left us of the fleet, linked together stern and bow,
For a prize to Plymouth Sound ?
Better run the ships aground !"
(Ended Damfreville his speech.)
Not a minute more to wait !
"Let the captains all and each
Shove ashore, then blow up, burn the vessels on the beach !
France must undergo her fate.

V.

Give the word !" But no such word
Was ever spoke or heard ;
For up stood, for out stepped, for in struck amid all these—
A captain ? A lieutenant ? A mate—first, second, third ?
No such man of mark, and meet
With his betters to compete !
But a simple Breton sailor pressed by Tourville for the fleet,
A poor coasting-pilot he, Herve Riel the Croisickese.

VI.

And "What mockery or malice have we here ?" cries Herve Riel :
"Are you mad, you Malouins ? Are you cowards, fools or rogues
Talk to me of rocks and shoals, me who took the soundings, tell
On my fingers every bank, every shallow, every swell
'Twixt the offing here and Greve, where the river disembogues ?
Are you bought by English gold ? Is it love the lying's for ?
Morn and eve, night and day,
Have I piloted your bay,
Entered free and anchored fast at the foot of Solidor.
Burn the fleet and ruin France ? That were worse than fifty
Hogues !

Sirs, they know I speak the truth! Sirs, believe me there's a way!
Only let me lead the line,
Have the biggest ship to steer,
Get this *Formidable* clear,
Make the others follow mine,
And I lead them, most and least, by a passage I know well,
Right to Solidor past Greve,
And there lay them safe and sound;
And if one ship misbehave,
Keel so much as grate the ground,
Why, I've nothing but my life—here's my head!" cries Herve Riel.

VII.

Not a minute more to wait.
"Steer us in, then, small and great!
Take the helm, lead the line, save the squadron!" cried its chief.
"Captains, give the sailor place!
He is Admiral, in brief."
Still the north-wind, by God's grace!
See the noble fellow's face
As the big ship, with a bound,
Clears the entry like a hound,
Keeps the passage as its inch of way were the wide sea's profound!
See, safe thro' shoal and rock,
How they follow in a flock,
Not a ship that misbehaves, not a keel that grates the ground,
Not a spar that comes to grief!
The peril, see, is past,
All are harbored to the last,
And just as Herve Riel hallos "Anchor!"—sure as fate
Up the English come, too late!

VIII.

So, the storm subsides to calm:
They see the green trees wave
On the heights o'erlooking Greve.

Hearts that bled are staunched with balm.
"Just our rapture to enhance,
  Let the English rake the bay,
Gnash their teeth and glare askance
  As they cannonade away!
'Neath rampired Solidor pleasant riding on the Rance!"
How hope succeeds despair on each captain's countenance!
Out burst all with one accord,
  "This is Paradise for Hell!
    Let France, let France's King
    Thank the man that did the thing!"
What a shout, and all one word,
  "Hervé Riel!"
As he stepped in front once more,
  Not a symptom of surprise
  In the frank, blue Breton eyes,
Just the same man as before.

IX.

Then said Damfreville, "My friend,
I must speak out at the end,
  Though I find the speaking hard.
Praise is deeper than the lips:
You have saved the King his ships,
  You must name your own reward.
'Faith, our sun was near eclipse!
Demand whate'er you will,
France remains your debtor still.
Ask to your heart's content and have! or my name's not Damfreville."

X.

Then a beam of fun outbroke
On the bearded mouth that spoke,
As the honest heart laughed through
Those frank eyes of Breton blue:
"Since I needs must say my say,

Since on board the duty's done,
And from Malo Roads to Croisic Point, what is it but a run?—
Since 'tis ask and have, I may—
Since the others go ashore—
Come! A good whole holiday!
Leave to go and see my wife, whom I call the Bell Aurore!"
That he asked and that he got—nothing more.

XI.

Name and deed alike are lost:
Not a pillar nor a post
In his Croisic keeps alive the feat as it befell;
Not a head in white and black
On a single fishing smack,
In memory of the man but for whom had gone to wrack
All that France saved from the fight whence England bore the bell.
Go to Paris: rank on rank
Search the heroes flung pell-mell
On the Louvre, face and flank!
You shall look long enough ere you come to Herve Riel.
So, for better and for worse,
Herve Riel, accept my verse!
In my verse, Herve Riel, do thou once more
Save the squadron, honor France, love thy wife the Belle Aurore!

ROBERT BROWNING.

THE BRITISH EMPIRE.

There is not a country in the history of the world that has undertaken what England in its traditional established policy and position has undertaken. There is no precedent in human history for a formation like the British Government. A small island at one extremity of the globe peoples the whole earth. But it is not satisfied with that; it goes among the ancient races of Asia and subjects 240,000,000 of people to its rule there. Along with all this it distributes over the world a commerce such as no imagination ever conceived in former times, and such as no poet ever painted. And all this it has to do with a strength that lies within the narrow limits of these shores—not a strength that I disparage; on the contrary, I wish to dissipate if I can the idle dreams of those who are always telling you that the strength of England depends upon its prestige, upon its extending its empire upon what it possesses beyond these shores. Rely upon it the strength of Great Britain and Ireland is within the United Kingdom. Whatever is to be done in defending and governing those vast colonies with their teeming millions, in protecting that unmeasured commerce, in relation to the enormous responsibility of India—whatever is to be done must be done by the force to be derived from you and your children, from you and your fellow-electors. And why? They are between some three and thirty millions of persons. They are a population less than the population of France, of Austria, of Germany or of

Russia; but the populations of France, Austria, Germany and Russia are quite able enough to settle their own matters within their own limits. We have undertaken to settle the affairs of a fourth or nearly a fourth of the entire human race scattered over the world; and is not that enough for the ambition of Lord Beaconsfield? It satisfied Mr. Pitt, Mr. Canning; it satisfied Sir Robert Peel; it satisfied Lord Palmerston, Lord Russell and the late Lord Derby; and why cannot it satisfy, I wish to know, Lord Beaconsfield and his colleagues? It seems to me they are all very much of one mind. They move with harmony among themselves. Is it not enough to satisfy the ambition of the members of the present Government? Strive as you will—I speak after the experience of a lifetime, of which a fair portion has been spent in office—strive and labor as you will in Parliament and office, human strength and human thought are not equal to the discharge of the whole duties appertaining to Government in this great, wonderful and world-wide Empire.

W. E. GLADSTONE.

GREAT BRITAIN AND AMERICA.

Let all good citizens in both England and America, all who desire the world's progress, strive to preserve peace and international good-will.

I appeal to you by the unity of our race—for, with two governments we are one people; by the unity of the grand old language we alike speak, with the thrilling names of father, mother, home, dear to us alike; by our common literature, our Shakespeare, who is your Shakespeare, our Milton, who is your Milton, our Longfellows and Tennysons, side by side in all our libraries; I appeal to you by the stirring memories of our common history, —by those ancestors of both our nations, who proved their prowess at Hastings, whether as sturdy Saxons defending the standard of King Harold, or as daring Normans spurring their chivalry to the trumpet of Duke William,—and who, afterward united on a better field, wrung from a reluctant tyrant that great charter which is the foundation of our liberties on both sides of the Atlantic; I appeal to you by the stirring times when those common ancestors lighted their beacons on every hill, and rallied around a lion-hearted queen, and launched forth—some of them in mere fishing vessels—against the proud Armada that dared to threaten their subjugation; I appeal to you by the struggles of the commonwealth, by the memories of those who put to rout the abettors of tyranny—Cromwell, Hampden, Sir Harry Vane; I appeal to you by those Pilgrim Fathers here, and by those Puritans and Covenanters who remained behind, by whose heroic sufferings both nations enjoy such freedom to worship God; I appeal to you by the graves in which our common ancestors repose,—not only, it may be, beneath the stately towers of Westminster, but in many an ancient village churchyard, where daisies grow on the turf-covered graves, and venerable yew-trees cast over them their solemn shade; I appeal to you by that Bible—precious to us both; by that gospel which our missionaries alike proclaim to the heathen world, and by that Saviour whom we both adore, never let there be strife between nations whose conflict would be the rushing together of two Niagaras, but whose union will be like the irresistible course of two great rivers flowing on majestically to fertilize and bless the world.

Never let our beautiful standards—yours of the stars and stripes, suggesting the lamps of night and the rays of day, and ours of the clustered crosses, telling of union in diversity, and reminding of the One Great Liberator and Peace-Maker, who, by the cross, gave life to the world—never let these glorious standards be arrayed in hostile ranks; but ever may they float side by side, leading on the van of the world's progress.

Oh, I can imagine that if we, the hereditary champions of freedom, were engaged in strife, all the despots of the earth would clap their hands, and all the demons in hell would exult, while angels would weep to see these two nations wasting the treasure and shedding the blood that should be reserved for the strife against the common foes of freedom.

Never give angels such cause of lamentation, never give despots and demons such cause for rejoicing; but ever Great Britain and America—the mother and the daughter, or, if you prefer it, the elder daughter and the younger—go forth hand in hand, angel guardians together of civilization, freedom and religion, their only rivalry the rivalry of love.

NEWMAN HALL.

POPULAR SOVEREIGNTY.

Our opponents have charged us with being the promoters of a dangerous excitement. They have the effrontery to say that I am the friend of public disorder. I am one of the people. Surely, if there be one thing in a free country more clear than another, it is that any one of the people may speak openly to the people. If I speak to the people of their rights, and indicate to them the way to secure them—if I speak of their danger to the monopolists of power—am I not a wise counsellor, both to the people and to their rulers?

Suppose I stood at the foot of Vesuvius, or Ætna, and, seeing a hamlet or a homestead planted on its slope, I said to the dwellers in that hamlet or in that homestead: "You see that vapor which ascends from the summit of the mountain, that vapor may become a dense, black smoke, that will obscure the sky. You see the trickling of lava from the crevices in the side of the mountain: that trickling of lava may become a river of fire. You hear that muttering in the bowels of the mountain; that muttering may become a bellowing thunder, the voice of a violent convulsion, that may shake half a continent. You know that at your feet is the grave of great cities, for which there is no resurrection, as histories tell us that dynasties and aristocracies have passed away, and their names have been known no more forever."

If I say this to the dwellers upon the slope of the mountain, and if there comes hereafter a catastrophe which makes the world to shudder, am I responsible for that catastrophe? I did not build the mountain, or fill it with explosive materials. I merely warned the men that were in danger. So, now, it is not I who am stimulating men to the violent pursuit of their acknowledged constitutional rights.

The class which has hitherto ruled in this country has failed miserably. It revels in power and wealth, whilst at its feet, a terrible peril for its future, lies the multitude which it has neglected. If a class has failed, let us try the nation.

That is our faith, that is our purpose, that is our cry. Let us try the nation. This it is which has called together these countless numbers of the people to demand a change; and from these gatherings, sublime in in their vastness and their resolution. I think I see, as it were, above the hilltops of time, the glimmerings of the dawn of a better and nobler day for the country and for the people I love so well.

JOHN BRIGHT.

OUR RELATIONS TO ENGLAND.

Who does not feel, what reflecting American does not acknowledge, the incalculable advantages derived by this land out of the deep fountains of civil, intellectual and moral truth, from which we have drawn in England? What American does not fell proud that his fathers were the countrymen of Bacon, of Newton, and of Locke? Who does not know that, while every pulse of civil liberty in the heart of the British empire beat warm and full in the bosom of our ancestors, the sobriety, the firmness, and the dignity, with which the cause of free principles struggled into existence here, constantly found encouragement and countenance from the friends of liberty there? Who does not remember that, when the pilgrims went over the sea, the prayers of the faithful British confessors, in all the quarters of their dispersion, went over with them, while their aching eyes were strained till the star of hope should go up in the western skies? And who will ever forget that, in that eventful struggle which severed these youthful republics from the British Crown, there was not heard, throughout our continent in arms, a voice which spoke louder for the rights of America than that of Burke, or of Chatham, within the walls of the British Parliament, and at the foot of the British Throne?

I am not—I need not say I am not—the panegyrist of England. I am not dazzled by her riches, nor awed by her power. The sceptre, the mitre, and the coronet,—

stars, garters, and blue ribbons,—seem to me poor things for great men to contend for. Nor is my admiration awakened by her armies, mustered for the battles of Europe; her navies, overshadowing the ocean; nor her empire, grasping the farthest East. It is these, and the price of guilt and blood by which they are too often maintained, which are the cause why no friend of liberty can salute her with undivided affections. But it is the cradle and the refuge of free principles, though often persecuted; the school of religious liberty, the more precious for the struggles through which it has passed; the tombs of those who have reflected honor on all who speak the English tongue; it is the birthplace of our fathers, the home of the Pilgrims; it is these which I love and venerate in England. I should feel ashamed of an enthusiasm for Italy and Greece, did I not also feel it for a land like this. In an American, it would seem to me degenerate and ungrateful to hang with passion upon the traces of Homer and Virgil, and follow, without emotion, the nearer and plainer footsteps of Shakespeare and Milton. I should think him cold in his love for his native land who felt no melting in his heart for that other native country which holds the ashes of his forefathers.

EDWARD EVERETT.

UNIVERSAL EMANCIPATION.

I put it to your oaths :—Do you think that a blessing of that kind—that a victory obtained by justice, over bigotry and oppression—should have a stigma cast upon it by an ignominious sentence upon men, bold and honest enough to propose that measure?—to propose the redeeming of Religion from the abuses of the Church, the reclaiming of three millions of men from bondage, and giving liberty to all who had a right to demand it? —giving, I say, in the so much censured words of this paper, giving "Universal Emancipation!" I speak in the spirit of the British law, which makes liberty commensurate with, and inseparable from, British soil;—which proclaims, even to the stranger and sojourner the moment he sets his foot upon British earth, that the ground upon which he treads is holy, and consecrated by the genius of Universal Emancipation. No matter in what language his doom may have been pronounced—no matter what complexion, incompatible with freedom, an Indian or an African sun may have burnt upon him; no matter in what disastrous battle his liberty may have been cloven down; no matter with what solemnities he may have been devoted upon the altar of slavery; the first moment he touches the sacred soil of Britain, the altar and the god sink together in the dust; his soul walks abroad in her own majesty; his body swells beyond the measure of the chains that burst from around him; and he stands—redeemed, regenerated and disenthralled by the irresistible genius of "Universal Emancipation."

CURRAN.

KOSSUTH'S FAREWELL TO HIS COUNTRY.

Farewell, my beloved country. Farewell, land of the Magyar. Farewell, thou land of sorrow. I shall never more behold the summit of thy mountains. I shall never again give the name of my country to that cherished soil where I drank from my mother's bosom the milk of justice and liberty. Pardon, oh, pardon him who is henceforth condemned to wander far from thee, because he combated for thy happiness. Pardon one who can only call free that spot of thy soil where he now kneels with a few of the faithful children of conquered Hungary. My last looks are fixed on my country, and I see thee overwhelmed with anguish. I look into the future; but that future is overshadowed. Thy plains are covered with blood, the redness of which pitiless destruction will change to black, the emblem of mourning for the victories thy sons have gained over the sacrilegious enemies of thy sacred soil.

How many grateful hearts have sent their prayers to the throne of the Almighty. How many tears have been gushed from their very depth to implore pity. How much blood has been shed to testify that the Magyar idolizes his country, and that he knows how to die for it. And yet, land of my love, thou art in slavery. From thy very bosom will be forged the chains to bind all that is sacred, and aid all that is sacrilegious. Oh, Almighty Creator, if thou lovest thy people to whom thou didst give victory under our heroic ancester, Arapad, I implore thee not to sink them in degradation. I speak to thee, my country, thus from the abyss of my despair, and whilst yet lingering on the threshold of thy soil. Pardon me that a great number of thy sons have shed their blood for thee on my account. I pleaded for thee—I hoped for thee, even in the dark moment when on thy brow was written the withering word "despair." I lifted my voice in thy behalf when men said, "Be thou a slave." I girt the sword about my loins, and I grasped the bloody plume, even when they said, "Thou art no longer a nation on the soil of the Magyar."

Time has written thy destiny on the pages of thy story in yellow and black letters—death. The Colossus of the North has set his seal to the sentence. But the glowing iron of the East shall melt that seal.

For thee, my country, that has shed so much blood, there is no pity; for does not the tyrant eat his bread on the hills formed of the bones of thy children?

My country, it is not the iron of the stranger that hath dug thy grave; it is not the thunder of fourteen nations, all arrayed against thee, that hath destroyed thee; and it is not the fifteenth nation, traversing the Carpathians, that has caused thee to drop thy arms. No, thou hast been betrayed—thou hast been sold, my country; thy death sentence has been written, beloved of my heart, by him whose love for thee I never dared to doubt. Yes, in the fervor of my boldest thought I should have almost as soon doubted of the existence of the Omnipotent, as have believed that he could ever be a traitor to his country. Thou hast been betrayed by him into whose hands I had but a little space before deposited the power of our country, which he swore to defend, even to the last drop of his heart's blood. He has done treason to his mother; for the glitter of gold hath been for him more seductive than that of the blood shed to save his country. Base gain had more value in his eyes than his country, and his God has abandoned him, as he has abandoned his God for his allies of hell.

I desire a free nation, free, man cannot be made but by God. And thou art fallen; faded as the lily, but which in another season puts forth its flower still more lovely than before. Thou art dead; for hath not thy winter come on? but it will not endure so long as that of thy companion under the frozen sky of Siberia. No. Fifteen nations have dug thy tomb. But the hosts of the sixteenth will come to save thee. Be faithful, as thou hast been even to the present. Lift up thy heart in prayer for the departed, but do not raise thy own hymn until thou hearest the thunders of the liberating people echo along thy mountains, and bellow in the depth of thy valleys.

Farewell, beloved companions. Farewell, comrades, countrymen. May the thought of God, and may the angels of liberty forever be with you. I will proclaim you to the civilized world as heroes; and the cause of an heroic people will be cherished by the freest nation on earth, the freest of all free people.

Farewell, thou land dyed with the blood of the brave. Guard those red marks, they will one day bear testimony on thy behalf.

And thou, farewell, O, youthful monarch of the Hungarians. Forget not that my nation is not destined for thee. Heaven inspires me with the confidence that the day will dawn when it shall be proved to thee even on the ruined walls of Buda.

May the Almighty bless thee, my beloved country. Believe, hope and love.

NEGRO SLAVERY.

I trust, that, at length, the time has come, when parliament will no longer bear to be told that slave-owners are the best lawgivers on slavery; no longer suffer our voices to roll across the Atlantic, in empty warnings and fruitless orders. Tell me not of rights—talk not of the property of the planter in his slaves. I deny his right—I acknowledge not his property. The principles, the feelings of our common nature, rise in rebellion against it. Be the appeal made to the understanding or to the heart, the sentence is the same—each rejects it! In vain you tell me of laws that sanction such a claim! There is a law, above all the enactments of the human codes—the same throughout the world—the same in all times: such as it was, before the daring genius of Columbus pierced the night of ages, and opened to one world the sources of power, wealth and knowledge; to another, all unutterable woes,—such is it at this day; it is the law written by the finger of God on the heart of man; and by that law, unchangeable and eternal—while men despise fraud and loathe rapine and hate blood—they shall reject, with indignation, the wild and guilty fantasy that man can hold property in man!

In vain you hold to treaties—to covenants between nations. The covenants of the Almighty, whether the old covenant or the new, denounce such unholy pretensions. To these laws did they of old refer, who maintained the African trade. Such treaties did they cite—and not untruly; for, by one shameful compact, you bartered the glories of Blenheim for the traffic in blood. Yet, in despite of law and treaty, that infernal traffic is now destroyed, and its votaries put to death like other pirates. How came this change to pass? Not, assuredly, by parliament leading the way; but the country at length awoke; the indignation of the people was kindled; it descended in thunder and smote the traffic, and scattered the guilty profits to the winds. Now, then, let the planters beware—let the government at home beware—let their assemblies beware—let the parliament beware! The same country is once more awake—awake to the condition of negro slavery; the same indignation kindles in the bosom of the same people; the same cloud is gathering that annihilated the slave trade; and if it shall descend again, they on whom its crash may fall will not be destroyed before I have warned them; but I pray that their destruction may turn away from us the more terrible judgments of God!

BROUGHAM.

THE LAST SPEECH OF ROBESPIERRE.

(A.D. 1794.)

The enemies of the Republic call me tyrant! Were I such, they would grovel at my feet. I should gorge them with gold—I should grant them impunity for their crimes—and they would be grateful. Were I such, the kings we have vanquished, far from denouncing Robespierre, would lend me their guilty support. There would be a covenant between them and me. Tyranny must have tools. But the enemies of tyranny—whither does their path tend? To the tomb, and to immortality! What tyrant is my protector? To what faction do I belong? Yourselves! What faction, since the beginning of the Revolution, has crushed and annihilated so many detected traitors? You—the people—our principles—are that faction!—a faction to which I am devoted, and against which all the scoundrelism of the day is banded!

The confirmation of the Republic has been my object; and I know that the Republic can be established only on the eternal basis of morality. Against me, and against those who hold kindred principles, the league is formed. My life? Oh! my life I abandon without a regret! I have seen the Past; and I foresee the Future.

What friend of his country would wish to survive the moment when he could no longer serve it—when he could no longer defend innocence against oppression? Wherefore should I continue in an order of things where intrigue eternally triumphs over truth; where justice is mocked; where passions the most abject, or fears the most absurd, override the sacred interests of humanity? In witnessing the multitude of vices which the torrent of the Revolution has rolled in turbid communion with its civic virtues, I confess that I have sometimes feared that I should be sullied, in the eyes of posterity, by the impure neighborhood of unprincipled men, who had thrust themselves into association with the sincere friends of humanity; and I rejoice that these conspirators against my country have now, by their reckless rage, traced the deep line of demarcation between themselves and all true men.

Question history, and learn how all the defenders of liberty, in all times, have been overwhelmed by calumny. But their traducers died also. The good and bad disappear alike from the earth; but in very different conditions. O Frenchmen! O my countrymen! let not your enemies, with their desolating doctrines, degrade your souls and enervate your virtues! No, Chaumette, no! Death is not "an eternal sleep!" Citizens! efface from the tomb that motto, graven by sacrilegious hands, which spreads all over nature a funeral crape, takes from oppressed innocence its support, and affronts the beneficent dispensation of death! Inscribe rather thereon these words: "Death is the commencement of immortality!" I leave to the oppressors of the people a terrible testament, which I proclaim with the independence befitting one whose career is so nearly ended: it is the awful truth, "Thou shalt die!"

From Translation by EPES SARGENT.

THE VALOR OF THE IRISH SOLDIER.

There is, however, one man (Lord Lyndhurst), of great abilities, not a member of this House, but whose talents and whose boldness have placed him in the topmost place in his party—who, disdaining all imposture, and thinking it the best course to appeal directly to the religious and national antipathies of the people of this country—abandoning all reserve, and flinging off the slender veil by which his political associates affect to cover, although they cannot hide, their motives—distinctly and audaciously tells the Irish people that they are not entitled to the same privileges as Englishmen; and pronounces them, in any particular which could enter his minute enumeration of the circumstances by which fellow-citizenship is created in race, identity and religion, to be aliens—to be aliens in race, to be aliens in country, to be aliens in religion. Aliens! was Arthur, Duke of Wellington, in the House of Lords, and did he not start up and exclaim, "Hold! I have seen the aliens do their duty?" The Duke of Wellington is not a man of an excitable temperament. His mind is of a cast too martial to be easily moved; but, notwithstanding his habitual inflexibility, I cannot help thinking that when he heard his Roman Catholic countrymen (for we are his countrymen) designated by a phrase as offensive as the abundant vocabulary of his eloquent confederate could supply, I cannot help thinking that he ought to have recollected the many fields of fight in which we have been contributors to his renown. "The battles, sieges, fortunes that he has passed," ought to have come back upon him. He ought to have remembered that, from the earliest achievement in which he displayed that military genius which has placed him foremost in the annals of modern warfare, down to that last and surpassing combat which has made his name imperishable—from Assaye to Waterloo—the Irish soldiers, with whom your armies are filled, were the inseparable auxiliaries to the glory with which his unparalleled successes have been crowned. Whose were the arms that drove your bayonets at Vimiera through the phalanxes that never reeled in the shock of war before? What desperate valor climbed the steeps and filled the moats at Badajos? All his victories should have rushed and crowded back upon his memory —Vimiera, Badajos, Salamanca, Albuera, Toulouse, and, last of all, the greatest—tell me, for you were there—I appeal to the gallant soldier before me (Sir Henry Hardinge), from whose opinions I differ, but who bears I know, a generous heart in an intrepid breast—tell me for you must needs remember—on that day when the destinies of mankind were trembling in the balance—while death fell in showers—when the artillery of France was levelled with a precision of the most deadly science—when her legions, incited by the voice, and inspired by the example of their mighty leader, rushed again and again to the onset—tell me, if for an instant, when, to hesitate for an instant was to be lost the "aliens" blenched? And when at length the moment for the last and decisive movement had arrived, and the valor which had so long been wisely checked, was at last let loose—when, with words familiar, but immortal, the great captain commanded the great assault—tell me, if Catholic Ireland, with less heroic valor than the natives of this your own glorious country, precipitated herself upon the foe? The blood of England, Scotland and of Ireland, flowed in the same stream, and drenched the same field. When the chill morning dawned, their dead lay cold and stark together; in the same deep pit their bodies were deposited—the green corn of spring is now breaking from their commingled dust—the dew falls from heaven upon their union in the grave. Partakers in every peril—in the glory shall we not be permitted to participate; and shall we be told, as a requital, that we are estranged from the noble country for whose salvation our life-blood was poured out?

RICHARD LALOR SHIEL.

THE LAST CHARGE OF NEY.

The whole continental struggle exhibited no sublimer spectacle than the last great effort of Napoleon to save his sinking empire. Europe had been put upon the plains of Waterloo to be battled for. The greatest military energy and skill the world possessed had been tasked to the utmost during the day. Thrones were tottering on the ensanguined field, and the shadows of fugitive kings flitted through the smoke of battle. Bonaparte's star trembled in the zenith, now blazing out in its ancient splendor, now suddenly paling before his anxious eye.

At length, when the Prussians appeared on the field he resolved to stake Europe on one bold throw. He committed himself and France to Ney, and saw his empire rest on a single charge. The intense anxiety with which he watched the advance of the column, the terrible suspense he suffered when the smoke of battle concealed it from sight, and the utter despair of his great heart when the curtain lifted over a fugitive army, and the despairing shriek rang on every side, "La garde recule, La garde recule," make us, for the moment, forget all the carnage, in sympathy with his distress.

Ney felt the pressure of the immense responsibility on his brave heart, and resolved not to prove unworthy of the great trust committed to his care. Nothing could be more imposing than the movement of the grand column to the assault. The guard had never yet recoiled before a human foe; and the allied forces beheld with awe its firm and terrible advance to the final charge.

For a moment the batteries stopped playing, and the firing ceased along the British lines, as without the beating of a drum, or the blast of a bugle, they moved in dead silence over the plain. The next moment the artillery opened, and the head of the gallant column seemed to sink down; yet they neither stopped nor faltered. Dissolving squadrons and whole battalions disappearing, one after another, in the destructive fire, affected not their steady courage. The ranks closed up as before, and each treading over his fallen comrade pressed firmly on The horse which Ney rode fell under him, and he had scarcely mounted another, before it also sank to the earth. Again and again did that unflinching man feel his steed sink down, till five had been shot under him. Then with his uniform riddled with bullets, and his face singed and blackened with powder, he marched on foot, with drawn sabre, at the head of his men.

In vain did the artillery hurl its storm of fire and lead into that living mass; up to the very muzzles they pressed, and driving the artillery-men from their places, pushed on through the English lines. But at that moment a file of soldiers, who had lain flat on the ground behind a low ridge of earth, suddenly rose and poured a volley into their very faces. Another and another followed, till one broad sheet of flame rolled on their bosoms, and in such a fierce and unexpected flow, that human courage could not withstand it. They reeled, shook, staggered back, then turned and fled.

The fate of Napoleon was writ. The star that had blazed so brightly over the world went down in blood; and the Bravest of the Brave had fought his last battle.

J. J. HEADLY.

LABOR.

I honor the toil-worn craftsman that with earth-made implement laboriously conquers the earth and makes her man's. Venerable to me is the hand, hard and coarse; wherein notwithstanding lies a cunning virtue, indefeasibly loyal as of this planet. Venerable, too, is the rugged face all weather-tanned, besoiled, with his rude intelligence; for it is the face of a man living man-like. Oh, but the more venerable for thy rudeness, and even because we must pity as well as love thee. Hardly entreated brother. For us was thy back so bent, for us were thy straight limbs and fingers so deformed; thou wert our conscript on whom the lot fell, and fighting our battles wert so marred. For in thee, too, lay a God-created form but it was not to be unfolded; encrusted must it stand with the thick adhesions and defacements of labor; and thy body like thy soul, was not to know freedom. Yet, toil on, toil on, thou art in thy duty, be out of it who may; thou toilest for the altogether indispensable daily bread.

There is a perennial nobleness, and even sacredness, in work. Were he ever so benighted, or forgetful of his high calling, there is always hope in a man that actually and earnestly works; in idleness alone there is perpetual despair. Consider how, even in the meanest sorts of labor, the whole soul of a man is composed into real harmony. He bends himself with free valor against his task: and doubt, desire, sorrow, remorse, indignation, despair itself shrink, murmuring far off into their caves. The glow of labor in him is a purifying fire, wherein all poison is burnt up; and of smoke itself there is made a bright and blessed flame.

Blessed is he who has found his work; let him ask no other blessedness; he has a life purpose. Labor is life. From the heart of the worker rises the celestial force, breathed into him by Almighty God, awakening him to all nobleness, to all knowledge. Hast thou valued patience, courage, openness to light, or readiness to own thy mistakes? In wrestling with the dim brute powers of fact, thou wilt continually learn. For every noble work the possibilities are diffused through immensity, undiscoverable, except to faith.

Man, son of Heaven, is there not in thine inmost heart a spirit of active method, giving thee no rest till thou unfold it? Complain not. Look up, wearied brother. See thy fellow-workmen surviving through eternity, the sacred bands of immortals.

THOMAS CARLYLE.

HORRORS OF CIVIL WAR.

(1844.)

Sir, these topics are perilous, but I do not fear to touch them. It is my thorough conviction that England would be able to put down any insurrectionary movement, with her gigantic force, even although maddened and frantic Ireland might be aided by calculating France. But at what a terrible cost of treasure and of life would treason be subdued! Well might the Duke of Wellington, although familiar with the fields of death, express his horror at the contemplation of civil war. War in Ireland would be worse than civil. A demon would take possession of the nation's heart,—every feeling of humanity would be extinguished,—neither to sex nor to age would mercy be given. The country would be deluged with blood; and when that deluge had subsided, it would be a sorry consolation to a British statesman, when he gazed upon the spectacle of desolation which Ireland would then present to him, that he beheld the spires of your Established Church still standing secure amidst the desert with which they would be encompassed. You have adjured us, in the name of the oath which we have sworn on the gospel of God,—I adjure you, in the name of every precept contained in that holy book,—in the name of that religion which is the perfection of humanity,—in the name of every obligation, divine and human, as you are men and Christians, to save my country from those evils to which I point, and to remember, that if you shall be the means of precipitating that country into perdition, posterity will deliver its great finding against you, and that you will not only be answerable to posterity, but responsible to that Judge, in whose presence, clothed with the blood of civil warfare, it will be more than dreadful to appear. But God forbid that these evils should ever have any other existence except in my own affrighted imaginings, and that those visions of disaster should be embodied in reality! God grant that the men to whom the destinies of England are confided by their sovereign may have the virtue and the wisdom to save her from those fearful ills that so darkly and so densely lower upon her! For my own part, I do not despair of witnessing the time when Ireland will cease to be the battle-field of faction; when our mutual acrimonies will be laid aside; when our fatal antipathies will be sacrificed to the good genius of our country; and, so far from wishing for a dismemberment of this majestic empire, I would offer up a prayer, as fervent as ever passed from the heart to the lips of any one of you, that the greatness of that empire may be imperishable, and that the power, and the affluence, and the glory, and, above all, the liberties of England may endure forever.

RICHARD LALOR SHIEL.

THE MEN TO MAKE A STATE.

The Men, to Make a State, must be Intelligent Men.—The right of suffrage is a fearful thing. It calls for wisdom, and discretion, and intelligence, of no ordinary standard. It takes in, at every exercise, the interests of all the nation. Its results reach forward through time into eternity. Its discharge must be accounted for among the dread responsibilities of the great day of judgment. Who will go to it blindly? Who will go to it passionately? Who will go to it as a sycophant, a tool, a slave? How many do! These are not the men to make a state.

The Men, to Make a State, must be Honest Men.—I do not mean men that would never steal. I do not mean men that would scorn to cheat in making change. I mean men with a single face. I mean men with a single eye. I mean men with a single tongue. I mean men that consider always what is right, and do it at whatever cost. I mean men whom no king on earth can buy. Men that are in the market for the highest bidder; men that make politics their trade, and look to office for a living; men that will crawl, where they cannot climb,—these are not the men to make a state.

The Men, to Make a State, must be Brave Men.—I mean the men that walk with open face and unprotected breast. I mean the men that do, but do not talk. I mean the men that dare to stand alone. I mean the men that are to-day where they were yesterday, and will be there to-morrow. I mean the men that can stand still and take the storm. I mean the men that are afraid to kill, but not afraid to die. The man that calls hard names and uses threats; the man that stabs, in secret, with his tongue or with his pen; the man that moves a mob to deeds of violence and self-destruction; the man that freely offers his last drop of blood, but never sheds the first,—these are not the men to make a state.

THE MEN, TO MAKE A STATE, MUST BE RELIGIOUS MEN.—To leave God out of states, is to be atheists. I do not mean that men must cant. I do not mean that men must wear long faces. I do not mean that men must talk of conscience, while they take your spoons. I speak of men who have it in their heart as well as on their brow. The men that own no future, the men that trample on the Bible, the men that never pray, are not the men to make a state.

THE MEN, TO MAKE A STATE, ARE MADE BY FAITH.—A man that has no faith is so much flesh. His heart is a muscle; nothing more. He has no past, for reverence; no future, for reliance. Such men can never make a state. There must be faith to look through clouds and storms up to the sun that shines as cheerily, on high, as on creation's morn. There must be faith that can afford to sink the present in the future; and let time go, in its strong grasp upon eternity. This is the way that men are made, to make a state.

THE MEN, TO MAKE A STATE, ARE MADE BY SELF-DENIAL.—The willow dallies with the water, draws its waves up in continual pulses of refreshment and delight; and is a willow, after all. An acorn has been loosened, some autumnal morning, by a squirrel's foot. It finds a nest in some rude cleft of an old granite rock, where there is scarcely earth to cover it. It knows no shelter, and it feels no shade. It asks no favor, and gives none. It grapples with the rock. It crowds up towards the sun. It is an oak. It has been seventy years an oak. It will be an oak for seven times seventy years; unless you need a man-of-war to thunder at the foe that shows a flag upon the shore, where freemen dwell: and then you take no willow in its daintiness and gracefulness; but that old, hardy, storm-stayed and storm-strengthened oak. So are the men made that will make a state.

THE MEN, TO MAKE A STATE, ARE THEMSELVES MADE BY OBEDIENCE.—Obedience is the health of human hearts: obedience to God; obedience to father and to mother, who are, to children, in the place of God; obedience to teachers and to masters, who are in the place of father and of mother; obedience to spiritual pastors, who are God's ministers; and to the powers that be, which are ordained of God. Obedience is but self-government in action; and he can never govern men who does not govern first himself. Only such men can make a state.

DOANE.

PART IV.

ARBOR DAY.

PART IV.

ARBOR DAY.

A TALK WITH TEACHERS.

The teacher should anticipate Arbor Day by half-hour conversations daily, for several weeks, on trees and flowers, particularly such as grow in Canada. Every pupil in a Canadian school should know the principal trees of our forests at sight, and a stroll through the woods in early spring, where convenient, would be an excellent way of observing their form and the variations of bark and leaf and stem.

In these conversations the following might be considered :

(1) *Extent of Canadian forests* : Once the home of the Indian, the deer, the elk, the wolf and the bear ; the forests of Canada compared with the forests of other countries, and how these forests are peopled ; the solitude of the forest. Selections of poetry and prose might be read descriptive of the forests.

(2) *The task of clearing the Canadian forests* : How trees are cut down ; how disposed of ; their conversion into fire-wood, saw logs, rails for fencing, shingles for roofing ; the experience of early settlers in the forests, dangers from wild beasts ; anecdotes and adventures ; the pursuit of game.

(3) *Remarkable forests* : The pine forests of Canada and the Northern States ; forests reserved for Park purposes ; some of the great English forests ; Epping Forest ;

Windsor Park; Bois de Boulogne, Paris; the forests of Central Europe, of India, Africa and the Amazon.

(4) *The commercial value of forests:* The oak and fir for ship building; the pine, spruce, elm, etc., for house building; the ash, hickory, basswood, etc., for carriage building; the walnut, chestnut, birch, etc., for furniture; description of lumbering and of a lumbering camp, of a saw mill, of a furniture factory.

(5) *Trees of the Bible:* The cedars of Lebanon, the olive, the pomegranate, the oak, the palm, the willow, the fig tree, the poplar, the elm, the myrtle, etc. Where and in what connection these trees are mentioned

(6) *Curious trees:* The cow tree, the bread fruit tree, the candle-nut tree, the banyan-tree, and the upas tree.

(7) *Nut bearing trees:* The hickory, oak, walnut, butternut, etc., of Canada; the cocoanut tree, the almond nut tree, and other trees of foreign countries.

(8) *Fruit trees:* Apple, peach, pear, cherry, plum, etc., of Canada; the fig, date, orange, lemon trees, etc., of other countries.

(9) *Beautiful trees:* The Canadian maple, the elm, the oak, the birch, etc.

(10) *Evergreen trees:* Pine, cedar, Canadian spruce, laurel, etc.

Flowers may be treated in a similar way. Canadian wild flowers might first be considered and pupils encouraged to collect specimens of them in early spring. The most common flowers for house planting or for bedding or for making borders, might be taken up.

A few days previous to Arbor Day, arrangements should be made for the planting of such trees and shrubs in the school grounds as may be necessary. The teacher might form a committee of the larger boys to attend to the tree planting, and of the girls to attend to flower beds. A committee should also be formed to arrange for raking up the school yard, looking after the repairs of the fences, and for removing all offensive material from the school premises. The committee on tree planting should provide the requisite number of trees, and also arrange for such assistance in planting them as may be necessary. Great care should be taken in the removal of the trees from their native bed. The roots should be fully protected and ample accommodation made for them in their new home. It may be well to call in the assistance of some resident of the section who has had some experience in matters of that kind. The committee on flower beds should also arrange for the laying of the necessary sodding and for the selection of such shrubs and flowers as are best adapted to the soil into which it is proposed to transplant them. A few general directions from the teacher in such cases might be helpful. The committee on school grounds should wait upon the trustees and secure, if possible, their co-operation in repairing fences and in attending to other matters coming under their direction. Every school yard in Canada should be a model of neatness, and with such an abundance of beautiful trees indigenous to the country there is no excuse for the want of shade which characterizes so many schools. With a little tact on the part of the teacher all objections on this score would quickly disappear.

Arbor Day should be made a busy, joyous holiday, one to which the pupils would look forward with enthusiasm and one that would each year add additional interest to Canadian forests and fields. Besides the decoration of the school grounds, Arbor Day should also be made to contribute to the æsthetic and intellectual culture of pupils. For that purpose suitable selections of poetry and prose may be memorized and an entertainment given in which the beauties of Nature, as displayed in her great forests and her myriad tinted flowers, are the principal theme. From the selections that follow, the teacher would have no difficulty in preparing a suitable programme.

1. CHOICE OF TREES.—Trees for school grounds and yards, along roadsides and streets, must be such as are least liable to suffer from injuries; they should be compact and symmetrical in shape, free from objectionable habits, such as bad odors, root-sprouting, frequent dropping of parts, etc., and from insect pests, and if planted for shade, should have a broad crown and a dense foliage, budding early in spring and retaining leaves long into the fall. Absence of skilful hands at tree planting on Arbor Days would also limit the selection to those which are transplanted easily and require the least care.

Trees native to the region in which the planting is done usually have more promise of success and are generally less costly than exotics. Trees from well-managed nurseries are preferable to those grown in the forest, because their root-system is better prepared for transplanting. Rapidly-growing trees, although giving shade soonest, are mostly short lived and become soonest unsightly.

2. SIZE.—Although as a rule small plants have a better promise of success, other considerations recommend the choice of larger sizes for roadside and ornamental plant-

ing. Trees of any size can be successfully transplanted, but in proportion to the size grows the difficulty, the amount of work and the care necessary. As a rule the largest size should not exceed two to three inches in diameter at the base and ten to fifteen feet in height. Those one-half that size will probably make better growth, because less of their root-system will be curtailed in taking them up for transplanting.

3. CONSIDERATIONS IN TRANSPLANTING.—(*a*) An abundance of fibrous roots. Not the turnip-like main or tap-root but the little fibres sustain the life of a tree. See that there are plenty of them, compactly grown within a small compass, and that they are not stripped of their bark or torn at their ends or dried up.

(*b*) A normal form and well-proportioned development of shaft and crown. The shaft should be clean and straight, neither thick set and short, or thread-like and over elongated, but gradually tapering and strong enough to hold up its head without support. The normal crown is characterized by vigorous full-sized leaves, or else by a large number of thick and full buds; it covers the main stem one-third to one-half its length, with a symmetric spread evenly branched, and has only one leader, of moderate length. The length and vigor of the last year's shoots, number and thickness of buds, and appearance of the bark afford means of judging the healthy constitution of the tree.

(*c*) The position from which the tree came has some influence on its further development. Trees from the forest have generally a wide spreading root system, which is difficult to take up and transplant. Those which have grown in the shade of the forest as a rule do not start easily in the open sunlight; those from cool north sides are apt to sicken when placed on hot exposures and *vice versa.* A healthy tree from poor soil transferred into better conditions will show itself grateful by vigorous development.

4. TREATMENT BEFORE TRANSPLANTING.—Transplanting is at best a forcible operation, and injury to the roots, although it may be small, is almost unavoidable. The roots are the life of the tree, and need, therefore, the most attention. In taking up a tree for transplanting the greatest care must be exercised to secure as much of the root-system intact as possible, especially of the small fibrous roots.

(*a*) *Never allow roots to become dry, from the time of taking up the tree until it is transplanted.* A healthy-looking tree may have the certainty of death in it if the root fibrils are dried out. To prevent drying during transportation, cover the roots with moist straw or moss or bags, or leave on them as much soil of the original bed as possible. At the place where the tree is to be planted, if the planting cannot be done at once, "heel in" the roots, i. e., cover them and part of the lower stem with fresh earth, or place the tree in the plant hole, throwing several spadefuls of earth on the roots.

(*b*) Pruning roots and branches is almost always necessary, but must be done with great care, especially as to root pruning. The cutting at the roots should be as little as possible, only removing with a clean sharp cut the bruised and broken parts. Extra long tap-roots may be cut away, but all the small fibres should be preserved. The cutting at the top is done to bring crown and root into proportion; the more loss at the root-system has been experienced the more need of reducing the crown system. Larger trees, therefore, require severer pruning, especially on poor soils; yet if there be fibrous roots enough to sustain great evaporation from the crown, the less cut the better. With large trees severe pruning is less dangerous than too little. A clean cut as close as possible to the stem or remaining branch will facilitate the healing of the wound. No stumps should be left (except with conifers, which suffer but little pruning). Shortening of the end shoots to one-half or two-thirds of their length may be done a little above a bud which is to take the lead. As a rule, the pruning for symmetry should have been done a year or so before transplanting, but may be done a year after.

5. Method in Planting a Tree.—(1) Holes are best made before the trees are brought to the ground. They should be a little deeper than the depth of the root-system, but twice as large around as seems necessary, to facilitate penetration of rains and development of rootlets through the loosened soil. Place the top soil, which is better (being richer in easily assimilated plant food) to one side, the raw soil from the bottom to the other side; in filling back bring the richer soil to the bottom. If it

be practicable, improve a heavy loamy soil by adding to and mixing with it looser sandy soil, or a loose poor soil by enriching it with loam or compost. Keep all stones out of the bottom; they may be used above the roots, or better on the surface. Providing proper drainage is the best means of improving ground for tree planting. Use no manure except as a top dressing.

(2) Planting is best done by two or three persons. A, who manipulates the tree, is the planter and responsible for the result; B and C do the spading under his direction, A places the tree in the hole, to ascertain whether this is of proper size; a board or stick laid across the hole aids in judging the depth. Trees should not be set deeper than they stood before, excepting in loose, poor soil. More trees are killed by too deep planting than the reverse. If the root-system is developed sideways but not centrally, as is often the case, a hill is raised in the hole to fill out the hollow space in the root-system, and the earth of the hill is patted down with the spade. When the hole is in proper order, A holds the tree perpendicularly in the middle of the hole, with the side bearing the fullest branches towards the south or south-west, for better protection of the shaft against the sun. B and C spread the roots into a natural position, then fill in the soil, using the good soil first—small spadefuls deliberately thrown over the roots in all directions—while A, by a slight shaking and pumping up and down of the stem, aids the earth in settling around the rootlets. A close contact of the soil with the rootlets is the secret of success in plant-

ing. Only fine mellow soil, not too moist, and free from stones, will permit such close adjustment to the rootlets, which should also be aided by hand and fingers filling in every crevice. A, while setting the tree, must exercise care to keep it in proper position and perpendicular, until the soil is packed so as to keep the tree in place; then B and C rapidly fill the holes, A treading down the soil firmly after a sufficient quantity is filled in, finishing off a little above the general level to allow for settling, and finally placing the stones or any mulching around the stem.

6. WATERING.—The practice of using water while planting can hardly be said to be a good one, unless the water is very carefully applied with a "rose" after the soil is well filled in and packed around the fibrous roots. Especially with a soil which has a tendency to clog, there is great danger of an uneven distribution and settling, with consequent empty spaces between the roots. More trees are probably killed by too much water in transplanting than by too little. Water after the transplanting (and perhaps before the last shovels of earth are filled in) especially if the soil was dry, is useful and should be applied during the hot season, choosing the late afternoon or evening for applying it.

7. AFTER CARE.—Any mulch of waste material, hay, straw, or better, wood shavings or chips, sawdust, or even stones simply placed around the foot of the tree, is of excellent service in checking evaporation.

Keeping the ground free from weeds and grass, and preventing it from baking, by occasional hoeing and raking, is advisable. To prevent the trees from being swayed by the wind, if of larger size, they should be staked firmly; a loose post is worse than none. The tying should be so done as not to cut or injure the tree; a tree-box insures more safety against accidents. With the development of the crown it becomes necessary to trim it, so as to carry the top above reach. Trees are not benefited by being used for hitching-posts, or climbing poles or other frolic.

Summarizing the elements of success in tree planting, they are:

(1) Trees suitable to soil and surrounding conditions;

(2) A well developed root-system kept in living condition;

(3) Wide holes and mellow soil;

(4) Firm packing of soil around the roots.

8 CHOICE OF KINDS.—Leaving out conifers—which require more careful handling and better situations than are as a rule to be had on occasions like that in view—there are over one hundred indigenous species to choose from for planting on the Atlantic side; of these thirty to forty might deserve attention for Arbor Day tree planting, according to climate, soil, and situation, or object. It is best to limit the choice for this occasion to trees of recognized merit native to your locality; opportunities will vary the choice. It is only possible here to name

the following selections, which admit of a wide application in Canada :

THREE TREES TO BE PLANTED WHERE NOTHING ELSE WILL GROW; easily transplanted, growing rapidly, but short-lived, liable to injuries, root-sprouting, soon scraggy looking unless specially attended : Silver Maple, Carolina Poplar, Box Elder.

FOUR TREES, AMONG THE BEST FOR STREET AND LAWN : Sugar Maple, Red Maple, Linden, Elm.

FIVE TREES DESIRABLE FOR LAWN AND YARD : Tulip Tree, Red Oak, Willow Oak, Black Cherry, Basswood.

TREES SUITABLE FOR SPECIAL POSITIONS : Sycamore, Black Birch, Mountain Ash, Black Walnut, Chestnut, Beech, Horse Chestnut.

THE LOVE OF NATURE.

The sounding cataract
Haunted me like a passion ; the tall rock,
The mountain, and the deep and gloomy wood,
Their colors and their forms, were then to me
An appetite,—a feeling and a love
That had no need of a remoter charm
By thought supplied, or any interest
Unborrowed from the eye.

That time is past,
And all its aching joys are now no more,
And all its dizzy raptures. Not for this
Faint I, nor mourn, nor murmur ; other gifts
Have followed, for such loss, I would believe,
Abundant recompense. For I have learned
To look on nature, not as in the hour
Of thoughtless youth, but hearing oftimes
The still sad music of humanity,
Nor harsh, nor grating, though of ample power
To chasten and subdue.

And I have felt
A presence that disturbs me with the joy
Of elevated thoughts ; a sense sublime
Of something far more deeply interfused,
Whose dwelling is the light of setting suns,
And the round ocean, and the living air,
And the blue sky, and in the mind of man ;
A motion and a spirit that impels
All thinking things, all objects of all thought,
And rolls through all things.

Therefore am I still
A lover of the meadows and the woods
And mountains, and of all that we behold
From this green earth ; of all the mighty world
Of eye and ear, both what they have create
And what perceive ; well pleased to recognize
In nature, and the language of the sense,
The anchor of my purest thoughts, the nurse,
The guide, the guardian of my heart, and soul
Of all my moral being.

WORDSWORTH.

A FOREST HYMN.

The groves were God's first temples. Ere man learned
To hew the shaft, and lay the architrave,
And spread the roof above them—ere he framed
The lofty vault, to gather and roll back
The sound of anthems; in the darkling wood,
Amid the cool and silence, he knelt down,
And offered to the Mightiest solemn thanks
And supplication. For his simple heart
Might not resist the sacred influence
Which, from the stilly twilight of the place,
And from the gray old trunks that high in heaven
Mingled their mossy boughs, and from the sound
Of the invisible breath that swayed at once
All their green tops, stole over him, and bowed
His spirit with the thought of boundless power
And inaccessible majesty. Ah why,
Should we, in the world's riper years, neglect
God's ancient sanctuaries, and adore
Only among the crowd, and under roofs
That our frail hands have raised? Let me at least,
Here in the shadow of this aged wood,
Offer one hymn—thrice happy, if it find
Acceptance in His ear.

Father, thy hand
Hath reared these venerable columns. Thou
Didst weave this verdant roof. Thou didst look down
Upon the naked earth, and, forthwith, rose
All these fair ranks of trees. They, in thy sun,
Budded, and shook their green leaves in thy breeze,

And shot toward heaven. The century-living crow
Whose birth was in their tops, grew old and died
Among their branches, till at last they stood,
As now they stand, massy, and tall, and dark,
Fit shrine for humble worshipper to hold
Communion with his Maker.

Thou hast not left
Thyself without a witness in these shades,
Of thy perfections. Grandeur, strength and grace
Are here to speak of Thee. This mighty oak—
By whose immovable stem I stand and seem
Almost annihilated—not a prince,
In all that proud old world beyond the deep,
E'er wore his crown as loftily as he
Wears the green coronal of leaves with which
Thy hand has graced him. Nestled at his root
Is beauty, such as blooms not in the glare
Of the broad sun. That delicate forest flower,
With scented breath and look so like a smile,
Seems, as it issues from the shapeless mould,
An emanation of the indwelling Life,
A visible token of the upholding Love,
That are the soul of this wide universe.

BRYANT.

THE FOREST TREES.

Up with your heads, ye sylvan lords,
  Wave proudly in the breeze,
For our cradle bands and coffin boards
  Must come from the forest trees.

We bless ye for your summer shade,
  When our weak limbs fail and tire ;
Our thanks are due for your winter aid,
  When we pile the bright log fire.

Oh ! where would be our rule on the sea,
  And the fame of the sailor band,
Were it not for the oak and cloud-crowned pine,
  That spring on the quiet land ?

When the ribs and masts of the good ship live,
  And weather the gale with ease,
Take his glass from the tar who will not give
  A health to the forest trees.

Ye lend to life its earliest joy,
  And wait on its latest page ;
In the circling hoop for the rosy boy,
  And the easy chair for age.

The old man totters on his way,
  With footsteps short and slow ;
But without the stick for his help and stay
  Not a yard's length could he go.

The hazel twig in the stripling's hand
  Hath magic power to please ;
And the trusty staff and slender wand
  Are plucked from the forest trees.

Ye are seen in the shape of the old hand loom
  And the merry ringing flail ;
Ye shine in the dome of the monarch's home
  And the sacred altar rail.

In the rustic porch, the wainscotted wall,
  In the gay triumphal car ;
In the rude built hut or the banquet hall,
  No matter ! there ye are !

Then up with your heads, ye sylvan lords !
  Wave proudly in the breeze ;
From our cradle bands to our coffin boards
  We're in debt to the forest trees.

ELIZA COOK.

PLANT A TREE.

He who plants a tree
Plants a hope.
Rootlets up through fibres blindly grope ;
Leaves unfold into horizons free.
So man's life must climb
From the clouds of time
Unto heavens sublime.
Canst thou prophesy, thou little tree,
What the glory of thy boughs shall be?

He who plants a tree
Plants a joy ;
Plants a comfort that will never cloy.
Every day a fresh reality.
Beautiful and strong,
To whose shelter throng
Creatures blithe with song.
If thou couldst but know thou happy tree,
Of the bliss that shall inhabit thee.

He who plants a tree
He plants peace.
Under its green curtains jargons cease,
Leaf and zephyr murmur soothingly ;
Shadows soft with sleep
Down tired eyelids creep,
Balm of slumber deep.
Never hast thou dreamed, thou blessed tree,
Of the benediction thou shalt be.

He who plants a tree
He plants youth ;
Vigor won for centuries in sooth ;
Life of time, that hints eternity !
Boughs their strength uprear,
New shoots every year
On old growths appear.
Thou shalt teach the ages, sturdy tree,
Youth of soul is immortality.

He who plants a tree
He plants love ;
Tents of coolness spreading out above
Wayfarers, he may not live to see
Gifts that grow are best ;
Hands that bless are blest ;
Plant,—life does the rest !
Heaven and earth help him who plants a tree,
And his work its own reward shall be.

LUCY LARCOM.

THE OAK.

A glorious tree is the old gray oak ;
He has stood for a thousand years—
Has stood and frowned
On the trees around,
Like a king among his peers ;
As around their king they stand, so now,
When the flowers their pale leaves fold
The tall trees round him stand, arrayed
In their robes of purple and gold.
He has stood like a tower
Through sun and shower,
And dared the winds to battle ;
He has heard the hail,
As from plates of mail,
From his own limbs shaken, rattle ;
He has tossed them about, and shorn the tops
(When the storm has roused his might)
Of the forest trees, as a strong man doth
The heads of his foes in fight.

GEORGE HILL.

WOODMAN, SPARE THAT TREE.

Woodman, spare that tree!
    Touch not a single bough!
In youth it sheltered me,
    And I'll protect it now.
'Twas my forefather's hand
    That placed it near his cot,
There, woodman, let it stand;
    Thy axe shall harm it not!

The old familiar tree,
    Whose glory and renown
Are spread o'er land and sea,—
    And wouldst thou hack it down?
Woodman, forbear thy stroke!
    Cut not its earth-bound ties;
Oh, spare that aged oak,
    Now towering to the skies!

When but an idle boy
    I sought its grateful shade;
In all their gushing joy,
    Here, too, my sisters played.
My mother kissed me here;
    My father pressed my hand—
Forgive the foolish tear;
    But let that old oak stand.

My heart-strings round thee cling,
    Close as thy bark, old friend;
Here shall the wild-bird sing,
    And still thy branches, bend.
Old tree! the storm still brave!
    And, woodman, leave the spot;
While I've a hand to save,
    Thy axe shall harm it not.

GEORGE P. MORRIS.

FOREST SONG.

A song for the beautiful trees!
    A song for the forest grand,
    The garden of God's own land,
The pride of His centuries.
Hurrah! for the kingly oak,
    For the maple, the sylvan queen,
For the lords of the emerald cloak,
    For the ladies in living green.

For the beautiful trees a song,
    The peers of a glorious realm,
    Linden, the ash, and the elm,
The poplar stately and strong
Hurrah! for the beech-tree trim,
    For the hickory stanch at core,
For the locust thorny and grim,
    For the silvery sycamore.

A song from the palm,—the pine,
    And for every tree that grows
    From the desolate zone of snows
To the zone of the burning line.
Hurrah! for the warders proud
    Of the mountain-side and vale,
That challenge the thunder-cloud,
    And buffet the stormy gale.

A song for the forest aisled,
    With its gothic roof sublime,
    The solemn temple of time,
Where man becometh a child,
As he lists to the anthem-roll
    Of the wind in the solitude,
The hymn which telleth his soul
    That God is the voice of the wood.

So long as the rivers flow,
    So long as the mountains rise,
    May the forest sing to the skies,
And shelter the earth below.
Hurrah! for the beautiful trees,
    Hurrah! for the forest grand,
The pride of His centuries.
    The garden of God's own land.

W. H. Venable.

INVITATION.

Oh, come away to the grave old woods
  Ere the skies are tinged with light,
Ere the slumbering leaves of the gloomy trees
  Have thrown off the mists of night;
    Ere the birds are up,
    Or the floweret's cup
  Is drained of its fresh'ning dew,
    Or the bubbling rill
    Kissing the hill
  Breaks on the distant view;
    Oh, such is the hour
    To feel the power
  Of the quiet, grave old woods!
    Then, while sluggards dream,
    Of some dismal theme,
      Let us stroll,
      With prayerful soul,
Through the depths of the grave old woods.

Oh, come away to the bright old woods,
  As the sun ascends the skies,
While the birdlings sing their morning hymn,
  And each leaf in the grove replies;
    When the golden-zoned bee
    Flies from flower to tree
  Seeking sweets for its honeyed cell,
    And the voice of praise
    Sounds its varied lays
  From the depths of each quiet dell:
    Oh, such is the hour
    To feel the power
  Of the magic bright old woods!
    Then, while sluggards dream
    Of some trifling theme,
      Let us stroll,
      With studious soul,
Through the depths of the bright old woods.

CHARLES SANGSTER.

PLANTING FOR THE FUTURE.

In youth's glad morning hour,
  All life a holiday doth seem ;
We glance adown time's vista long
  Beholding but the sunny gleam.

The happy hearts that meet to-day,
  In a loving band are drawn more near
By the loving end that crowns our work,
  Planting trees for a future year.

O tender trees ! ye may thrive and grow,
  And spread your branches to the sun,
When the youthful band assembled here,
  Has reaped life's harvest, every one.

When the shining eye shall lose its fire,
  When the rosy cheek shall fade away,
Thou'lt drink of the dew and bask in the light
  Forgetful of this Arbor Day.

The bounding heart, the active limb,
  The merry laugh and sparkling jest,
Be mingled with the things of earth,
  And sink to solitude and rest.

But o'er this ground with branching arms,
  These trees shall cast their leafy shade,
And other hearts as light and gay,
  Shall reap the shelter we have made.

So let our planting ever be,
  Something in store for a future year,
When homeward with our harvest bound,
  We'll meet the Master without fear.

HARRIET B. WRIGHT.

THE HEART OF THE TREE.

What does he plant who plants a tree?
He plants a friend of sun and sky;
He plants the flag of breezes free;
The shaft of beauty, towering high;
He plants a home to heaven anigh
For song and mother-croon of bird
In hushed and happy twilight heard—
The treble of heaven's harmony—
These things he plants who plants a tree.

What does he plant who plants a tree?
He plants cool shade and tender rain,
And seed and bud of days to be,
And years that fade and flush again;
He plants the glory of the plain;
He plants the forest's heritage;
The harvest of a coming age;
The joy that unborn eyes shall see—
These things he plants who plants a tree.

What does he plant who plants a tree?
He plants, in sap and leaf and wood,
In love of home and loyalty
And far-cast thought of civic good—
His blessing on the neighborhood
Who in the hollow of His hand
Holds all the growth of all our land—
A nation's growth from sea to sea
Stirs in his heart who plants a tree.

THE CENTURY.

THE IVY GREEN.

Oh, a dainty plant is the ivy green,
  That creepeth o'er ruins old!
Of right choice food are his meals I ween,
  In his cell so lone and cold.
The walls must be crumbled, the stones decayed,
  To pleasure his dainty whim;
And the mold'ring dust that years have made
  Is a merry meal for him.
    Creeping where no life is seen,
    A rare old plant is the ivy green.

Fast he stealeth on, though he wears no wings,
  And a staunch old heart has he!
How closely he twineth, how tightly he clings,
  To his friend, the huge oak tree!
And slyly he traileth along the ground,
  And his leaves he gently waves,
And he joyously twines and hugs around
  The rich mould of dead men's graves.
    Creeping where no life is seen,
    A rare old plant is the ivy green.

Whole ages have fled, and their works decayed,
  And nations scattered been;
But the stout old ivy shall never fade
  From its hale and hearty green.
The brave old plant in its lonely days
  Shall fatten upon the past;
For the stateliest building man can raise
  Is the ivy's food at last.
    Creeping where no life is seen,
    A rare old plant is the ivy green.

CHARLES DICKENS.

MAY.

Can it be that it is snowing,
  On this clear and sunny day?
Are the snow-flakes thickly falling
  In the pleasant month of May?

No, it is the apple blossoms
  Falling, falling from the trees,
Dancing in a whirl of rapture
  To the music of the breeze.

Till the orchard grass is covered
  With a carpet pure and white;
Like the crystal snow of winter
  Dipped in rosy sunset light.

May, the month of song and story,
  Singing birds and fairest flowers;
May, the month of nature's glory,
  Sunshine bright and gentle showers.

Listen to the robins singing
  'Mid the branches of the trees;
Listen to the blue-birds' carol
  And the drowsy hum of bees.

All the land is filled with sunshine,
  Every heart is light and gay,
Nature smiles upon her children
  For it is the month of May.

May, the month of song and story,
  Singing birds and fairest flowers;
May, the month of nature's glory,
  Sunshine bright and gentle showers.

Wm. G. Park.

A BUTTERCUP.

A little yellow buttercup
  Stood laughing in the sun ;
The grass all green around it,
  The summer just begun !
Its saucy little head abrim
  With happiness and fun.

Near by—grown old and gone to seed,
  A dandelion grew,
To right and left with every breeze
  His snowy tissues flew.
He shook his saucy head and said :
  "I've some advice for you.

"Don't think because you're yellow now,
  That golden days will last ;
I was as gay as you are, once ;
  But now my youth is past.
This day will be my last to bloom ;
  The hours are going fast.

"Perhaps your fun may last a week,
  But then you'll have to die."
The dandelion ceased to speak,—
  A breeze that capered by
Snatched all the white hairs from his head ;
  And wafted them on high.

His yellow neighbor first looked sad,
  Then, cheering up, he said :
"If one's to live in fear of death,
  One might as well be dead.".
The little buttercup laughed on,
  And waved his golden head.

K. C.

FLOWERS.

Spake full well, in language quaint and olden,
One who dwelleth by the castled Rhine,
When he called the flowers, so blue and golden,
Stars, that in earth's firmament do shine.

Wondrous truths, and manifold as wondrous,
God hath written in those stars above ;
But not less in the bright flowerets under us
Stand the revelation of His love.

Bright and glorious is that revelation,
Written all over this great world of ours ;
Making evident our own creation,
In these stars of earth, these golden flowers.

Everywhere about us they are glowing,
Some like stars, to tell us spring is born ;
Others, their blue eyes with tears o'erflowing,
Stand like Ruth amid the golden corn.

In all places then, and in all seasons,
Flowers expand their light and soul-like wings,
Teaching us, by most persuasive reasons,
How akin they are to human things.

And with childlike, credulous affection
We behold their tender buds expand ;
Emblems of our own great resurrection,
Emblems of the bright and better land.

LONGFELLOW.

BRING FLOWERS.

Bring flowers to strew in the conqueror's path!
He hath shaken thrones with his stormy wrath;
He comes with spoils of nations back,
The vines lie crushed in his chariot's track,
The turf looks red where he won the day.
Bring flowers to die in the conqueror's way!

Bring flowers to the captive's lonely cell!
They have tales of the joyous woods to tell,—
Of the free blue streams; and the glowing sky,
And the bright world shut from his languid eye;
They will bear him a thought of the sunny hours,
And the dream of his youth. Bring him flowers, wild flowers.

Bring flowers, fresh flowers, for the bride to wear!
They were born to blush in her shining hair.
She is leaving the home of her childhood's mirth,
She hath bid farewell to her father's hearth,
Her place is now by another's side.
Bring flowers, for the locks of the fair young bride!

Bring flowers, pale flowers, o'er the bier to shed,
A crown for the brow of the early dead!
For this through its leaves hath the white rose burst,
For this in the woods was the violet nursed!
Though they smile in vain for what once was ours,
They are love's last gift. Bring ye flowers, pale flowers!

Bring flowers to the shrine where we kneel in prayer,—
They are nature's offering, their place is there!
They speak of hope to the fainting heart,
With a voice of promise they come and part,
They sleep in dust through the wintry hours,
They break forth in glory. Bring flowers, bright flowers!

MRS. HEMANS.

THE BLUEBIRD'S SONG.

I know the song that the bluebird is singing,
Out in the apple tree where he is swinging.
Brave little fellow ! the skies may be dreary—
Nothing cares he while his heart is so cheery !

Hark ! how the music leaps out from his throat !
Hark ! was there ever so merry a note?
Listen awhile, and you'll hear what he's saying,
Up in the apple tree swinging and swaying.

"Dear little blossoms down under the snow,
You must be weary of winter I know ;
Hark, while I sing you a message of cheer !
Summer is coming ! and spring time is here !"

"Little white snowdrop ! I pray you arise ;
Bright yellow crocus ! come open your eyes ;
Sweet little violets, hid from the cold,
Put on your mantles of purple and gold ,
Daffodils ! daffodils ! say do you hear ?
Summer is coming ! and spring time is here !"

Anon.

MAY DAY.

Oh, the merry May has pleasant hours,
  And dreamily they glide,
As if they floated like the leaves
  Upon a silver tide.
The trees are full of crimson buds,
  And the woods are full of birds ;
And the waters flow to music,
  Like a tune with pleasant words.

The verdure of the meadow land
  Is creeping to the hills ;
The sweet, blue-blossomed violets
  Are blowing by the rills ;
The lilac has a leaf of balm
  For every wind that stirs ;
And the larch stands green and beautiful
  Amid the sombre firs.

There's perfume upon every wind—
  Music in every tree—
Dew for the moisture-loving flowers—
  Sweets for the sucking bee.
The sick come forth for the healing sun ;
  The young are gathering flowers ;
And life is a tale of poetry,
  That is told by golden hours.

NATHANIEL PARKER WILLIS.

NATURE'S GARDEN.

O Painter of the fruits and flowers!
  We thank Thee for thy wise design
Whereby these human hands of ours
  In Nature's garden work with Thine.

And thanks that from our daily need
  The joy of simple faith was born;
That he who smites the summer weed,
  May trust Thee for the autumn corn.

Give fools their gold, and knaves their power;
  Let fortune's bubbles rise and fall;
Who sows a field or trains a flower,
  Or plants a tree, is more than all.

For he who blesses most is blest;
  And God and man shall own his worth
Who toils to leave as his bequest
  An added beauty to the earth.

And, soon or late, to all that sow,
  The time of harvest shall be given;
The flowers shall bloom, the fruit shall grow,
  If not on earth, at last in heaven.

WHITTIER.

THE CLASS TREE.

TUNE—*God save the Queen.*

Grow thou and flourish well
Ever the story tell
Of this glad day ;
Long may thy branches raise
To heaven our grateful praise,
Waft them on sunlight rays
To God away.

Deep in the earth to-day,
Safely thy roots we lay
Tree of our love ;
Grow thou and flourish long ;
Ever our grateful song
Shall its glad notes prolong
To God above.

Let music swell the breeze,
And ring from all the trees,
On this glad day ;
Bless thou each student band
O'er all our happy land ;
Teach them Thy love's command
Great God, we pray.

ARBOR DAY MANUAL.

BUILDING THE BIRCH CANOE.

FIRST PUPIL:—

"Give me of your bark, O birch tree!
Of your yellow bark, O birch tree!
Growing by the rushing river,
Tall and stately in the valley!
I a light canoe will build me,
Build a swift Cheemaun for sailing,
That shalt float upon the river,
Like a yellow leaf in autumn,
Like a yellow water lily!"

SECOND PUPIL:—

And the tree with all its branches
Rustled in the breeze of morning,
Saying with a sigh of patience,
"Take my cloak, O Hiawatha!"

THIRD PUPIL:—

"Give me of thy boughs, O cedar!
Of your strong and pliant branches,
My canoe to make more steady,
Make more strong and firm beneath me!
Through the summit of the cedar
Went a sound, a cry of horror,
Went a murmur of resistance,
But it whispered, bending downward,
'Take my boughs, O Hiawatha!'
Down he hewed the boughs of cedar,
Shaped them straightway to a framework,
Like two bows he formed and shaped them,
Like two bended bows together."

FOURTH PUPIL :—

"Give me of your roots, O Tamarack !
Of your fibrous roots, O larch tree !
My canoe to bind together
That the water may not enter,
That the river may not wet me !"

FIFTH PUPIL :—

And the larch, with all its fibres,
Shivered in the air of morning,
Touched his forehead with his tassels
Said, with one long sigh of sorrow,
"Take them all, O Hiawatha !"

SIXTH PUPIL :—

"Give me of your balm, O fir tree !
Of your balsam and your resin,
So to close the seams together
That the water may not enter,
That the river may not wet me."

SEVENTH PUPIL :—

And the fir tree, tall and sombre,
Sobbed through all its robes of darkness,
Rattled like a shore of pebbles,
Answered wailing, answered weeping,
"Take my balm, O Hiawatha !"

ALL :—

Thus the birch canoe was builded
In the valley, by the river,
In the bosom of the forest ;
And the forest life was in it,
All its mystery and magic,
All the lightness of the birch tree,
All the toughness of the cedar.
All the larch's supple sinews ;
And it floated on the river,
Like a yellow leaf in autumn,
Like a yellow water lily.

LONGFELLOW.

EXERCISE FOR SIX PUPILS.

1\. In the merry month of May
Comes our gladsome Arbor Day,
And with cheerful voice we raise
Hearty notes of grateful praise.

2\. All the buds and bees are singing ;
All the lily bells are ringing ;
All the brooks run full of laughter,
And the winds come whispering after,
What is this they sing and say ?
It is May !

3\. Hail beauteous May ! that dost inspire
Mirth and youth and warm desire ;
Woods and groves are of thy dressing,
Hill and dale doth boast thy blessing.

4\. Robins in the tree-tops
Blossoms in the grass ;
Green things a-growing
Everywhere you pass.

5\. Sudden little breezes ;
Showers of silver dew ;
Black bough and bent twig
Budding out anew !

6\. Pine tree and willow tree,
Fringed elm and larch
Don't you think that May time's
Pleasanter than March ?

———

ODES TO THE FLOWERS.

[The children are to stand in a semi-circle, each child holding her respective flower, and talking to it. The flower may be given to the teacher or some one in the audience.]

To a Daisy:—

Oh! little flower so bright and fair,
We find you blooming everywhere.
My dear,— your merry little eyes
Are always looking to the skies.

Your dress is white and red and pink,—
The sweetest is the white,—I think.
Around your pretty yellow head,
Your dainty ruffled cap is spread.

You are the "day's eye," people say,
And so you're wide awake all day;—
And when the sun is hid from sight,
You shut your eyes like mine, so tight,
And bid the world a "sweet good-night."

Presentation: So here's my daisy wide awake,
I've brought it here for you to take.

To a Pansy:—

Oh! little flower, you drink the dew,
And bathe in Heaven's own rain-drops too,
Your food is sunshine bright and fair,
You breathe like us the balmy air.

Your dress of purple velvet hue,
Your over-dress, of lilac, too,
And in between each dainty fold,
Your pretty suit is trimmed with gold.

Kind people you are sure to please,
For sometimes you are called "heart's-ease."
And just like us when shadows creep,
You shut your eyes and go to sleep.

And in your little bed you lie,
Till bright the sun shines in the sky.
I know who is your cousin, too,
The violet with eyes so blue.

Your name means happy thoughts and true,
I wish *I* were as sweet as you.
Presentation: I'm going to give my flower to you,
With happy thoughts and kisses too.

To a Violet:—

Dear,—you've a name we can't forget,
The sweetest one, of violet.
We love you best, of all the flowers,
Others may claim, but you are ours.

Sweet-heart, when I'm older grown,
I'll have a garden all my own,
And have it growing through and through,
With pretty lit le plants like you.

Dearie, your darling little head
Hangs down as if you were afraid.
So modest and so sweet are you,—
So pretty are your eyes of blue,

That I don't wonder you're a pet!
You dainty, precious violet!
Presentation: Hoping you'll not me forget,
Here is my little violet.

To a Rose:—

The sweetest flower of all that grows,
To me's the fragrant-scented rose.
This is the queen of all the rest,
In robes of royal velvet dressed.

She has a gown of red so bright,
And bridal robe of gauzy white,
And one of pink and cream and buff,
Now don't you think that is enough?

I know now what they mean who speak,
Of roses blooming in each cheek.
They say I'll have a cheek of rose,
If like that flower I'll live outdoors.

See, here's a rose of every hue,—
I've made them in a bunch for you.
[*Presents roses to one of the audience.*]

TO A SNOWDROP:—

My dear, you are the *sweetest* sight,
So small and fair, so pure and white!
When all is cold and chill around,
You lift your head above the ground.

I found you out in all the snow,
And brought you in to warm, you know,
And say good-bye to the Snow-King,
And ring the bells to coming Spring.

I know where every snow-drop dwells,
For I have listened to the bells.
I know how many on a stem,
For I have counted all of them.

I am my mamma's snow-drop too,
For I am small and white like you.
I wonder how you ever grow
Out there in all the cold and snow?

Tho' I am big and eight years old,
I could not live in all that cold.
Presentation: Here are my snow-drops—won't you take
And keep them for ——— sake?

In concert: Now don't you think this school of ours
Is raising pretty little flowers.

AN EXERCISE FOR ARBOR DAY.

Adapted from Arbor Day Manual and Other Exercises.

One tree at least should be planted each year by the scholars; and, if possible, on the school grounds. In cities, this will be impossible, of course. Planting must be arranged in parks. In these cases, it is usual to have some prominent public man make an address. The children march and sing. But as these will be few compared with the vast number they may plant on their own grounds, the teacher will want exercises fitted for a "tree planting" on his own premises.

1. There will be exercises in the school building; then these being finished,

2. There will be exercises at the spot selected for the planting.

At a signal the school will rise, and march in this order:

1. The speaker and teacher.
2. The pupils who will plant the tree.
3. Those who will perform any part.
4. Those who will sing, etc.
5. Guests.
6. The rest of the pupils.

This part of the exercise should be practised until it can be well done.

(The tree should be at the spot, the opening made in the ground, the shovels and dirt in place.)

There should be a platform decorated with evergreens and flowers. On coming to order the speaker chosen will make an address. Programme follows.

EXERCISE IN THE SCHOOL-ROOM.

THE TEACHER :—

To-day is the "Tree Planting Day." We are going to plant something to-day that will live long after we are gone. A great many persons have thought about trees. I will ask you to tell us what you have found.

1ST PUPIL :—

The first one to plant trees was the great Creator. He commanded the earth to bring forth "the fruit tree yielding fruit after his kind." And when the Creator saw it, He "saw that it was good. When He made the garden in Eden He caused to grow "every tree that is pleasant to the sight." This shows us that the Creator felt that trees were necessary for the happiness of mankind

2ND PUPIL :—

Without doubt, better trees there might be than even the most noble and beautiful now. I suppose God has in His thoughts, much better ones than He has ever planted on this globe. They are reserved for the glorious land. Beneath them we may walk !

H. W. BEECHER.

3RD PUPIL :—

When we plant a tree we are doing what we can to make our planet a more wholesome and happier dwelling place for those who are to come after us, if not for ourselves. As you drop the seed, as you plant the sapling, your left hand hardly knows what your right hand is doing. But Nature knows, and in due time the Power that sees and works in secret will reward you openly. You have been warned against hiding your talent in a napkin; but if your talent takes the form of a maple-key or an acorn, and your napkin is a shred of the apron that covers the lap of the earth, you may hide it there unblamed; and when you render in your account you will find that your deposit has been drawing compound interest all the time.

O. W. HOLMES.

4TH PUPIL:—

If it is something to make two blades of grass grow where only one was growing, it is much more to have been the occasion of planting an oak which shall defy twenty scores of winters, or an elm which shall canopy with its green cloud of foliage half as many generations of mortal immortalities. I have written many verses, but the best poems I have produced are the trees I planted on the hillside which overlooks the broad meadows, scalloped and rounded at their edges by loops of the sinuous Housatonic.

O. W. HOLMES.

5TH PUPIL:—

What are these maples and beeches and birches but odes and idyls and madrigals? What are those pines and firs and spruces but holy hymns, too solemn for the many-hued raiment of their gay, deciduous neighbors?

O. W. HOLMES.

6TH PUPIL :—

"We may obtain some idea of the usefulness of trees when we learn that we obtain from the forests of Canada over $40,000,000 worth of products every year. Among these products are lumber, timber, railroad ties, telegraph poles, fuel, charcoal, fencing stuff, tan-bark, etc. In fact, no other crop equals that of the forest in money value."

7TH PUPIL :—

"Our supply of some of the best kinds of timber is being rapidly exhausted. Forest fires alone do damage each year to the extent of thousands of dollars. These fires are caused in different ways—by the sparks from locomotives, the carelessness of farmers in clearing their land, and from camp-fires left by hunters. Such fires are the chief discouragement to timber culture. In addition to the loss by fire, there are droughts, floods, changes of climate, etc., and from all of these our forests suffer."

8TH PUPIL :—

"Many parts of the old world, which were once fertile and thickly peopled, have become so impoverished through the destruction of forests that they are barren and uninhabited. Large regions in south-western France, which were once marshy and sandy, are now giving a living to dense populations, because trees were planted and cultivated."

TEACHER :—

"We are going to plant a tree to-day, and I want you to tell me which is your favorite tree, and if possible quote something about it."

1ST PUPIL (boy) :—

"I choose the apple tree. It is a good tree for shade, for its branches spread so far, and then it is useful as well as ornamental. I don't know what we should do without apples, and I think we ought to plant as many apple trees as we can. It was a favorite tree with Bryant, the poet. He says:

"'What plant we in this apple tree?
Sweets for a hundred flowering springs
To load the May-wind's restless wings,
When from the orchard's row, he pours
Its fragrance through the open doors:
A world of blossoms for the bee,
Flowers for the sick girl's silent room,
For the glad infant sprigs of bloom,
We plant with the apple-tree.'"

2ND PUPIL (girl) :—

"Apples are very nice of course, but I love the blossoms better. I found a quotation from Henry Ward Beecher, and although it is not poetry, I think it very appropriate:

"'But we must not neglect the blossoms of fruit trees. What a great heart an apple tree must have! What generous work it makes of blossoming! It is not content with a single bloom for each apple that is to be; but a profusion, a prodigality of blossoms, there must be. The tree is but a huge bouquet; it gives you twenty times as much as there is need for, and evidently because it loves to blossom.'"

3RD PUPIL (boy):—

"I love the pine. It stands up so straight and tall, that it looks like a king among trees. I have two verses to the pine by James Russell Lowell:

"'Thou alone know'st the splendor of winter
'Mid thy snow-silvered, hushed precipices,
Hearing crags of green ice groan and splinter,
And then plunge down the muffled abysses,
In the quiet of midnight.

"'Thou above know'st the glory of summer,
Gazing down on thy broad seas of forest;
On thy subjects that send a proud murmur
Up to thee, to their sachem, who towerest
From thy bleak throne to heaven.'"

4TH PUPIL (boy):—

"I think the hemlock quite as handsome as the pine. It is green in winter as well as summer. Longfellow has written some very pretty lines about it:

"'O hemlock tree! O hemlock tree! how faithful are thy branches;
Green not alone in summer time,
But in the winter's frost and rime!
O hemlock tree! O hemlock tree! how faithful are thy branches!'"

5TH PUPIL (girl):—

"I love the aspen. I can't help pitying the poor tree, for it trembles, trembles, all the time, as if it had been frightened. I have some lines about the aspen. They were written by John Leyden:

"'Beneath a shivering canopy reclined
Of aspen leaves that wave without a wind,
I love to lie, when lulling breezes stir
The spiry cones that tremble on the fir."'

6TH PUPIL (boy):—

"Nobody seems to think of the oak, which I call the grandest of trees. Only think how large it grows and how long it lives! A little while ago, somebody called the pine the king of trees; but I think you will agree with me that the name belongs to the oak. I found a great deal of poetry about the oak, but I like these lines by H. F. Chorley best of all:

"'A song to the oak, the brave old oak,
Who hath ruled in the greenwood long;
Here's health and renown to his broad, green crown,
And his fifty arms so strong.
There's fear in his frown when the sun goes down,
And the fire in the West fades out;
And he showeth his might on a wild midnight,
When the storms through his branches shout.'"

7TH PUPIL (boy):—

"I say, let us plant a hickory tree. We may never eat the nuts ourselves, but perhaps our grand-children will have fun going nutting in the autumn. I am glad somebody had the good sense to plant hickory trees for us, and I guess the squirrels are glad too:

"'When the autumn comes its round
Rich, sweet walnuts will be found,
Covering thickly all the ground
Where my boughs are spread.
Ask the boys that visit me,
Full of happiness and glee,
If they'd mourn the hickory tree
Were it felled and dead.'"

8TH PUPIL (girl):—

"I love the lilac tree, its blossoms are so sweet in the spring! Don't you remember what pretty bouquets we made of lilacs last year. We set the vases in the windows, and the bees came and helped themselves to honey. I think we ought to remember the bees as well as the squirrels. Mrs. Stebbins has written some lines about the lilac:

"'I am thinking of the lilac trees,
That shook their purple plumes,
And when the sash was open,
Shed fragrance through the rooms.'"

9TH PUPIL (boy):—

"The willow is my favorite tree. Perhaps I like it so well because it shows signs of life so early in the spring.

"The willow is almost the earliest to gladden us with the promise and reality of beauty in its graceful and delicate foliage, and the last to scatter its yellow yet scarcely withered leaves upon the ground. All through the winter, too, its yellow twigs give it a seeming aspect, which is not without a cheering influence, even in the grayest and gloomiest day. Beneath a clouded sky it faithfully remembers the sunshine."

10TH PUPIL (girl):—

"I think the ash is a beautiful tree. I can't make a speech about it, but I can tell you what Mr. Lowell says:

"'The ash her purple drops forgivingly,
And sadly, breaking not the general hush;
The maple swamps glow like a sunset sea,
Each leaf a ripple with its separate flash;
All round the woods' edge creeps the skirting blaze,
Of bushes low; as, when on cloudy days,
Ere the rain falls the cautious farmer burns his brush.'"

11TH PUPIL (boy):—

"No one has cast a vote for the maple. I think it the most beautiful of all trees, and besides it is the national tree of Canada. Hear what has been said of it:

All hail to the broad-leaved Maple!
With her fair and changeful dress—
A type of our youthful country
In its pride and loveliness;
Whether in Spring or Summer,
Or in the dreary Fall,
'Mid Nature's forest children,
She's fairest of them all.

Down sunny slopes and valleys
Her graceful form is seen,
Her wide, umbrageous branches
The sunburnt reaper screen;
'Mid the dark-browed firs and cedars
Her livelier colors shine,
Like the dawn of the brighter future
On the settler's hut of pine.

She crowns the pleasant hill-top,
Whispers on breezy downs,
And casts refreshing shadows
O'er the streets of our busy towns;
She gladdens the aching eye-ball,
Shelters the weary head,
And scatters her crimson glories
On the graves of the silent dead.

When Winter's frosts are yielding
To the sun's returning sway,
And merry groups are speeding
To sugar-woods away;
The sweet and welling juices,
Which form their welcome spoil,
Tell of the teeming plenty,
Which here waits honest toil.

When sweet-toned Spring, soft-breathing,
Breaks Nature's icy sleep,
And the forest boughs are swaying
Like the green waves of the deep ;
In her fair and budding beauty,
A fitting emblem she
Of this our land of promise,
Of hope, of liberty.

And when her leaves, all crimson,
Droop silently and fall,
Like drops of life-blood welling
From a warrior brave and tall ;
They tell how fast and freely
Would her children's blood be shed,
Ere the soil of our faith and freedom
Should echo a foeman's tread.

Then hail to the broad-leaved Maple ?
With her fair and changeful dress—
A type of our youthful country
In its pride and loveliness ;
Whether in Spring or Summer,
Or in the dreary Fall,
'Mid Nature's forest children,
She's fairest of them all.

H. F. Darnell, D.D.

SCRIPTURE SELECTIONS.

May be arranged for a responsive service.

GENESIS.

I, 11. And God said, Let the earth bring forth the fruit tree, yielding fruit after his kind.

12. And the earth brought forth the tree, yielding fruit whose seed was in itself after his kind. And God saw that it was good.

29. And God said, Behold I have given you every tree in which is the fruit of a tree yielding seed; to you it shall be for meat.

II, 8. And the Lord God planted a garden eastward in Eden, and there He put the man whom He had formed.

9. And out of the ground made the Lord God to grow every tree that is pleasant to the sight, and good for food; the tree of life also in the midst of the garden, and the tree of knowledge of good and evil.

DEUTERONOMY.

VIII, 7, 8, 9. For the Lord thy God bringeth thee into a good land; a land of brooks of water, of fountains and depths that spring out of valleys and hills; a land of wheat, and barley, and vines, and fig trees, and pomegranates; a land of oil olive, and honey; a land wherein thou shalt eat bread without scarceness, thou shalt not lack anything in it; a land whose stones are iron, and out of whose hills thou mayest dig brass.

XX, 19. For the tree of the field is man's life.

I KINGS.

IV, 29. And God gave Solomon wisdom and understanding exceedingly much.

33. And he spake of trees from the cedar tree that is in Lebanon even unto the hyssop that springeth out of the wall.

X, 11. And the navy also of Hiram that brought gold from Ophir brought in from Ophir great plenty of almug trees and precious stones.

12. And the king made of the almug trees pillars for the house of the Lord, and for the king's house, harps also, and psalteries for singers; there came no such almug trees, nor were seen unto this day.

27. Solomon made cedars to be as the sycamore trees that are in the vale or abundance.

PSALMS.

I, 1, 2, 3. Blessed is the man whose delight is in the law of the Lord. He shall be like a tree planted by the streams of water that bringeth its fruit in its season, whose leaf also does not wither, and whatsoever he doeth shall prosper.

XXXVII, 35. I have seen the wicked in great power, and spreading himself like a green bay tree.

36. Yet he passed away, and, lo! he was not; yea, I sought him, but he could not be found.

XCII, 12. The righteous shall flourish like the palm tree; he shall grow like a cedar in Lebanon.

CIV, 16, 17. The trees of the Lord are full of sap; the cedars of Lebanon which he hath planted; where the birds make their nests; as for the stork, the fir trees are her house.

ISAIAH.

VI, 13. As a teil tree and as an oak whose substance is in them when they cast their leaves; so the holy seed shall be the substance thereof.

XLI, 19. I will plant in the wilderness the cedar tree, and the myrtle, and the oil tree; I will set in the desert the fir tree, and the pine and the box tree together.

XLIV, 4. They shall spring up as among the grass, as willows by the water courses.

14. He heweth him down cedars, and taketh the cypress and the oak, which he strengtheneth for himself among the trees of the forest; he planteth an ash and the rain doth nourish it.

LV, 12. All the trees of the field shall clap their hands;

13. Instead of the thorn shall come up the fir tree, and instead of the brier shall come up the myrtle tree, and it shall be to the Lord for a name.

LX, 13. The glory of Lebanon shall come unto thee, the fir tree, the pine tree and the box together.

LXI, 3. That they might be called trees of righteousness, the planting of the Lord, that he might be glorified.

JEREMIAH.

XVII, 7, 8. Blessed is the man that trusteth in the Lord, and whose hope the Lord is. For he shall be like a tree planted by the water, and spreadeth out his roots by the river, and shall not fear when heat cometh, but her leaf shall be green, and shall not be careful in the year of drouth, neither shall cease from yielding fruit.

EZEKIEL.

XXXI, 3. Behold the Assyrian was a cedar in Lebanon with fair branches and . . . his top was among the thick boughs.

4. The waters made him great, the deep set him up on high, with the rivers running round about his plants, and sent out her little rivers unto all the trees of the field.

5. Therefore his height was exalted above all the trees of the field, and his boughs were multiplied, and his branches became long, because of the multitude of waters, when he shot forth.

6. All the fowls of heaven made their nests in his boughs.

7. Thus was he fair in his greatness in the length of his branches; for his root was by great waters.

8. The cedars in the garden of God could not hide him; the fir trees were not like his boughs, and the chestnut trees were not like his branches; nor any tree in the garden of God was like unto him in its beauty.

9. I have made him fair by the multitude of his branches; so that all the trees of Eden, that were in the garden of God, envied him.

XXXIV, 27. And the tree of the field shall yield her fruit, and the earth shall yield her increase, and they shall be safe in their land, and shall know that I am the Lord.

XLVII, 12. And by the river by the bank thereof, on this side and on that side shall grow all the trees for meat, whose leaf shall not fade, neither shall the fruit thereof be consumed; it shall bring forth new fruit, according to his months. . . . and the fruit thereof shall be for meat, and the leaf thereof for medicine.

MATTHEW.

VII, 17. Even so every good tree bringeth forth good fruit; but a corrupt tree bringeth forth evil fruit.

18. A good tree cannot bring forth evil fruit, neither can a corrupt tree bring forth good fruit.

19. Every tree that bringeth not forth good fruit is hewn down, and cast into the fire.

20. Wherefore by their fruits ye shall know them.

XII, 33. Either make the tree good, and his fruit good; or else make the tree corrupt, and his fruit corrupt; for the tree is known by his fruit.

REVELATION.

II, 7. . . . To him that overcometh will I give to eat of the tree of life, which is in the midst of the paradise of God.

XXI, 10. And he carried me away in the spirit to a great and high mountain, and showed me that great city, the holy Jerusalem. . . .

XXII, 2. In the midst of the street of it, and on either side of the river, was there the tree of life, which bare twelve manner of fruits, and yielded her fruit every month; and the leaves of the tree were for the healing of the nations.

SPECIMEN PROGRAMME.

Adapted from Arbor Day Manual.

(This programme is intended to be merely suggestive, and may be varied as tastes, circumstances and opportunities may permit. The ingenuity of teachers is relied upon to make such changes as may be necessary to interest in some way all grades of pupils, care being taken to make the exercises as full of life as possible.)

SUGGESTIONS: The order of recitations noted below may be greatly varied. Different scholars may recite one verse each of a stated poem, all reciting the last verse in concert.

A very appropriate exercise for younger children may be made under the head "Breezes from the Forest," or "Voices of the Trees," in which many children may take part, each pupil reciting a verse especially prepared. The first may begin: "I am the sugar maple," etc., other pupils speaking as other trees. The following is given as an illustration of this plan:

"I am the sugar maple and a favorite ornamental tree. People love me because I am possessed of sweetness. I claim to have made more boys and girls happy than any other tree. I have many changes of dress—wearing in spring the softest shade of every color, in the summer the purest emerald, and in the autumn the most brilliant yellow. My wood is used for furniture, floors, and for furnishing the interior of houses, and after the houses are finished, few can warm them better than I."

The expression in the opening sentence may be varied, as "I am known as"—"They call me," etc.

Older pupils might interest themselves in organizing as a "*Convention of Trees*," each pupil representing a tree familiar in the locality, and to be called by its name. Officers to be chosen by name of trees, and remarks and discussions participated in by members of the Convention, to be recognized by names of trees.

Compositions may be prepared by older students upon various subjects connected with trees; as, for example, their uses for shade, for ornament, for producing fuel, lumber, etc.; their influence in increasing the rainfall, retaining moisture, modifying the temperature, etc.; their value in furnishing food, materials for clothing, ropes, medicines, oils, homes for the birds, houses, furniture, etc.; their value as defence against storms, from avalanches in Switzerland, and in preserving health by counteracting the influences of malaria, etc.

Compositions may also be written on the size of trees, trees in history, care of trees, enemies of trees, the kinds and habits of native trees, kinds of ornamental trees; also, a description of the tree chosen for planting, its characteristics, usefulness, etc, ; upon varieties of shrubs that are valuable for landscape gardening, their habits of growth, flowering, etc. The same exercises may be extended to include the vines of flower seeds or flowering plants that may be selected for cultivation.

1. Devotional Exercises :

Note.—See Scripture lesson given elsewhere. This may be read by one person, or different scholars may each repeat a verse or a sentence. Or it may be made a responsive service, the teacher repeating one sentence, and the scholars the next.

2. Reading of the Law Establishing Arbor Day.

3. Reading of Letters in Reference to Arbor Day.

Note.—Many teachers and others in charge of exercises may choose to invite letters appropriate to the occasion, from prominent persons in the different localities who are unable to be present.

4. Song.

5. Recitations.—By different pupils.

First Pupil :

"The groves were God's first temples,
Ere man learned
To hew the shaft, and lay the architrave
And spread the roof above them—ere he framed
The lofty vault, to gather and roll back
The round of anthems, in the darkling wood,
Amidst the cool and silence, he knelt down
And offered to the Mightiest solemn thanks
And supplications."

Bryant.

Second Pupil :

"I shall speak of trees, as we see them, love them, adore them in the fields where they are alive, holding their green sunshades over our heads, talking to us with their hundred thousand whispering tongues, looking down on us with that sweet meekness which belongs to huge but limited organisms—which one sees most in the patient posture, the outstretched arms, and the heavy, drooping robes of these vast beings, endowed with life, but not with soul—which outgrow us and outlive us, but stand helpless, poor things—while nature dresses and undresses them." Holmes.

THIRD PUPIL:

"Give fools their gold and knaves their power;
Let fortune's bubbles rise and fall;
Who sows a field, or trains a flower,
Or plants a tree, is more than all.

For he who blesses most is blest;
And God and man shall own his worth,
Who toils to leave as his bequest
An added beauty to the earth."

WHITTIER.

FOURTH PUPIL:

"There is something nobly simple and pure in a taste for the cultivation of forest trees. It argues, I think, a sweet and generous nature to have this strong relish for the beauties of vegetation, and this friendship for the hardy and glorious sons of the forest. There is a grandeur of thought connected with this part of rural economy. * * * He who plants an oak looks forward to future ages, and plants for posterity. Nothing can be less selfish than this."

IRVING.

FIFTH PUPIL:

"What conqueror in any part of 'Life's broad field of battle' could desire a more beautiful, a more noble, or a more patriotic monument than a tree planted by the hands of pure and joyous children, as a memorial of his achievements."

LOSSING.

SIXTH PUPIL:

"Oh! Rosalind, these trees shall be my books,
And in their barks my thoughts I'll character,
That every eye which in this forest looks,
Shall see thy virtue witnessed everywhere."

SHAKESPEARE.

SEVENTH PUPIL:

"There is something unspeakably cheerful in a spot of ground covered with trees, that smiles amidst all the rigors of winter, and gives us a view of the most gay season in the midst of that which is the most dead and melancholy."

ADDISON.

EIGHTH PUPIL:

"As the leaves of trees are said to absorb all noxious qualities of the air, and to breathe forth a purer atmosphere, so it seems to me as if they drew from us all sordid and angry passions, and breathed forth peace and philanthropy."

—IRVING.

NINTH PUPIL:

"I care not how men trace their ancestry,
To ape or Adam; let them please their whim;
But I in June am midway to believe
A tree among my far progenitors,
Such sympathy is mine with all the race,
Such mutual recognition vaguely sweet
There is between us."

LOWELL.

TENTH PUPIL:

"Trees have about them something beautiful and attractive even to the fancy. Since they cannot change their plan, are witnesses of all the changes that take place around them; and as some reach a great age, they become, as it were, historical monuments, and, like ourselves, they have a life growing and passing away, not being inanimate and unvarying like the fields and rivers. One sees them passing through various stages, and at last, step by step, approaching death, which makes them look still more like ourselves.

HUMBOLDT.

ELEVENTH PUPIL:

"Summer or winter, day or night,
The woods are an ever new delight;
They give us peace, and they make us strong,
Such wonderful balms to them belong;
So, living or dying, I'll take my ease
Under the trees, under the trees."

STODDARD.

6. READING OR DECLAMATION.

7. SONG.

8. ADDRESS.—"Our School-houses and our Homes, How to beautify them."

NOTE.—Any other appropriate subject may be selected.

9. SONG.

10. BRIEF ESSAYS.—By different scholars.

First scholar may choose for subject, "My Favorite Tree is an Oak,' and give reasons. Other scholars may follow, taking for subjects the Elm, Maple, Beech, Birch, Ash, etc. These essays should be very short.

11. SONG.

12. VOTING ON THE QUESTION.—"What is the Favorite Tree."

13. READING OR RECITATION.

14. SONG.

15. ORGANIZATION OF LOCAL "Shade Tree Planting Association."

NOTE.—The scholars should at least appoint a committee to serve for a year to see that trees planted are properly cared for.

16. God Save the Queen.

www.ingramcontent.com/pod-product-compliance
Lightning Source LLC
Chambersburg PA
CBHW030901270326
41929CB00008B/528

* 9 7 8 3 3 3 7 3 0 3 8 5 3 *